A Policy Travelogue

A POLICY TRAVELOGUE

Tracing Welfare Reform in Aotearoa/New Zealand and Canada

Catherine Kingfisher

berghahn
NEW YORK · OXFORD
www.berghahnbooks.com

Published in 2013 by

Berghahn Books

www.berghahnbooks.com

Library of Congress Cataloging-in-Publication Data

Kingfisher, Catherine Pélissier.
A policy travelogue : tracing welfare reform in Aotearoa/New Zealand and Canada /
Catherine Kingfisher.
    pages cm
    Includes bibliographical references and index.
    ISBN 978-1-78238-005-4 (hardback) — ISBN 978-1-78533-221-0 (paperback) —
ISBN 978-1-78238-006-1 (ebook)
    1. Public welfare—New Zealand. 2. Public welfare—Alberta. 3. Social
service—New Zealand. 4. Social service—Alberta. 5. New Zealand—Social policy.
6. Alberta—Social policy. I. Title.
HV515.5.K56 2013
362.5'568097123—dc23

                                                                2013005574

British Library Cataloguing in Publication Data

A catalogue record for this book is available from the British Library

ISBN 978-1-78238-005-4 hardback
ISBN 978-1-78533-221-0 paperback
ISBN 978-1-78238-006-1 ebook

En hommage à ma mère, Emma Loubière Pélissier, dont la joie de vivre, l'humour, la bonté, et l'amour ont embelli notre monde.

Contents

ACKNOWLEDGMENTS

This book would not have been possible without the poor single mothers, community service providers, and welfare workers who so generously shared their experiences and thoughts with me. I was both amazed and humbled by their indulgent responses to my snooping presence and endless questions, especially in light of the time and resource limitations from which they suffer. Gatekeepers to the welfare system and to various community service agencies, as well as several politicians and official policy makers in Aotearoa/New Zealand, were also crucial to the success of this project. I am grateful for their willingness to provide access to their organizations and for their insights into the policy process.

The productive criticism of colleagues has been equally essential. I am especially indebted to Jeff Maskovsky and A. R. Vasavi for their comprehensive, considered, and gently demanding feedback. In addition, I thank Janine Brodie, Norman Buchignani, John Clarke, Alvin Finkel, Richard Freeman, Michael Goldsmith, Judith Goode, Lois Harder, Trevor Harrison, Doreen Indra, Wendy Larner, Claudia Malacrida, Sybille Manneschmidt, Sandi Morgen, Maria Ng, Melanie Nolan, Jamie Peck, Cris Shore, Rachel Simon-Kumar, Alan Smart, Marilyn Strathern, Carol Williams, and Patrick Wilson for the many ways in which they enriched aspects of my thinking and writing. I thank Allison Dobek, Catherine Gannon, Michael McCarthy, and Cindy Venhuis for their superb research assistance; and Paul Klein and Jenny Oseen for their outstanding editorial contributions. At Berghahn Books, I am grateful to Ann Przyzycki DeVita, Adam Capitanio, Elizabeth Berg, Melissa Spinelli, and other members of the production team for their timely and professional work.

In Aotearoa/New Zealand, Michael Goldsmith and Beryl Fletcher kindly hosted me in 2004 and 2005. We joked about their basement suite (a.k.a., the "pit of despair") but I am eternally grateful to them for putting it at my disposal, and for their excellent company. Other friends and family, including Andrea Cuèllar, Dagmar Dahle, Priya Kurian, John Pélissier, Bernadette Pélissier, Marguerite Pélissier, Jacqueline Preyde, Denise van Schothorst, Laura Lee Slayton, Michael Stingl, and, above all, Levi Kingfisher, gave me much-needed encouragement.

Finally, I thank Karen Campbell, whose fine artwork, elegantly depicting fields of shift and change, graces the cover of this book.

Funds for this research were generously provided by the Wenner-Gren Foundation for Anthropological Research, the Social Science and Humanities Research Council of Canada, and the University of Lethbridge Research Fund.

TRACING POLICY

Translation and Assemblage

∞

This book explores the social life of policy. According to mainstream policy science, social policy is produced by policy experts on the basis of rational, scientific knowledge. Some of this knowledge is locally produced, and some of it is drawn from elsewhere, where similarly situated policy experts have worked to deal with related problems. Once developed, policy is implemented by policy providers, who operate as conduits for its administration in institutions designed to serve and manage various populations and their problems. Finally, social policy is received by the targets of policy, whose lives are accordingly altered for the better.

This story about social policy serves to produce and support modernist interpretations of governance that extend the metaphor of body as machine to minds and personalities as well as to society; that cover up the messiness of official policy production; that fail to take into account the reality that all those who engage with social policy—not only policy elites, but also providers and recipients—are active and knowledgeable insiders who in fact make and transform policy in their interactions with it; and, finally, that fall short of providing an adequate accounting of the realities and nuances of power as it is embedded in policy, always engaged with and sometimes thwarted by the range of actors who encounter it.

Initially, anthropologists were at least partially aligned with this mainstream story, certainly with regard to official policy production. When policy studies emerged as an academic and practical enterprise in the mid-twentieth century, US political scientist Harold Lasswell (1951: 3) under-scored the "intelligence needs" of policy, that is, the need to improve "the concrete content of the information and the interpretations available to policy makers." In response to this call, and in a volume co-edited by Lasswell, anthropologists Margaret Mead (1951) and Clyde Kluckhohn (1951) argued that policy makers needed to understand *culture* in order to make good policy: both Culture (with a big "C") as a feature of the hu-man species, and culture (with a little "c") as the specific parameters of practice and meaning-making characteristic of particular groups. As an argument against abstraction—armchair policy making, as it were—and in favor of policy making based on concrete, situated knowledges of cul-tural and social realities, this provided a useful intervention, an early in-stance of applied anthropology.

This intervention has not gone out of date. Indeed, contemporary practices of fast policy transfer (Peck 2002; Peck and Theodore 2001, 2010) fly in the face of this insight by framing policies developed in one location as applicable to all locations, engaging in precisely the kind of acultural universalizing that Mead and Kluckhohn challenged. However, while recent interpretive approaches to policy, emerging in political sci-ence as well as in anthropology (Belshaw 1976; Fischer 2003; Shore and Wright 1997, 2011; Shore, Wright, and Però 2011; Wedel et al. 2005), have continued to build on Mead's and Kluckhohn's contributions, they have also turned them on their head to argue that culture does not just have an impact on how policies play out, but also the reverse: that policy is one of the key mechanisms by which we "do" culture. In this reading, while it may be the case that we need to understand culture in order to make good policy, it is also the case that we need to understand policy in order to understand culture. Policy as a mechanism for social engineering is thus itself an artifact of the social, giving lie to the belief that there ex-ists an outside-of-culture space of social scientific rationality.

From this interpretive stance, policies reflect particular kinds of knowl-edge of the problems we attend to and of how to best approach them. As such, they are charters for social action: they tell us what we need to do (Malinowski 1926; see Shore and Wright 1997). This telling, however, is built on a range of other knowledges, tacit as well as explicit, that go be-yond the brief of any specific policy to index worldviews and ideologies—that is, understandings of the nature of human being, of social interaction, and of social organization, in both actual and idealized forms. The ideo-logical agendas that mainstream policy analysts concede may influence policy (e.g., Evans 2004a, 2004b, 2004c) are accordingly seen as neither peripheral nor accidental in an interpretive framework. Instead, policy projects are envisioned as from the beginning interested and invested;

they involve constructing, rather than just responding to problems and categories of person in need of intervention (Clarke 2004; Fischer 2003; Innes 2002; Jenkins 2007; Kingfisher 2007a; Lendvai and Stubbs 2006, 2007; Shore and Wright 1997; Shore and Wright 2011; Stubbs 2005; Wedel et al. 2005). Analyses of policy must therefore begin with an examination of "the assumptions and framing of policy debates" (Wedel et al. 2005: 33)—of "its enabling discourses, mobilizing metaphors, and underlying ideologies and uses" (Wedel et al. 2005: 34)—in order to discern how policy buttresses the work of governance. In this framework, then, policy is not only an artifact and architect of cultural meaning; it is also a site of power struggles—over definitions, diagnoses, identities, the proper configuration of society, and sometimes over life and death.

These interpretive claims about the nature of policy are usefully set alongside analyses of the policy process that have discerned the *productive* aspects of what has typically been thought of as *implementation*. Observations of policy delivery in sites where policy providers meet with clients indicate that providers are not, in fact, neutral conduits through which policies flow intact and unmediated. Rather, providers' interactions with policy mandates and clients in the space between bureaucracies and target populations actually determine what policies are, in fact, in operation, certainly in terms of their particular shapes and valences. The route from policy conception to realization is, accordingly, more convoluted than direct, and the distinction between official formation and implementation less clear than some may think, or wish (e.g., Lipsky 1980; Prottas 1979; Wirth 1991; see also Freeman 2006; Jenkins 2007; Kingfisher 2001; Pressman and Wildavsky 1984). Similarly, a number of ethnographic studies with the targets of policy have shown that recipients, too, far from being the passive receptacles that seem to people official policy makers' imaginations, are actively engaged in interpreting, accommodating, resisting, and manipulating policy for their own ends (e.g., Freeman 2006; Goode 2002; Jenkins 2007; Kingfisher 1996a, 2001; Lipsky 1980; Prottas 1979; Stack 1974; Susser 1982; Valentine 1968).

These two insights—policy as a power-laden artifact and architect of culture, and policy as produced not only officially but also in myriad unofficial ways—serve to displace models of policy as rational, neutral, and acultural, as well as to trouble visions of policy as something that can be implemented in any kind of straightforward, top-down, unmediated, and transparent manner. Instead, these insights invite us to envision the life of social policy—a process rather than a thing—as complex and convoluted, tracing and leaving traces of meaning and power as it travels across sites and through persons. These tracings and traces are not accidents or imperfections—places or instances where something has gone awry, the result of incomplete or poor information—but are, rather, inherent to the policy process itself.

A Case Study

My interest in tracing policy began in the summer of 2000, when I was writing grant applications to work with welfare mothers in southern Alberta, where I had recently moved from Aotearoa/New Zealand.[1] I discovered that in the early 1990s the Alberta provincial government of premier Ralph Klein, in the process of reforming its governing structures and welfare systems, had been heavily influenced by Roger Douglas, the former finance minister of New Zealand. Douglas had been a key architect of the New Zealand Model (hereafter referred to as the NZ Model), a dramatic project of neoliberal welfare state restructuring emphasizing privatization, marketization, and personal responsibility that emerged in the 1980s and 1990s. Although awarded little scrutiny in the social science literature relative to the development and export of US and British models of restructuring, the NZ Model, given its emphasis on a simultaneously comprehensive and speedy dismantling of the welfare state, nevertheless drew the interest of proponents of structural adjustment at the IMF and World Bank, as well as of conservatives in several Western welfare states (Baker and Tippin 1999; Kelsey 1995, 1999)—including some in Canada, whose federal government had put in motion a rescaling of the welfare state beginning in the early 1990s that laid the groundwork for provincial experimentation in the organization and provision of social services. Policy elites in Alberta became particularly interested in the NZ Model as they looked externally for legitimization as well as guidance on how to approach reform. This connection became the starting point for an ethnographic exploration that took me to a range of sites in Aotearoa/New Zealand and Alberta between 2001 and 2006.

The New Zealand–Alberta story provides a particular set of theoretical and ethnographic opportunities. First, it foregrounds forms of policy travel that fall outside of the two frames that have tended to dominate scholarly analyses of policy movements across jurisdictions. In contrast to diffusionist models, which posit policy knowledge as radiating out from centers to margins—from the United States or Britain, for example, to Aotearoa/New Zealand or Australia; or from so-called developed to developing countries (for critiques, see Czarniawska and Sevón 2005; Freeman 2006; Newman 2006; Schön 1973)—the New Zealand–Alberta connection indicates that policy can also travel along the margins. If, as I argue throughout this book, policy making is a process of assemblage, then policy travels across jurisdictions will be similarly less linear and more multidirectional, polyvocal, messy, and "irrational" than diffusionist models would suggest. This connection within the periphery provides a different perspective on globalization, decentering the United States and other big policy players in our analytical imaginations, thereby allowing for a more nuanced understanding of the many players in the global emergence and circulation of neoliberal forms of governance.

The New Zealand–Alberta case also buttresses challenges to methodological nationalism (e.g., Jenkins 2007; Lendvai and Stubbs 2006; Newman 2006; Stone 2002, 2004), which envisions policy production and movement as the exclusive purview of national states. This is a problem that has plagued globalization studies in general (Sassen 2007), as well as studies of policy transfer in particular, given that, in a number of cases, neoliberal restructuring has served to devolve policy making to smaller bodies, such as, in Canada, provinces. There is, in addition, growing recognition of the importance of think tanks and independent policy experts in policy formation and travel (Dolowitz and Marsh 1996, 2000; Lendvai and Stubbs 2006; Stone 2000, 2002, 2004). The New Zealand–Alberta connection provides an instructive example in this regard: not only did policy cross national and provincial boundaries, but, given that the key agent of transfer, Roger Douglas, was no longer a New Zealand official but a private consultant at the time, policy traversed, and rendered fuzzy, the distinction between the official and the unofficial.

Further, since policy travels unfold through time, the New Zealand–Alberta story provides an opportunity to trace the temporal dimensions of policy. Less than a decade after the NZ Model found a home away from home in Alberta, the Labor-Coalition government of Helen Clark, elected in 1999, took a different route, disassembling key features of the Model. Since the election of John Key in 2008, however, the more progressive era of Helen Clark has given way to a resurrection of a form of the NZ Model, marked by both the redeployment of blame-the-victim discourses and the tabling of policy proposals that would tighten access to state support. In Alberta, in the meantime, although Ralph Klein is now long out of office, the welfare reforms his administration instituted remain firmly in place, buttressed by discourses of economic crisis and austerity even in an oil- and gas-rich province. These permutations and iterations provide an opportunity to trace how particular policy frames work themselves out in specific communities of practice over time. Given these ongoing unfoldings, moreover, the New Zealand–Alberta case also speaks to contemporary policy contexts, marked by progressively accelerated fast policy transfer in situations increasingly characterized by a frenetic sense of urgency, and in which official policy responses of the sort

I describe here are framed in terms of inevitability, as the only options possible. The New Zealand–Alberta story thus sheds light on historical patterns that continue to unfold in current policy realities.

Finally, and most generally, despite long-standing theorizations of globalization as the travel of ideas across geographic and cultural space, there are few detailed analyses of these processes with regard to policy. Studies of the movement of policy frames from one jurisdiction to another—what in mainstream policy sciences is referred to as *transfer*—come the closest to this, but, as I argue later in this chapter, the rubric of transfer is inadequate to the task. Nor do studies of transfer explore what happens to policy as it moves through various sites of policy delivery and reception; rather, they tend to confine themselves to spaces of official policy making. Analyses of global pressures on national policy making (Esping-Andersen 1996; Mishra 1999; Taylor-Gooby 2001) and cross-national comparisons of particular policy arenas (e.g., Cochrane, Clarke, and Gewirtz 2001; Daly and Rake 2003; O'Connor, Orloff, and Shaver 1996; Sainsbury 1996, 2000) similarly tend to restrict themselves to state-level analyses. In neglecting to follow policy beyond sites of official policy making through to sites of implementation and reception, these approaches, however fruitful, reveal only part of the terrain of policy travels. In this light, the New Zealand–Alberta connection provides an opportunity to empirically trace the simultaneous movement of policy up, down, and sideways.

Neoliberalism and Welfare for Poor Single Mothers

Neither unique nor aberrant, welfare state restructurings in Aotearoa/New Zealand and Alberta were in keeping with, and contributed to, wider global shifts toward neoliberal forms of governance. Emerging neoliberalisms entailed a radical departure from liberal progressive forms of governance, which conceptualized and responded to social ills structurally and collectively. Instead, they embodied forms of governance that highlighted individual causalities and decentralized and individualized remedies for social problems (Brodie 2002). Attacks on the welfare state were a central element of these projects in the advanced capitalist countries of North America, Europe, and the Pacific Rim, where government officials and neoliberal pundits constructed social provisioning as prohibitively expensive in the context of international economic competition, and the receipt of state support as disempowering of recipients in its fostering of dependence (Kingfisher 2002a). The ensuing reforms had ramifications for education, housing, health care, employment, the environment, and public versus private ownership of resources and delivery of services, among others. Although any of these would serve as an instructive empirical referent for a study of the New Zealand–Alberta connection, my focus here is on financial assistance (hereafter referred to as welfare) for poor single mothers.

I have chosen this focus for several reasons. Although seemingly gender neutral, the shift to neoliberalism entails a particular double bind for welfare mothers, who serve as a "litmus test ... of gendered social rights" (Hobson 1994: 171). In particular, in both Aotearoa/New Zealand and Alberta, welfare state restructuring brought in new rules regarding engagement in paid labor; and although the rules differed, in both cases poor single mothers were redefined as potential able-bodied workers—as unemployed rather than unemployable. Rejecting constructions of (poor) women as mothers and housewives in favor of their constitution as potential able-bodied workers (see, e.g., Kingfisher 2002b; Kingfisher and Goldsmith 2001; Mason 2003), the restructurings served to render motherhood a less acceptable reason for reliance on the state. The emphasis on employment, however, did not mean that poor single mothers were relieved of, or adequately supported in, their responsibility for their dependent children. The reforms accordingly placed welfare mothers in a double bind: they were simultaneously mothers and low-paid workers who did not have the resources to pay someone else to look after their children. My focus on welfare for poor single mothers is intended to highlight the extreme social and economic vulnerability that this double bind engenders.

It is also worth noting that, in contrast to their powerless position as a global force, poor single mothers nevertheless play a pivotal, albeit unmarked, role in global imaginaries and practices. This may seem counterintuitive. Globalization has been variously described as the increasing international interdependence of economic, political, and social forces; as the movement of finance, technology, people, and ideas across national borders; as the development of circuits of travel for technology, finance, people, and ideas that are outside of the control of national states; and as the decentering of state and interstate relations as the primary loci of activity. Poor single mothers do not leap to the forefront of any of these frames. They do not figure in the glittery high speed and high-powered transnational movements and developments applauded by pundits of globalization. Nor do they have a place in below- or above-the-state global social movements: they are not part of the antiglobalization movement, they do not demonstrate at WTO or G20 meetings, there is no poor mothers' movement akin to the global indigenous or gay movements.

However, just as the practices of high-powered businessmen are often made possible by the housewives behind the scenes who do the child care and entertaining and sustaining, so high-powered global finance and technology are made possible by territorially situated armies of low-paid and insecure workers—the metaphorical housewives of globalization who in a number of cases also happen to be actual women (Sassen 1996, 1998). Poor single mothers, then, may be seen as located in one particular space of globalization: that occupied by those who either people the ranks of low-paid labor or who are penalized for their inability to do so. The workfare ideologies and programs to which welfare mothers are subjected can thus be seen as one element of the global spread of neoliberal forms of labor market regulation; welfare reform here becomes one of the ways in which local economies are made to be more globally competitive. Thus welfare mothers are enticed/coerced into being the housewives of a global free market.

Poor single mothers are also an ideological keystone of the global travel of neoliberal constructs of the person. *Ideoscapes*, as Appadurai (1996: 36; emphasis in original) describes them, are traveling images that are "[o]ften directly political and frequently have to do with the ideologies of states and the counterideologies of movements explicitly oriented to capturing state power or a piece of it. These ideoscapes are composed of elements of the Enlightenment worldview, which consists of a chain of ideas, terms, and images, including *freedom, welfare, rights, sovereignty, representation,* and the master term *democracy*." Appadurai's focus is on a particularly positive set of keywords, to which I would add the term *individual*, which, in an Enlightenment frame, refers to the *self-possessed* (that is, sovereign) and *self-actualized* bearer of rights and participant in democracy. This model of the person is closely tied to the idea of *freedom*, which, in the context of neoliberal globalization, concerns the freedom/right to participate in markets without hindrance of state interference (Clarke 2004; see also Harvey 2005; Kingfisher and Maskovsky 2008; Smith 2007). Robertson (1992) argues in this respect that the increasing global circulation and influence of a definition of persons as self-sufficient, autonomous entities comprises a key feature of the current era of globalization. The force of this ideology is not necessarily revolutionary or liberatory, however, but may also—may, in fact, frequently—entail imposition. Workfare, as I discuss throughout this book, provides one example of the imposition of particularly pernicious forms of "individualism" and "freedom."

Thus, just as an increasingly insecure and poorly paid segment of the labor force provides the foundation for the valorized aspects of economic globalization, so the poor single mother provides the (negative) foundation for the valorized aspects of the (globalized) neoliberal individual. In the context of the increasing movement and spread of free-market forms of social and economic organization, poor single mothers in pre-reform welfare systems are retrospectively reconstructed as "dependent" on the state, and, by virtue of that dependence, as neither sovereign nor self-actualized. They represent one embodiment of the non-neoliberal subject, the nonenterprising, the non-self-sufficient (Kingfisher 2007a, 2007b); they travel as a negative image (Kingfisher 1999). The simultaneous travel of ideas of how to transform welfare mothers into ideal subjects—sovereign, independent, and free—is testimony to both the purchase and the asserted "naturalness" of the neoliberal model of the person, as well as to the labor involved in pressing such naturalness.

Neoliberalism's Ideal Self

Welfare for poor single mothers thus provides an opportunity to trace the "active society" model, a keystone of neoliberal cultural formations, as it moves, via policy, across sites and through persons. Articulated by the OECD in 1990, this approach to state-market-individual relations entailed "fostering economic opportunity and activity for everyone in order to combat poverty, dependency and social exclusion" (OECD 1990: xi, cited in Walters 1997: 224). Where the welfare society distinguishes between those who have to engage in paid labor and those who do not, in an active society framework, "the market is the only true source for satisfaction of human desires and needs, just as participation in paid employment is the key to personal fulfillment, self-development and membership in society" (Walters 1997: 224). This represents a shift away from a conception of society in which the market has a place within a larger overall scheme, and towards one in which everything has to be put into market space—in which the market *is* the overall scheme. Governments drawing on this framework accordingly work to alter both the institutional and cultural terrain of action (Larner 2000; Schwartz 1997) in an attempt to rewrite relations between state, market, and society, as well as to change individual behavior and, by extension, notions of proper personhood and citizenship.

Building on the philosophies of Friedrich Hayek and Milton Friedman, the active society model asserts that "the wellbeing of both political and social existence is to be ensured not by centralized planning and bureaucracy, but through the 'enterprising' activities and choices of autonomous entities—businesses, organizations, persons—each striving to maximize its own advantage by inventing and promoting new projects by means of individual and local calculations of strategies and tactics, costs and benefits" (Rose 1992: 145). In this framework, the person is reconfigured as an active entrepreneurial agent, an expert in making self-interested choices and mitigating risk (Dean 2007; Fairclough 1991; Heelas 1991;

Miller and Rose 2008; Rose 1992). This neoliberal, active self, "[tuned] for production ... is ... highly motivated and energized, competitive, ambitious, goal-setting and strongly oriented towards free market rewards; and underlying all these are the ideas of individual autonomy and independence" (Heelas 1991: 77).

As I have noted elsewhere (Kingfisher 2002b; see also Kingfisher and Goldsmith 2001), the neoliberal, active-society model of the person is profoundly gendered, raced, classed, and historically and culturally specific. Insofar as they challenge the supposedly natural and universal status of this construct, poor single women—as women, as poor persons, and often as either members of racialized minorities or attributed their constructed negative characteristics—become targets for reform, for efforts to remake the person. As Heelas (1991: 72) claims, "Radical government must surely go to the heart of the matter—character reform." In this sense, disciplining some, via welfare reform, provides a way of governing the whole; policing those on the margins becomes one mechanism for the construction and assertion of the normative. The harsher reforms of the 1990s instituted by the New Zealand and Alberta governments—complete with condemnations of the supposedly parasitic poor, rhetorics of responsibilization, work tests, and procedures enabling/coercing welfare recipients to engage in their own self-transformation while simultaneously providing mechanisms for the surveillance of that effort—are thus prime examples of active society approaches to the governance of the "marginalized," as opposed to the "civilized," who, in contrast, are capable of managing their own risk and therefore do not require policing and intervention (Dean 1995: 580). Later New Zealand reforms, which instituted a case management approach and highlighted the "expertise" that beneficiaries had vis-à-vis their own lives, did not represent a radical departure from this model, but rather put in place a softer version of the same trend. Here, case managers took on a pastoral role (Dean 1995: 575), assessing, guiding, counseling, and mediating.

The difference between these "harder" and "softer" approaches to welfare reform mirrors Dean's (1999: 161–62) distinction between left-leaning "active society" models that "encompass but go beyond participation in the market to include participation in other social spheres," and right-leaning "enterprise culture" models that are about the revival and extension of "the norms and values associated with the market." These two forms represent different situated articulations of neoliberalism—as a philosophy, as a cultural system, as a model for social organization, and as a mode of governance—that build on the actively and self-directedly engaged person. Neoliberal models of the independent individual thus take on different forms and valences in different contexts; there is no

Neoliberalism, but only neoliberalisms. I return to this point below with respect to the idea of a global neoliberal policy regime, but first take a detour to outline, as concepts and methods, *translation* and *assemblage*—the processes by means of which the neoliberal independent individual of the active society emerges in particular forms in particular places among particular actors.

Translation and Assemblage

Collier and Ong (2005: 11) assert that global forms—here, neoliberal approaches to welfare reform—"have a distinctive capacity for decontextualization and recontextualization, abstractability and movement, across diverse social and cultural situations and spheres of life." Such forms, they continue, "are able to assimilate themselves to new environments, to code heterogeneous contexts and objects in terms that are amenable to control and valuation" (2005: 11; see also Collier 2006: 400). How this assimilation is constructed—but also deconstructed and reconstructed—in specific contexts of engagement is the focus of this book.

Traveling policy, like globalization, is nothing new; nevertheless, it has been accelerating in recent decades to such an extent that it is now ubiquitous, almost mundane (Lendvai and Stubbs 2009). This increasingly frequent movement of policy across jurisdictions has generated a burgeoning literature devoted to its analysis. One strand of this literature, in keeping with mainstream policy science approaches, posits policy transfer as rational and technical, the artifact of systematic and deliberate learning and application (e.g., Dolowitz and Marsh 1996, 2000; Evans 2004a, 2004b, 2004c). Thus the term *transfer*. Interpretive scholars, however, whose work comprises a different and significantly smaller strand of literature on policy travels, favor the term *translation*. While both *transfer* and *translation* capture the movement involved in policy travels, they conceptualize it in profoundly different ways.

In models of transfer, policy packages are mechanically moved from one setting to another. Metaphors of conveyor belts (Lendvai and Stubs 2006: 2) and conduits (Johnson and Hagström 2011: 366) are common here: documents, institutional structures, and agents of transfer carry policies across sites the way luggage handlers and conveyor belts in airports carry suitcases from one airline to the next, sending them off to destinations across the globe. The contents of the "suitcases" are unaltered by the means by which they travel. Policy transfer thus takes on the valence of "merely telling" (Freeman 2009: 441), or, to use a different image, the recitation of recipes for exact replication. From a translation perspective, however, traveling policies are not the same as traveling suitcases, and they are not set recipes. Policies, rather, are about *ideas*, and ideas are complicated phenomena: they connect up with other ideas, have blurred boundaries, take on different valences in different contexts, shift and change. They are processes as much as things, belonging to the messy realm of human imagination and action.

The pleasure and amusement of the children's party game "telephone" is that messages change as they pass through persons: "Patty walked the dog" magically becomes "Pardon the hog." Translation approaches underscore and draw attention to precisely these kinds of changes and transformations, to the kinds of blurrings, partialities, and shifts that accompany mediated "knowing at a distance" (Freeman 2009: 430). The imagery of translation is thus not of a mechanical passing of closed suitcases from one handler to another, but instead points to the packing and repacking of the contents of suitcases as travelers, rather than handlers, move along their trajectories. Nor does translation offer up imageries of the exact replication of recipes. Rather, what is invoked is an idea of cooking—of human doing—as improvisation.

While models of transfer eschew this kind of messiness, translation approaches embrace it—not in mindless celebration of diversity, but in recognition that "messiness" provides a somewhat closer approximation to reality. In transfer approaches, as my metaphor of baggage handlers implies, people are simply carriers. In translation frameworks, in contrast, carriers are reconfigured as interested, invested actors with specific agendas who interact with similarly interested and invested actors on the "receiving" end of policy travels. Policy messages are, accordingly, *mediated* (Freeman 2009; Lendvai and Stubbs 2006, 2007, 2009; Newman 2006). In crossing boundaries—between various official and expert bodies, between themselves and texts, between institutional demands and various arenas of "real life"—participants in policy travels thus engage not only in the movement of meaning, but also in its construction (Freeman 2009: 437).

Meaning (or equivalence of meaning) is thus not prior to translation, but emerges *in* translation (Freeman 2009: 437; Lendvai and Bainton, forthcoming). This reflects, first of all, the polysemy of signs. Signs do not carry the same meaning with them everywhere they go; rather, there are shadings and specificities that have to do with local readings and local contexts—with what particular terms, ideologies, and frames are articulating with in specific cases (Clarke 2004: 37–38; see also Czarniawska and Sevón 2005; Freeman 2006, 2009; Hall 1985; Schram 2006). As Freeman (2006: 381) puts it:

The relationship between a sign and what it signifies is neither determined nor mechanical. What things mean is a matter of convention (a social construct) and it is invariably inexact. Meaning may be shared, but it is not identical. This fundamental epistemological uncertainty, this requirement that every utterance be accompanied by some hermeneutic move on the part of the reader or listener, is a source of innovation and creativity as well as error and failure. Translation—the processing of what you say into terms that I understand—is ubiquitous and imperfect.

As I explore in the following chapters, "work," "mothering," and "family" have a range of meanings that shift across time and space: constructions of "work" in Aotearoa/New Zealand, for example, did not exactly match received constructions of "work" in Alberta; and policy experts' constructions of "mothering" and "the family" in both sites were different from those of recipients. Here, the dangers involved in assuming that a word or concept means the same thing to all speakers of a language match those of translation across languages.

The emergence of meaning in translation also indexes power relations (Freeman 2009; Lendvai and Stubbs 2006, 2007; Newman 2006; Stubbs 2005). If traveling policies are marketed by agents of persuasion, then they are being marketed as better than other possibilities. Similarly, if policy experts on the receiving end of policy travels are "seekers out," then they are "actively engaged in the *production* of the technologies associated with new vocabularies of power and ... [are] creative agents in the formation of new discursive ensembles" (Newman 2006: 13; emphasis in original). While not necessarily "seekers out," those charged with implementing policy, as well as those targeted by it, are also actively engaged in the power relations constructed via translation. Lendvai and Stubbs (2007: 4) accordingly remind us, drawing on postcolonial theory, that translation is "the very working of power" (see also Lendvai and Stubbs 2009); it is not just about meaning making, but about meaning making in the interest of claims making. A similar point has been made by anthropologists reflecting on the translation work of ethnography (see, e.g., Asad 1986; Clifford 1997; Crapanzano 1986; Rubel and Rosman 2003). Given that translation "is always complicit with the building, transforming or disrupting of power relations" (Sakai 2006: 72), it is thus always worth asking, "what gets transferred, who gets to translate, and who are the losers and winners within a particular policy transfer situation" (Lendvai and Bainton, forthcoming). In sum, what is happening when policies move is a process of appropriation—a taking over, as much as a carrying over, that is intentional and productive (Freeman 2009: 434–35; see also Lendvai and Stubbs 2006: 4). In this process, new things can be created, things can be lost or erased, and meanings are rarely permanently fixed (Freeman 2009: 432; Newman 2006: 2; Stubbs 2002: 322).

The work of translation involves processes of assemblage: understanding something newly emergent in light of what is received, framing an idea from elsewhere in terms of what is known here, connecting theoretical frames and practices in new ways—all in light of an array of agendas related to making sense of the world, devising programs of action, asserting power and control, or just getting through the day. Referring simultaneously to a pieced-together formation, or constellation, and to the processes of creating linkages across sites and formations (Phillips 2006: 18), assemblage thus comprises both the activity and product of translation; it is accordingly best characterized as "heterogeneous, contingent, unstable, partial, and situated" (Collier and Ong 2005: 12; see also Olds and Thrift 2005: 271; Ong 2005). The image of *collage* (Marcus and Saka 2006: 102) is particularly useful in capturing the situatedness and specificity of assemblages, although not so useful in capturing their instability, which, to draw on a popular concept from the globalization literature (Pieterse 2009), is perhaps better indexed by the concept of *hybridity*.

Deleuze and Guattari describe the general parameters of assemblage as follows:

> On a first, horizontal, axis, an assemblage comprises two segments, one of content, the other of expression. On the one hand it is a *machinic assemblage* of bodies, of actions and passions, an intermingling of bodies reacting to one another; on the other hand it is a *collective assemblage of enunciation*, of acts and statements, of incorporeal transformations attributed to bodies. Then on a vertical axis, the assemblage has both *territorial sides*, or reterritorialized sides, which stabilize it, and *cutting edges of deterritorialization*, which carry it away (1987: 88; emphasis in original).

Although mutually constitutive, the machinic and enunciative elements of assemblages—always in-the-making, always on-the-move—can be delinked from their connection in one domain and rearticulated with machinic or expressive elements from different domains to compose new assemblages; in other words, they can be combined and recombined in myriad ways. For instance, as I discuss in more detail in chapter 4, welfare mothers disassembled the linkages between discourses of "independence" and state practices designed to move women off of welfare and into work. Instead, they imported "independence" into their own arenas, translating it into independence from men rather than from the state. The point here is that particular systems of meaning and practice, seemingly sedimented, can be actively disarticulated and rearticulated in new ways.

The axis of territorialization/deterritorialization includes both spatial and nonspatial social processes that "stabilize or destabilize the identity of the assemblage" (DeLanda 2006: 19). In being lifted from Aotearoa/New Zealand and rearticulated in Alberta, the NZ Model is simultaneously reinforced and stabilized, via its spread and currency, and destabilized, as bits and pieces are disarticulated and either left behind or rearticulated with bits and pieces of other formations in new and different ways. Similarly, when providers and recipients draw on the shared meanings, stories, and categories of their interpersonal networks (DeLanda 2006: 56–57) to engage with policy, they do so in ways that both reinforce and threaten policy mandates and their underlying philosophies.

Together, *assemblage* and *translation* point to the cut-and-paste processes of piecing together that are involved as policies travel up, down, and sideways. It would be a mistake, however, to envision these processes as involving freewheeling cutting-and-pasting by sovereign agents in completely open and unconstrained environments populated by unmoored, empty signifiers. Nor are translation and assemblage haphazard, as my reference to the children's game "telephone" might imply. Although fluid and unstable, translation and assemblage are also constrained. Signs and practices can be disarticulated and set off on travels in any number of directions, and policy assemblages can indeed represent cut-and-paste experimentation, but what and how things are translated, cut-and-pasted, and experimented with is not completely arbitrary. There are always parameters, not the least of which is history: in this case, the history of how poverty and poor people have been conceptualized, of how social welfare systems have been structured, of how human nature has been characterized, and of economic practices. At the same time, constraints are not uniformly or predictably deterministic: "Structures exhibit tendencies— lines of force, openings and closures which constrain, shape, channel and in that sense 'determine.' But they cannot determine in the harder sense of fix absolutely, guarantee" (Hall 1985: 96). There may be tendencies, in other words, but they tell us more about past structures than about exactly where current practices and movements will lead (Hall 1986a: 41). Scholars of assemblage theory tend to agree with this orientation, underscoring the profound creativity and unpredictability of processes of assemblage (e.g., Deleuze and Guattari 1987; Marcus and Saka 2006; Ong and Collier 2005; Venn 2006), even in the face of both constraint and the propensity of traces of what came before to reemerge (Hall 1985: 111). It might be most useful, then, to think of processes of translation and assemblage as occurring within contexts that are simultaneously constraining and enabling—that is, within certain parameters the contours of which may be shifted via the very processes of assemblage.

Freeman's (2007) discussion of policy production as bricolage points precisely to such constraints and enablements. In analyzing how policy makers interpret how they engage in the knowledge construction on which policy formation is based, Freeman outlines the complex ways in which different theories of learning—rationalist, organizational, and constructivist—come into play simultaneously and in overlapping fashion in real-life policy-making situations. He accordingly positions policy makers as Lévi-Straussian bricoleurs, and policy as "put together," assembled from different bits and pieces, from different times and places, on the basis of a range of sometimes competing, sometimes overlapping epistemological frames—basically, a working with, building on, and making do with what is available. The *working with* is about possibility and creativity, while the *what is available* points to constraint.

Within these parameters of possibility and limitation, policy assemblages—like the translations of which they are composed—are always about one vision of persons and society as opposed to others, about one proposed solution to problems among myriad possibilities. In this sense, policy translation and assemblage represent attempts at hegemony—a cobbling together of practices and meanings with the goal of creating some kind of common sense regarding the nature of persons, the state, the market, or social support. Policy travels—translations and assemblages—are accordingly about power travels, whether with respect to officials and experts attempting to devise workable forms of governance, or to providers and recipients accommodating policy mandates or "talking back," constructing counterhegemonies.

In sum, in contrast to the mechanistic and abstract metaphor of *transfer*, which only minimally situates policy travels in the social, *translation* and *assemblage* provide entry points into the rich complexity of ethnographic realities in which participants interact to jointly construct, assert, struggle over, challenge, and modify particular readings of their worlds. Far from positing reasoned linearity or uncontested top-down imposition, they invite us to theorize policy production as piecemeal, always in the making, and always about unfolding and shifting struggle.

Convergence and Divergence, Neoliberalism and Its Limits: Global Policy Regimes Revisited

When applied to neoliberalism—as cultural system, governing practice, or policy regime–the theoretical and methodological frameworks of translation and assemblage serve to position it as an activity rather than as a finished product. In addition, neoliberalism is theorized as unfolding in specific, already-inhabited contexts, and as thus always already articulating with other cultural formations. Although it may be characterized by a particular "grammar" (Kingfisher 2002b), this grammar is constantly "disarticulating and rearticulating, disjunctive and contradictory" (Kingfisher and Maskovsky 2008: 120). Neoliberalism's existence thus takes shape only in the fluid and multiple translations on which it depends for its movement, and it accordingly rarely realizes its totalizing desires (Kingfisher and Maskovsky 2008; Maskovsky and Kingfisher 2001; see also Kingfisher 2002c). Since various neoliberal assemblages "cannot be analytically reduced to cases of a uniform global condition of 'Neoliberalism' writ large" (Ong 2006: 14; see also Collier and Ong 2005: 12), we are enjoined to attend to concrete specificities—to avoid taking the so-called global neoliberal policy regime for granted, and to instead treat it as something that "needs to be explained in particular places and with reference to particular peoples, territories, states and cultural formations" (Kingfisher and Maskovsky 2008: 123–24). The New Zealand–Alberta case provides just such an opportunity for analysis of particular unfoldings and articulations—unfoldings and articulations, moreover, that I argue simultaneously buttress and trouble ideas and practices of a global neoliberal policy regime.

In policy studies, the question of homogenization and heterogeneity that runs through the globalization literature is reframed to ask whether the increasing global circulation of policy elites working to create a singular vision of state, society, and individuals is producing global policy convergence (sometimes referred to as *harmonization*); or whether, in contrast, we are witnessing hybridizations and mélanges reflective of unique local cultural conditions—that is, divergence. Are any such differences really only variations on a theme, or are they serious differences of the sort that preclude the possibility of a frame that we can with confidence refer to as a global neoliberal policy regime? It is important here to think of convergence and divergence not only in reference to policy travels across jurisdictions, but also in relation to the range of engagements with policy that happen in sites of policy implementation and reception. These are also sites of convergence and divergence that contribute to, or undermine, the consolidation of policy regimes.

On the one hand, if policy production and travel entail translation and assemblage, convergence is impossible. Insofar as the concept of translation "attracts attention to the fact that a thing moved from one place to another cannot emerge unchanged"—that "to set something in a new place is to construct it anew" (Czarniawska and Sevón 2005: 8)—we are enjoined to recognize policy travels as entailing processes of transformation rather than replication. Johnson and Hagström (2011: 372; emphasis in original) go so far as to claim that translation "does not—*cannot*—lead to convergence, standardization or uniformity in any absolute sense." Similarly, Lendvai and Stubbs (2007: 175) indicate that "a series of interesting, and sometimes even surprising, disturbances can occur in the spaces between the 'creation,' the 'transmission' and the 'interpretation' or 'reception' of policy meanings." On the other hand, in tracing the emergence, travel, and various articulations of the NZ Model in Aotearoa/New Zealand and Alberta, I encountered some remarkable convergences: convergences in the social constructions that informed reform policies in both Aotearoa/New Zealand and Alberta, convergences in how providers in both sites approached policy, and convergences in how recipients in two small cities on opposite sides of globe translated and assembled knowledges of policy, men, work, and parenting. These convergences were in some cases so close that terms and concepts were not just shared, but almost identical in meaning and the uses to which they were put (cf. Freeman 2006: 381). Some of these convergences reflect the near hegemony of neoliberal models of the person, while others index particular bureaucratic arrangements and structures of interaction.

Throughout this book, then, I situate my analysis in the spaces of in-betweenness where convergence and divergence are negotiated and produced: between Aotearoa/New Zealand and Alberta, between policy mandates and providers, between providers and recipients. In so doing, I endeavor to draw attention to the ongoing tensions between similarity and difference, providing an opportunity to step outside of an either/or binary and into the complexities of a both/and reality. My argument, in other words—despite the emphasis on transformation, hybridity, mélange, and improvisation afforded by the theoretical frameworks of translation and assemblage—is that we need to always also attend to patterns of replication and reproduction.

Situating Translation and Assemblage: Outline of a Travelogue

In the following chapters, I use the frames of translation and assemblage to gain insight into a range of policy-related phenomena in particular spaces and contexts of occurrence. First, I explore the transformation of objects as they are moved from one philosophical and political framework—Keynesianism—into another—neoliberalism. Brodie (2002:100) points out in this regard that the privatization characteristic of neoliberalism "involves much more than simply removing things from one sector and placing them in another. ... the thing moved is itself transformed into something quite different. Objects become differently understood and regulated." Translation, then, occurs as new governing frameworks emerge at particular historical junctures to transform how the world is constructed. This means that we need to attend to translation and assemblage across time as well as space. In both Aotearoa/New Zealand and Alberta, old models were transformed into new ones as objects—poverty, mothering, work, the poor—were retranslated in the light of new knowledges, new understandings of the nature of being human and of how the world operates, or should operate. Second, I explore translation as it occurred in the spaces through which the NZ Model moved from Aotearoa/New Zealand to Alberta, focusing specifically on the selectivity and power plays engaged in by the various players on both sides.

These two lines of exploration provide the frame for chapter 1, in which I focus on official policy production, tracing it though policy documents, community service reports, media, and scholarly reflection and analysis. I explore the emergence of the NZ Model in Aotearoa/New Zealand, its travel from Aotearoa/New Zealand to Alberta, and the outcomes of this travel for policy formation in Alberta as processes of translation and assemblage across both time and space. Situating the emergence of the NZ Model in Aotearoa/New Zealand and its indigenization in Alberta in the context of the unique welfare histories and cultural formations of each site, as well as in relation to the agendas of those both selling and seeking out the NZ Model, I focus on the transformations that inevitably accompany policy travels and explore the simultaneous construction of divergence and convergence with respect to a global neoliberal policy regime.

My goal, however, is to "study through" (Reinhold 1994; Wedel et al. 2005; Wright and Reinhold 2011)—to "follow the policy" (Shore and Wright 2011: 12; Peck and Theodore 2012)—by holistically combining insights into the processes of official policy production with analyses of its implementation and reception. With this agenda in mind, I devote the remainder of my travelogue to the translation and assemblage work of welfare providers, community service providers, and welfare recipients. Each group, situated differently in circuits of policy, possesses different kinds of knowledge of policy and of the worlds it attempts to reflect and construct. Each also has different degrees of and zones of power in which to affect things. Each group thus interacts with policy in unique ways, translating and assembling it in light of their own knowledges, experiences, and agendas. Johnson and Hagström (2011: 384) accordingly point out that "[t]ranslation processes generally operate on several levels simultaneously: in the interaction between individuals at micro level; within the framework of individual organizations and in the interaction at meso level; and under the influence of various economic, political, and sociocultural structures at macro level."

In chapters 2 through 4, then, I move to more territorially solid spaces of policy production: welfare offices, community service organizations, and the lives of poor single mothers. I chose as my research sites two small cities: Kingston, in Aotearoa/New Zealand; and Riverview, in Alberta.[2] Neither site is a metropolitan center—Kingston has a population of roughly 120,000 and Riverview 90,000—and neither is a location of official policy making. Situating myself in Riverview and Kingston thus provided an opportunity to address a gap in the policy and welfare reform literature related to scale by exploring how policies constructed in urban centers articulate in midsize centers. This focus serves to balance the prevailing emphases on large metropolitan areas in current research on neoliberalism and restructuring.

In chapter 2, I focus on the work of policy providers employed in the Riverview and Kingston welfare offices. As the executors of policy, welfare providers are the means by which new policy practices and the ideas informing them are put into place. Located in the borderland between the bureaucracy and the population it is designed to serve (and police), welfare providers are situated differently from policy elites, who neither interact directly with clients nor administer policy; they thus have different kinds of knowledges of how the welfare bureaucracy operates and of some of the determining features and vicissitudes of clients' lives. Providers translate policy mandates in light of these knowledges, assembling approaches to policy and to their clients that reflect the articulation of policy with the requirements of their institutional locations. These assemblages depart from as much as replicate official mandates and frameworks.

Circuits of policy movement and translation are composed not only of government elites and official providers, however, but also of an unofficial, amorphous constellation of providers working in a range of nongovernmental organizations. Occupying a different kind of in-between space than welfare providers, community service providers assist clients in navigating the welfare bureaucracy and provide extra social and material support in an attempt to fill in the gaps left by deficient systems of official provision. In chapter 3, then, I explore community service providers' translations of welfare policy in the context of their institutional and societal locations. These locations provide unique positionings vis-à-vis both the state and welfare clients, offering different kinds of knowledge that articulate with agendas that serve to simultaneously criticize and buttress state interests.

Finally, in chapter 4, I turn to the translation and assemblage work of poor single mothers, exploring their engagements with dominant ideas embedded in policy concerning work, motherhood, independence, poverty, and the proper configurations of person, state, and society. I emphasize the women's uneven, contradictory articulation of the claims informing welfare reform and workfare, as they interact with policy on the basis of their own knowledges of parenting, employment, and relationships with men, coupled with the various (and often contradictory) interpretations of policy they receive from welfare and community service providers. I explore in particular how poor single mothers translated even that which they absorbed most uncritically (ideas about independent individuality, and about women's role as mothers) in ways reflective of their situated knowledges, in the process transforming the objects of absorption into something slightly, and, in some cases, radically different from what was intended by policy makers.

A Few Small but Important Caveats

The sequence I follow, from "horizontal" (Aotearoa/New Zealand to Alberta) to "vertical" (official policy-making centers, to welfare and community service providers, to recipients), and from more to less powerful actors simultaneously replicates and troubles top-down models of policy formation and implementation. It replicates them by following official lines of authority and dissemination, tracing policy as it is produced by powerful government actors and a range of policy experts and then administered by authorized agents of the state or of nongovernmental organizations, being received, finally, by supplicants for support. But in so tracing the movement of policy, top-down models are turned on their heads as various actors—officially authorized and not—not only replicate but sometimes also transform what they are receiving and transmitting. As it moves through various points of connection, then, policy shifts, such that at sites of "reception" its resemblance to "origins" reflects not intact replication, but instead ranges from family resemblance to diametric opposition.

Nor is the sequencing of chapters meant to indicate that national and provincial scales operate separately from—or, for that matter, unproblematically encompass—those of welfare and community service offices or of recipients' lives. There are temporal processes at work, to be sure, as new policy frames travel, but translation and assemblage are also ongoing processes occurring simultaneously at all scales, even as the translation and assemblage work of some players, at some scales, counts for more. Since movement itself tends to remains elusive, leaving us to work with traces of movement (Strathern 2004: 17), I have arranged the following chapters in a way that I think best allows for tracking processes of translation and assemblage that award agency to interlocutors while simultaneously situating them in the institutional and discursive universes within which they operate.

Finally, rather than providing a complete accounting of neoliberal welfare reform in its totality, my goal is to follow specific lines of thought and practice, traveling both historically and contemporarily to provide a few modest insights into how policy is made and lived. A handful of key bits and pieces of the story of welfare reform in Aotearoa/New Zealand and Alberta provide my mechanism for doing this. Thus I do not wish to give the impression that I intend to locate and delineate an original or singular source for global neoliberal welfare reform; neoliberalism was not born in Aotearoa/New Zealand, and both the New Zealand and Alberta governments drew on a number of schools of thought and practice, including those emanating from the United Kingdom and the United States, in designing their restructured welfare states. Nor is it my goal to exhaustively explain welfare reform in either Aotearoa/New Zealand or Alberta. Rather, I focus on a specific set of connections between Aotearoa/New Zealand and Alberta that provide a unique entry point into policy travels, emphasizing in the process various middle grounds—between the two sites, between previous welfare regimes and emerging ones, between gender regimes, between providers and the women they work with, and between women, men, and welfare systems. My focus, therefore, is on lines of articulation, and on heterogeneous and multiple forms, iterations, and manifestations of aspects of neoliberal welfare reform. This approach resonates with Deleuze and Guattari's (1987: 21) rhizomic analysis:

> Unlike trees or their roots, the rhizome connects any point to any other point, and its traits are not necessarily linked to traits of the same nature; it brings into play very different regimes of signs, and even nonsign states. The rhizome is reducible neither to the One nor the multiple. It is not the One that becomes Two or even directly three, four five, etc. It is not a multiple derived from the One, or to which One is added (n + 1). It is composed not of units but of dimensions, or rather directions in motion. It has neither beginning nor end, but always a middle (milieu) from which it grows and which it overspills. ... The rhizome operates by variation, expansion, conquest, capture, offshoots.

Rhizomes have multiple entryways and have neither genetic axes nor deep structures (1987: 12). If the interest is in the ontological status of a global policy regime, then the New Zealand–Alberta case provides one entry point (rather than a final answer). Structure—by which I mean some kind of organizational form and direction, rather than something absolutely determining and eternal—is emergent, heterogeneous, and always improvisational (see, e.g., Marcus and Saka 2006; Venn 2006).

And in these points-along-lines-of-connection that I explore here—the movement of policy frames from Aotearoa/New Zealand to Alberta, the translations and assemblages of policy made by various providers and poor single mothers—I am interested in dimensions and directions in motion. The *milieu* to which Deleuze and Guattari refer is about the middle, the in-between, but also about the environment: the conditions of possibility, the context, the air, that gives rise to and is produced by, in this case, neoliberal welfare reform, its permutations, and its limits.

This approach—tracing and following through particular threads while eschewing any attempt to provide a final, comprehensive, and thus closed analysis—serves to best capture the social life of policy as ongoing, open, and emergent translation and assemblage.

Notes

1. Throughout this book, I use *Aotearoa/New Zealand* when referring broadly to a place and a social system that includes, while simultaneously marking a tension between, both Maori and Pakeha (European) cultural formations, and *New Zealand* when referring more narrowly to the state and its practices.
2. Throughout this book I use pseudonyms for towns, community service organizations, and research participants. Although statistical and sociodemographic data are accurate, sources of official documents and reports on Riverview and Kingston have also been disguised.

Chapter 1

THE NEW ZEALAND MODEL
AT HOME AND ABROAD

∞

How do "new" policy concepts take on different inflections
as they are enrolled into different politico-cultural contexts
or governmental projects? (Newman 2006: 14)

The first "stop" in my travelogue is the NZ Model of welfare state restructuring. How was the NZ Model assembled at home, in Aotearoa/New
Zealand? How was it then globalized and asserted as common sense in
the context of Alberta's welfare state restructuring? I begin by tracing the
temporal travel of ideas in both places, outlining historical foundations as
a mechanism for the diagnosis of continuity and change. This approach
underscores the important (if somewhat obvious) point that policy shifts,
however dramatic, have historical antecedents; new policy regimes do not
so much replace previous ones as layer on top of them (Belgrave 2004: 38;
see also Thomson 1991). As I describe in more detail below, for instance,
historically entrenched gender regimes in Aotearoa/New Zealand and
Alberta had enormous impact on the shape of the neoliberal welfare reforms that policy elites in each place were able to launch in the 1980s and
1990s. Thus neither the NZ Model nor the reformed regime in Alberta
represented something entirely novel; rather, both were assemblages, cut-
and-pasted from the old, the new, and the elsewhere in an effort to graft,
in unique ways, contemporary agendas onto received systems of meaning
and structure.

Second, I trace the geographic travel of policy frames from Aotearoa/ New Zealand to Alberta. In working to capture the translation and assemblage work involved in that cross-national, cross-cultural enterprise, I tell two stories. The first is about how the NZ Model, as it was articulated by former New Zealand finance minister Roger Douglas, was used by the Klein administration to buttress and justify its intentions to push an already-existing approach to poor relief to its logical extremes. Evidently, the trends towards individualization and decollectivization characteristic of neoliberal forms of governance (Bourdieu 1999, 2003) are not necessarily replicated at the level of governments themselves, where attempted consolidation and convergence, as opposed to national uniqueness, seem to be the goal. In this sense, the felicitous congruence between the NZ Model and the Klein administration's desired pathway served as a building block of an emerging global neoliberal policy regime. At the same time, however, while some things traveled well from Aotearoa/New Zealand to Alberta, others did not. Far from straightforward and comprehensive, the translation of the NZ Model in Alberta was in fact partial and piecemeal, marked by tensions between convergence and divergence. Thus the very effort to produce policy harmonization simultaneously served to undercut its possibility, at least in any total sense. This is the second story.

The New Zealand Model

I begin with the shifts in Aotearoa/New Zealand from which Roger Douglas drew in writing his sales manuals—*There's Got to Be a Better Way!* (1980) and *Unfinished Business* (1993a)—and in constructing his sermons on reform for his Alberta audiences.

History

The dismantling of the New Zealand welfare state that began with the election of the Fourth Labour government in 1984 engendered profound dislocations in the social order and extreme hardship for many. This disassembling, however, built on already-existing social tensions. Despite romantic constructions of pre-1984 Aotearoa/New Zealand as a comprehensive cradle-to-grave welfare state, the New Zealand welfare state never "attained a rights-based welfare system" (Rudd 1993: 231): certain programs were always means tested, and there was always an undercurrent of public resentment for the "undeserving" poor. The post-1984 changes are thus most appropriately theorized as continuation, as well as rupture.

Up until the mid-nineteenth century, poor relief in Aotearoa/New Zealand was limited to charitable aid. Various ordinances introduced in the second half of the century[1] were skeletal in nature, providing mechanisms for placing official responsibility for the poor onto family members, and for the coordination of nongovernmental charitable aid agencies. The story of the New Zealand welfare state from the late nineteenth century to 1984 is one of struggles over which groups were eligible, or deserving, of aid, coupled with a gradual, albeit uneven, widening of the state safety net. Supports targeting mothers were first instituted in the 1911 Widows' Pension Act, with mothers whose husbands had deserted being made eligible in 1936. In 1938, on the heels of the Depression, the First Labour government introduced the Social Security Act, altering the scale of welfare provisioning by situating it as a centralized, national enterprise. Administered through the new Social Security Department, the Act "sought universal coverage for all relevant citizens ... [including] the elderly, widows, orphans, children, invalids, minors, the sick, the unemployed, those who had fought in the Land Wars [between Pakeha (European) and Maori], and an emergency benefit" (O'Brien and Wilkes 1993: 53–54). Deserted mothers were included in the category of widows with children, and never-married mothers sought assistance under the provisions of the emergency benefit.

The support of deserted and never-married mothers via the widows' benefit and the amorphous emergency benefit served to buttress a moral hierarchy, based on relationships with men, in which widows were at the top, followed by deserted wives, and then, at the bottom, the unmarried mothers for whom specific, named provisions were not instituted until 1973 (Beaglehole 1994: 83; Belgrave 2004; McClure 1998; Nolan 2000).[2] Thus the situation of poor single mothers through most of the twentieth century was marked by "poverty, dependence and powerlessness" (Beaglehole 1993: 30). This changed after the 1972 Royal Commission of Inquiry into Social Security called for increased state involvement in securing the needs of citizens, heralding a shift from absolute to relative poverty, and from the relief of destitution to the facilitation of participation in society. The government responded by consolidating a range of provisions previously grouped under the rubric of "domestic purposes benefit" (which included the emergency benefit and other benefits for women without male providers), into the statutory (as opposed to discretionary) Domestic Purposes Benefit (DPB), a means-tested program that provided poor single mothers with sufficient resources to be able to stay at home to look after their children until the youngest turned eighteen years of age.

Two patterns that mark the history of the New Zealand welfare state— the male breadwinner model and the tension between individualism and the collectivism—are crucial to situating the DPB. The New Zealand welfare state was built not on a foundation of income maintenance and social security, but on the "family wage" and full male employment (Shirley and St. John 1997: 39; see also Castles 1985; Schwartz 2000). In this model, women were not considered primary breadwinners, and so the family wage did not apply to them.[3] Instead, they were to be homemakers and mothers, financially dependent on their husbands' wages. Retaining the idea that women's primary role was as mothers, the DPB shifted the locus of support for mothering from men to the state.

This gendered division of labor sat alongside a tension between the individual and the collective in the societal assignment of responsibility for well-being that built on a distinction between the "deserving" and the "undeserving." Morally fit and industrious persons were by definition able to take care of themselves—if not directly, then through the efforts of husbands or other relatives. Only those who were unable to look after themselves for reasons out of their control were considered deserving of collective—that is, state and societal—sympathy and assistance. From the very beginning, then, debates about provisioning were marked by the fear that too-generous assistance would encourage parasitic tendencies (McClure 1998; O'Brien and Wilkes 1993). This deserving/undeserving distinction played out in relation to Maori as well as single mothers more generally, articulating a hierarchy of gendered morality with race relations to produce a history of unequal access for Maori, who had always been more scrutinized and vilified by both the state and dominant Pakeha society, who always had to accommodate Pakeha culture in their practices (rather than vice versa), and who consistently received lower welfare benefits than Pakeha through the first half of the twentieth century.[4] (Although the history of Pacific Island and immigrant women's relationship to welfare in Aotearoa/New Zealand has yet to be written, I suspect that it in many ways parallels that of Maori).

Over the years, the place occupied by poor single mothers[5] in the Aotearoa/New Zealand imagination has shifted: from morally bankrupt prior to the institutionalization of the DPB, to "responsible and courageous" (McClure 2004: 150) in the late 1960s and early 1970s, to, in the late 1970s and early 1980s, lazy and likely to cheat the system (McClure 1998: 2004).[6] Significantly, debates surrounding the DPB were in part debates concerning the relative moral statuses and rights of stay-at-home mothers in two-parent families, stay-at-home mothers on the benefit, and employed single mothers. Interestingly, as Nolan (2000: 270–73, 289–96) points out, and as my own data support, what was *not* at issue was whether mothering was women's primary role, or whether mothering constituted "work." As I discuss below, this maternalist cultural orientation had a significant impact on the particular form of workfare-related measures put into place during the reforms of the 1980s and 1990s. It was also, as I will show, lost in translation when the NZ Model traveled to Alberta.

Although the NZ "cradle-to-grave" welfare state never existed for some—particularly for Maori men in terms of full employment, and for Maori (and, I would suspect, Pacific Island and immigrant) women under pre-DPB discretionary regimes—and despite the moral controversies surrounding the DPB, for over a decade in Aotearoa/New Zealand poor single mothers had official access to a source of support that, from the vantage point of the mid-1990s, was quite generous: enough money (even if barely enough) to support themselves and their children, and state-subsidized housing and health care. Single mothers were able to (more or less) adequately care for their children, and some were even able to purchase homes and pursue tertiary education. By the mid-1980s, in other words, there was something to lose.

The particular lines of tension that run through the New Zealand welfare state indicate that its history is less one of steady evolutionary progress and more one of ongoing struggle; it was, in any case, far from a paradise of universal inclusivity. These tensions also indicate that the reforms of the 1980s and 1990s, albeit in many ways abrupt, built on philosophical and social strains that had historical resonance. Significantly, and in addition to fears about the moral status and behavior of single mothers, indications of concern about "public sector overload" were already present by the late 1970s (Bertram 1993), even though the discourse of reform did not emerge fully until the mid-1980s, and the material manifestations of that philosophical orientation took shape only in the early 1990s.

Tensions in New Zealand's welfare history also signal that assemblage is part and parcel of the policy-making process in general, rather than something that is unique to the kinds of travels exemplified by the New Zealand–Alberta case. At the very least, policy making involves struggle, as different voices vie for primacy of place; the outcomes of policy-making processes, as well as of policy applications, will thus always carry traces of those struggles and their (temporary, and often unstable) settlements. Thus the NZ Model, to which I now turn, was a composite—not only of historical trajectories and struggles, but also of various globalized localisms: the New Zealand state had a long history of turning to the United Kingdom for governing frameworks, and (neo)liberal economic models as well as discourses of welfare state reform emanating from the United States and the United Kingdom had an impact on the thinking of the New Zealand reformers (Belgrave 2004; Bertram 1993; McClure 2004). The NZ Model, in other words, drew on a range of approaches and practices in circulation at the time of its emergence. Nevertheless, in order to avoid an infinite regress of travels and hybridizations, where everything is everywhere and nowhere, in what follows I avoid detailed analyses of the "elsewhere's" in the NZ Model, and focus, rather, on the configurations of the model itself.

Crisis and Retrenchment: 1984 on

The Fourth Labor government inherited a highly regulated and protected economy that was in crisis. Protectionism, dependency on primary exports, increasing foreign debt, low growth, high inflation, and the insulation of large segments of the population from the vagaries of the market via universal employment and social programs were all held up to scrutiny, and all declared unsustainable (Belgrave 2004; Boston 1993; Kingfisher and Goldsmith 2001; Larner 1997; McClure 1998). In response, Roger Douglas, the new finance minister, assembled what came to be known as *Rogernomics*, an approach to economic restructuring focused on trade liberalization, deregulation of the economic and financial sectors, and the selling of state assets to local and international interests (Boston 1993; Jesson 1987; see also Easton 1997, 1999; Kelsey 1993, 1995, 1999; Larner 1997; Shirley and St. John 1997). A response to fiscal imperatives, Rogernomics reflected the increasing purchase of a range of public sector management theories that drew on aspects of market-oriented thinking and fed a "general ideological shift to the right" (Boston 1991: 1; see also McClure 1998). Rogernomics did not just appropriate bits and pieces of neoliberal philosophies of marketization, however; rather, it grafted these onto social democratic thought, claiming that efficiencies generated by an infusion of market principles in the public sector would benefit the wider community. Thus Treasury's briefing to the incoming government in 1984, *Economic Management*, paired equity with efficiency to claim that, "[i]f social objectives are to be achieved, improved economic performance is critical" (New Zealand Treasury 1984: 119; see Larner 1997 for detailed analysis of this document). Reflecting both divisions within caucus and popular sentiment (Belgrave 2004; Boston 1993; McClure 1998), Rogernomics nevertheless delinked the economic from the social in its governing practices, leaving social policy for the most part alone (Boston 1993; Kelsey 1995; Larner 1997; Schwartz 2000; Shirley and St. John 1997). It thus articulated practical conditions (or, particular readings of them) and philosophical and policy preferences in a unique assemblage.

Delinking, however, did not mean that the social remained untouched by economic restructuring. In selling off state-owned enterprises, for instance, the government removed itself from the business of creating jobs that had served to disguise unemployment (Schwartz 2000: 94). This fundamentally altered the labor market, which, in turn, dramatically increased pressures on welfare programs, so that, by 1989, "the state was supporting more rather than less of the community" (McClure 1998: 228). Rogernomics thus had profound negative implications for Labour's agenda of social democracy: recession, inflation (which jumped to 15.3 percent in 1985–86), and booming unemployment (which doubled between 1984 and 1990) left more and more people with less (Boston 1993; Shirley and St. John 1997). Median incomes declined by an astounding 19.2 percent between 1982 and 1991, by which time 611,000 people (17.8 percent of the population) found themselves living in poverty (Kelsey 1995: 275). Maori were particularly hard hit by unemployment, with 20 percent losing their jobs between 1987 and 1989, and unemployment for Maori between the ages of fifteen and twenty-four hitting 40 percent (double the rate for non-Maori) by 1991 (Shirley and St. John 1997: 44). As jobs dwindled, increasing numbers of single parents were forced to turn to the DPB (McClure 1998: 228).

The delinking of the economic from the social was, therefore, imaginary (Shirley and St. John 1997); marketization, once started, shifted the terrain within which actors—individual, organizational, and governmental—operated (Larner 1997). Thus while Labour did not engage with welfare policy directly, its economic policies, and their fallouts, laid the groundwork for the changes to social policy made by the National government that followed. This groundwork, moreover, went beyond the practical repercussions of economic restructuring to include valorizations of liberalization, deregulation, marketization, and privatization that entailed shifts in the very grounds of personhood and citizenship. Most notable here was a move from a focus on taxpayers (an identity that can work to bolster a shared sense of community), and unemployment (the prevention of which was formerly constructed as the job of the state), to a focus on the "consumer" (Larner 1997; Larner and Walters 2000). In this new frame, deregulation was couched in terms of reduced costs for consumers as opposed to better use of taxpayers' contributions, and unemployment was framed as the price to be paid in order to meet the needs of consumers for lower costs (although it was argued that this would eventually lead to economic growth, which would take care of unemployment). Society—formerly a collectivity—was reconfigured into a collection of individuals, each an active agent and expert in making self-interested choices and mitigating risk. Thus *Economic Management,* in which Treasury advocated for "maximum welfare gain at minimum cost" (New Zealand Treasury 1984: 250), argued, first, that "[i]n general, efficiently functioning markets can be expected to maximize opportunities for welfare gains;" and second, that "in general individuals ... can pursue their own interests satisfactorily, or at least as well as others could do for them" (1984: 251). The implication was that individual freedom of choice, as opposed to government interference and paternalism, would lead to the best possible outcomes (1984: 253; see also Peters 1997). Although *Economic Management* did not specifically address the DPB, it foregrounded targeting, claiming that "[o]ften assistance does not go to those for whom it is intended, or does not go to those with the greatest need," and calling for "urgent attention to better targeting and more efficient and more cost-effective policy implementation" (New Zealand Treasury 1984: 255).

When National was elected in 1990, Finance Minister Ruth Richardson explicitly relinked the economic and the social by applying market principles directly to social policy (Shirley and St. John 1997: 47; Schwartz 2000). Changes to social policy included in Richardson's 1991 budget—popularly referred to as "the mother of all budgets," or "Ruthanasia"—entailed major cuts to the value of welfare benefits, tighter targeting and eligibility requirements, the introduction of user fees for health care services, and the virtual elimination of housing subsidies (Belgrave 2004: 37; Waldegrave and Frater 1996: 163): means-tested programs were made meaner, and universal programs were severely undercut. DPB rates for a single adult with one child were reduced by $25.00/week—no small amount when situated in the wider context of simultaneous cuts to health care and housing assistance programs. Taken together, these changes led to the proliferation of food banks, and to dramatic increases in morbidity, crime, and suicide (Kelsey 1993; Shirley and St. John 1997). Kelsey (1995: 277) refers specifically to a "deepening [of] the feminisation of poverty;" and Dobbin (1995) indicates that among women, Maori and Pacific Islanders were particularly disadvantaged.

Although on one level systematic, Ruthanasia, like Rogernomics, entailed as much cut-and-paste experimentation as "rational" and "evidence-based" policy making. Kelsey (1995: 278) notes in this regard that "[t]he level of benefit cuts in 1991, supposedly designed to increase incentives, was pure guesswork by the Treasury. The Minister of Social Welfare admitted that decisions on benefit levels were based on instinct and expediency, not empirical research.... Important decisions ... were being made with inadequate data and no monitoring of their impact." Indeed, it was not until 1994 that the Department of Welfare decided to conduct research "as to whether beneficiaries receive enough money to live on" (1995: 278), and it was not until the late 1990s that benefit levels got back to what the 1972 Royal Commission on Social Security described as subsistence level (Boston, Dalziel, and St. John 1999: 301).

Finally, in 1996, the Tax Reduction and Social Policy Bill introduced work tests and work preparation requirements for DPB beneficiaries. Under the new policies, beneficiaries had to make themselves available for fifteen hours of work per week once their youngest child reached seven years of age; when the youngest child turned fourteen, work availability was increased to thirty hours a week. "Availability" meant that beneficiaries had to be willing to take any job offered to them, on penalty of losing their benefits. In 1998, the government tightened work test/work preparation requirements, and also mailed a "Code of Social and Family Responsibility" to every household in the country. The Code, which emphasized individual and family responsibility for economic, social, and physical well-being, supported the government's general approach to state-citizen relations, as well as its specific approach to welfare, clearly articulating the shifts in governance inaugurated by Rogernomics and Ruthanasia. This regime remained in place until the election of Helen Clark in 1999.

Cultural Shifts, or, the Return of the Repressed

The set of changes ushered in by Rogernomics and Ruthanasia—moves from relative back to absolute poverty, reconceptualizations of government (there should be less of it), retheorizations of poverty and inequality (it is the fault of those who suffer from it), and reconstitutions of personhood (as ideally individual and self-sufficient)—entailed two discursive shifts. The first was a move from discourses of state intervention to market discourses of efficiency, flexibility, and competition. This was then coupled with a shift from discourses of the collective good to moral discourses of independence and responsibility. Justifications for the welfare reforms of the 1990s accordingly highlighted *ethical* imperatives, as indicated in the opening sentence of then minister of welfare Jenny Shipley's 1991 *Welfare that Works: A Statement of Government Policy on Social Assistance*, which laid out the reforms required by Ruth Richardson's mother-of-all-budgets: "The Government's social and economic objective is to provide an environment where New Zealand families are able to take control of their own lives, freed from the dependence on state welfare that currently traps so many of our people" (Shipley 1991: 1). The emphasis on current entrapment signaled the deployment of imaginings of a past in which New Zealanders were not dependent. "National leaders," as McClure (1998: 233) sums it up, "invoked a return to their idealized vision of an earlier New Zealand before the coming of the welfare state, a place where the state did less, and individuals did more."

Given its historical tendency to focus for the most part on helping Pakeha men and elderly persons who fell on hard times through no fault of their own (McClure 2004: 143–47), it might well be the case that the cradle-to-grave New Zealand welfare state was a blip, an aberration, in the *longue durée* of a more residualist welfare state. The emphasis on the "consumer" that emerged as neoliberalism gained currency in Aotearoa/New Zealand would therefore have been able, with some ease, to displace the historically more shallow notion that citizens were entitled to state support (Belgrave 2004: 36). Post-Rogernomics, beneficiaries were no longer viewed in relation to the economy (the weakness of which could have explained their need to be on the benefit), but in relation to their own individual characters; citizenship, accordingly, shifted from a birthright to something that had to be earned via participation in the workforce, leading to a social division between "givers and takers" (McClure 2004: 152). At the same time, there was a shift away from the needs of people and toward those of budgets. For instance, the State Sector Act of 1988 was designed to ensure that "chief executives of government agencies were responsible primarily for delivering services within budgets and were not driven by the needs of those they serviced" (Belgrave 2004: 37–38). Similarly, the first of six "key points" that open the chapter on benefit reform in *Welfare that Works* claims that "the growing cost of benefits has been one of the factors depressing the economy, and a generous benefit system that has required constant borrowing has added to the problem it was meant to solve" (Shipley 1991: 23).

Rogernomics and Ruthanasia represented, respectively, particular articulations of neoliberal philosophies of marketization with social democratic inclinations, and of economic efficiency with a set of moral imperatives that harkened back to a pioneering self-sufficiency. Ideologies of free markets and self-sufficiency, however, were placed in check by an equally powerful formation: a gender regime, sedimented by the family wage, and supported, albeit meagerly, by the Family Benefit, that placed women in the home as primary care givers. The DPB was meant to uphold this primary place of women, despite the concerns about the demise of the male-headed household that accompanied it: even if the DPB did serve to sever women's dependence on men, women remained *mothers*. This primary/primordial role survived the welfare state restructurings of the 1980s and 1990s, albeit unevenly. On the one hand, poor single mothers were vilified as parasites and subjected to the discourse of worker citizenship as well as to the material hardships engendered by the draconian cuts of 1991. On the other hand, the discourse of worker citizenship, while enhanced by those cuts, was not accompanied by policy practices that explicitly required poor single mothers to engage in work-related activities. Until 1996, official pressure was indirect—in having to cover more needs with fewer resources, beneficiaries might be "encouraged" to seek paid employment—rather than taking the direct form of work tests. And, as I have already noted, the work tests introduced in 1996 required beneficiaries to seek part-time work only when their youngest child turned seven, and full-time work only when the youngest child turned fourteen. Thus the (re)emergence of the self-sufficient pioneer (the neoliberal individual) in the reforms of the 1980s and 1990s was limited by an enduring gender regime in which women were first and foremost mothers. Policy assemblages in Alberta, to which I now turn, were quite different.

Alberta, Canada: Federal History

The Canadian welfare state was never as comprehensive as New Zealand's: in Esping-Andersen's (1990) typology, pre-1984 New Zealand would have most closely resembled a social democratic regime with a hint of liberalism thrown in (in the form of means testing for some programs[7]); while Canada, prior to the 1990s, most closely approximated a liberal-residualist regime, characterized by means testing and relatively modest forms of social insurance. Broad typologies, however, can obfuscate as much as clarify the experiences of particular groups (Sainsbury 1996). In the New Zealand–Alberta case, certain similarities become evident when programs specifically targeting poor single mothers are attended to. Thus, just as in Aotearoa/New Zealand, single mothers and Indigenous persons in Canada and Alberta have historically been categorized as less "deserving" than others; and, as in a number of welfare states, evaluations of women's "deservedness" in both Canada/Alberta and Aotearoa/New Zealand were strongly inflected by judgments concerning sexual morality that were raced as well as gendered. Although the alignments developed in the 1990s across the broad differences between the New Zealand and Canadian/Albertan welfare states can be read as artifacts of a global convergence around neoliberal forms of governance, this convergence was built, at least in part, on certain similarities that already existed in the treatment of marginalized groups.

Until the 1940s, public welfare in Canada was considered the purview of provincial and municipal authorities rather than of the central state. Although the federal government began to play a role in economic regulation and social provision in 1940 with the passage of the Unemployment Insurance Act, it did not gather significant momentum in this role until the postwar years, when it enacted the Family Allowance in 1944 and the Canada Assistance Plan (CAP) in 1966. The Family Allowance was Canada's first universal welfare program, designed to provide a universal basic income to every child under the age of sixteen. Although responding to postwar challenges to men's earning power, benefits were provided directly to mothers. CAP, in contrast, was designed to organize the provision of means-tested programs for those living in poverty, and signaled a move away from "deservedness" towards "need" (Muscovitch 1996; Reichwein 2002). As a centralized framing and funding mechanism for provincially administered welfare programs, CAP provided poor single mothers with the means to support themselves and their children; it thus represents the single most important piece of legislation for poor single mothers in twentieth-century Canada.

Over the course of the 1980s, however, rhetorics of economic inevitability in the face of global competition began to challenge CAP's expansionist approach to the welfare state. In addition, arguments that public relief fostered unhealthy dependence and was therefore disempowering rather than liberatory gained increasing credibility, indicating that neoliberal valorizations of the individual were taking hold despite the longstanding Canadian mix of Tory (conservative) paternalism and socialism (Goldberg 1990; see also Baker 1997; Denis 1995). In the early 1990s, the federal government began to impose ceilings on CAP spending and introduced targeting to the Family Allowance. It also began making the case that increases in the percentage of the population receiving social assistance, shifts in family structure and labor force participation, and the size of the budget deficit would necessitate major changes to the architecture of the welfare state (Human Resources and Development Canada 1994).

In 1996, CAP was replaced by Canada Health and Social Transfer (CHST), which devolved social services to the provincial level, reduced transfer funds (thus requiring provinces to contribute more of their own funding), and eliminated all national standards except those regarding residency requirements. Although altering the landscape and scale of provisioning considerably, in some ways the shift ushered in by CHST was not as abrupt as it may appear; it was, rather, an imprimatur of practices regarding reform—and workfare, in particular—that were already well under way at the provincial level, as the story of reform in Alberta indicates.

Provincial History

From 1905, when Alberta became a province, until 1935, when it established a Bureau of Relief and Public Welfare under the umbrella of Public

Health (a free-standing Department of Public Welfare was not established until 1944), relief efforts were piecemeal and poorly coordinated,
although Worker's Compensation and Mother's Allowance were introduced in 1909 and 1919, respectively (Alberta Family and Social Services
1990; Reichwein 2002). Indeed, until the 1966 passage of CAP—and despite a the introduction of a Social Allowance for poor single mothers and
other unemployables in 1961—Alberta had a national reputation "as a
remaining living example of a welfare system dominated by the restrictive
and punitive philosophy of poor law traditions" (Reichwein 2002: 26; see
also Murphy 1997).[8] Mother's Allowance, for instance, provided funding
exclusively for widows and women married to men with disabilities; it was
also accompanied by strict surveillance practices designed to inculcate
middle-class values of industry and independence. These concerns about
dependency and worthiness, on the one hand, and proper (heteronormative, nuclear) family formation, on the other—concerns common across
Canada (Strong-Boag 1995; see also Langford 2011; Little 1994, 1998;
Sangster 2001; Strange and Loo 1997)—endured, more or less officially,
until CAP replaced the "deserving" model with a needs-based one.

It was in the context of this historical approach to relief that the provincial government of Donald Getty, capitalizing on debates and frameworks emerging at the national level, replaced Social Allowance with
Supports for Independence (SFI) in 1990. Arguing that Social Allowance
had "built-in disincentives which promote dependence on government
funding rather than independence based on an ability to work" (Alberta
Family and Social Services 1990: 5), and that "[w]elfare can never provide enough money to meet all needs, and life on welfare promotes a
low expectation of the need or ability to grow into independent and self-
sufficient adults" (1990: 11), the government was determined to shift what
it referred to as the "philosophy" of welfare to emphasize employment
over the receipt of assistance. It accomplished this philosophical shift by
lowering allowance rates and introducing incentives to work. Many poor
single mothers previously considered unemployable were now deemed
employable (Boychuk 1998: 75). As the government put it:

> In 1971, almost all single parents were considered unavailable for employ-
> ment because of child care responsibilities. Under Supports for Indepen-
> dence, 57 per cent are considered employable. This is primarily due to poli-
> cy changes which placed a work expectation on some single parents. Those
> with only one child are expected to work once the child is more than 4
> months old. Those with two children are expected to work if both children
> are in school. All other single parents have been considered exempt from a
> work expectation. (Alberta Family and Social Services 1990: 9)

Interestingly, the report provides no information concerning the grounds on which decisions were made about what constitutes employability. What is clear in the report is that employment had to be made more "attractive": "The difference between Social Allowance benefits and wage income for entry level jobs is, for some clients, not enough to provide an incentive to leave the program" (Alberta Family and Social Services 1990: 11). Most important for my purposes here, the requirement that recipients make themselves available for work once their youngest child turned four months old is a clear indicator that harsh workfare requirements were emerging well before Ralph Klein became premier and before Roger Douglas made his visits to Alberta. Although this requirement had been shifted by the time Klein took office so that recipients would not have to return to work until their youngest child was two years old, the trend was clearly set.

Enter Ralph Klein

On 25 January 1993, Ralph Klein, the newly elected premier who won on a platform of fiscal austerity and government downsizing as the best responses to recession and government debt (Harrison 2010; Murphy 1997), made his first reference to welfare in the provincial legislative assembly. His intention, he said, was to create "social programs for those who cannot fend for themselves but with an emphasis on breaking the poverty cycle and encouraging individuals that self-reliance is still the best way to achieve dignity and pride" (Government of Alberta Hansard, 25 January 1993). Shortly thereafter, on 1 February, Mike Cardinal, the minister of family and social services, gave further indication of the government's orientation to poverty: "Our provincial economy is changing, restructuring itself in response to global pressures of international trade and economic competitiveness. Our work force is literally being shaken out by these changes. Those lacking skills are ending up on low-paying or part-time jobs, and many individuals who are unable to get back into the work force are finding themselves needing assistance from the government" (Government of Alberta Hansard, 1 February 1993). Two days later, Cardinal indicated that the reforms that he would shortly introduce would focus on "ensuring that the program is efficient and that the limited amount of money we have is directed to those who truly need it"; he also stressed the need to work across government departments to "focus on developing a continuum of services all aimed at independence and self-sufficiency" (Government of Alberta Hansard, 3 February 1993).

The Klein administration's approach was formally laid out in its strategic plans, *A Better Way* (1994) and *A Better Way II* (1995). In *A Better Way: A Plan for Securing Alberta's Future*, the government asserted that "individuals and families are responsible for meeting their basic needs and for the safety and security of their children" (Government of Alberta 1994: 9–10). Welfare reforms would accordingly be designed to operationalize a shift "from a passive system to an active-re-employment program" (Alberta Family and Social Services 1994: 5). In keeping with this model, the new government's key goals included reductions to caseloads and the rechanneling of funds from maintenance to employment initiatives (Alberta Family and Social Services 1994: 5).[9]

Similar objectives were listed in the Department of Family and Social Services' 1995 Business Plan. Mirroring the emphasis on targeting articulated in *A Better Way II*, the Business Plan emphasized using the money saved by cuts to maintenance support to help those "most in need" (Alberta Family and Social Services 1995: 7). Accordingly, SFI was to be a program of "last resort." "Administrative harassment" (Armitage 2003: 83) would become one of the key mechanisms for ensuring that SFI would remain less attractive than employment.

The reforms rolled out in 1993 and 1994 did not simply reiterate the sentiments and approaches outlined in the 1990 SFI package of the Getty administration; they also operationalized them in stark, draconian fashion: benefit levels were cut, coverage for health care was reduced, changes were made in exemption levels for those who engaged in paid labor, and new workfare requirements were applied to recipients once their youngest child reached six months of age (Alberta Family and Social Services 1996; Canada West Foundation 1997). The impacts of these changes were significant. Between 1993 and 1995, benefits for single parents with one child were cut by $138.00 per month, a reduction of 13.4 percent (Alberta Family and Social Services 1996: 4). In 1992, the annual benefit for a single parent with one child was $12,357.00; by 1997 it had been reduced to $10,538.00. Welfare caseloads were cut from 94,087 in 1993 to 49,001 in 1995, a reduction of 47.9 percent (1996: 2); by 1997, caseloads were down to 42,747. By 1995, welfare expenditures had been slashed by 42 percent, while employment initiatives increased by 300 percent (1996: 3). In 1996, three years after Klein's election victory, 52.9 percent of lone parent families in the province lived in poverty (Lee and Engler 2000: 11–12); and, as in Aotearoa/New Zealand, the impact of cuts to the welfare system was accentuated by cuts in other sectors, such as health care (see, e.g., Black and Stanford 2005; Harder and Trimble 2005; Murphy 1997; National Council of Welfare 1997).

Two years after the reforms, Denis (1995: 380) argued that Klein's new policies were best viewed as cultural policies of moral regulation:

> As far as the established [Keynesian] welfare paradigm goes, well … this was a symptom of the wrong values taking over society: dependency upon the state, lack of initiative, a willingness to live beyond one's means. Seen from within the culture of hyperliberalism, cutbacks, in this case, are a positive good: welfare recipients—no less than offenders—had to be reformed, had to take responsibility for their own lives. By forcibly putting them on the road to recovery, the government shows all Albertans the way home … so that Alberta may become itself again.

The Klein administration's restructurings were thus designed to devolve responsibility for well-being to individuals who, no longer burdened by state-imposed dependency, would rise to the occasion and eventually revel in their newfound independence. Alberta would become itself again—a do-it-yourself province populated by rugged, pull-yourself-up-by-your-bootstraps pioneering entrepreneurs. Among those who had the most to gain were those who were the most confined, restricted, and imprisoned by the welfare system: poor single mothers.

Enter Roger Douglas and the NZ Model

Although the Fourth Labour government delinked the economic from the social, as I described earlier, this did not mean that Roger Douglas was averse to applying his approach across the board—quite the contrary. Indeed, in 1988 Douglas was pushed out of government because Prime Minister David Lange "lost his nerve," according to some, in instituting Douglas's proposed reforms (*The Economist*, 16 October 1993, quoted in the *Edmonton Journal*, 6 November 1993). This "loss of nerve" served to fuel Douglas's view that the only way to successfully restructure government was to push reform through across the board, as quickly and comprehensively as possible, before resistance could be mobilized. This view became his primary message as a policy entrepreneur. Quickly transforming himself from finance minister into private consultant (he became managing director of his own firm, Douglas Associates), Douglas joined a cadre of former New Zealand government officials, academics, and activists crisscrossing the globe to sell—or warn of the dangers of—the NZ Model. (Douglas remained active on the consulting circuit until 2008, when he was reelected to the New Zealand Parliament from the party list for the right-wing Association of Consumers and Taxpayers, or ACT.)

Bemoaning the "unfinished business" (also the title of his 1993 book) left undone when he was pushed out as finance minister, Douglas became a strong advocate for restructuring social welfare. In addition to reflecting on his own experiences in economic reform, by 1991 Ruth Richardson's social reforms were also available for him to point to. Echoing the sentiments expressed in Welfare Minister Jenny Shipley's *Welfare that Works*, referred to above, Douglas wrote that "[p]ersonal and family responsibility and support should be placed first once more" (1993a: 55). Highly critical of benefit systems that discouraged welfare recipients from seeking employment, Douglas's assessment of the problem was straightforward:

> The personal goals of underprivileged people are essentially the same as those of the rest of the community. They want the opportunity, security and dignity which come from fair treatment, productive employment, rising living standards and personal choice. At present they are worse off than others in society because they lack skills, information, motivation and the spur to achieve. Their condition makes them vulnerable to social and economic pressure. They find it hard to survive without help. However, *if the help we provide locks them into the role of passive recipients, all the State and society does is turn their vulnerability and dependency into a permanent condition.* (1993a: 197; emphasis added)[10]

This message was eagerly adopted by the Klein administration. But why Douglas? And why a model so geographically removed? It was certainly not the case that US approaches, much closer to home, were uninfluential. Indeed, analysis of reportage in the province's two major newspapers—the *Calgary Herald* and the *Edmonton Journal*—indicates that members of the Klein administration were quite interested in developments in the United States, and particularly in the work of David Osborne and Ted Gaebler, authors of *Reinventing Government* (1992). Gaebler, like Douglas, also made a number of visits to Alberta, and the press noted that, "a well marked copy of *Reinventing Government* sits on the desk of Treasurer Jim Dinning. And the book is often quoted as gospel by government MLAs" (*Calgary Herald*, 12 March 1994). Nor was a turn to developments in the United States new in the history of Alberta welfare reform: in its overview of the 1990 SFI program, for instance, Alberta Family and Social Services (1990: 13) noted: "Welfare reform in American and Canadian jurisdictions has increasingly focused on independence through employment and training. These experiments indicate that an emphasis on employment services reduces welfare caseloads and costs over the long term. In the United States in particular, this approach was shown to be far more significant than attempts to reduce welfare dependency by tightening eligibility and restricting and reducing benefits."[11]

My goal, however, is not to provide a comprehensive analysis of welfare reform in Alberta, complete with a catalogue of the entire range of influences at play (for that matter, I could also point to the US influence on Roger Douglas, who cited Charles Murray in *Unfinished Business*). Rather, my intention is to trace in some detail one element on which the Alberta assemblage drew—the NZ Model.[12]

My argument for why Douglas and the NZ Model became influential in Alberta is as follows. First, while there is nothing surprising about the influence of US thinking and practice on Canada, the uneven relationship between the two countries has made some Canadian politicians hesitant to align themselves too closely to US models or interests. Thus one reporter noted, "It would be politically incorrect [for Klein] to give the impression of lifting contentious government policy from a New York textbook [*Reinventing Government*]" (*Calgary Herald*, 12 March 1994). This kind of remark was never made in reference to *Unfinished Business*, which, like *Reinventing Government*, was also reported to be high on the government's reading list (*Edmonton Journal*, 6 March 1994a). My point is that the United States may not have provided the best (overtly acknowledged) model for a Canadian province that, however conservative, was nevertheless part of a more communitarian social formation that has struggled for years to maintain an identity separate from its more powerful neighbor to the south. In addition, although Canada had never been as generous in its welfare provisioning as Aotearoa/New Zealand, Canada and Aotearoa/New Zealand shared, at the most general level, a political culture in which state-sponsored social services were considered reasonable; in other words, Aotearoa/New Zealand's historically communitarian ethos was more in keeping with Canada's post-Depression liberal progressivism than with US-style individualism. Changes in Aotearoa/New Zealand, then, a fellow Commonwealth member and almost socialist in its historical orientation to welfare, could only lend credibility to the kinds of shifts the Klein administration was undertaking.

Second, while a US-style workfare state may have been what the Klein administration had in mind, the NZ Model provided a perfect "first world" blueprint for how to transform a relatively more expansive welfare state (which is what was in place in Alberta at the time) into a deeply neoliberal and residualist one—and quickly. If the US reforms represented extreme expressions of neoliberal models of the person and of the proper configurations of state, market, and individual/community, they were situated in the context of an already markedly residualist welfare state. The New Zealand welfare state, on the other hand, was, at least between 1938 and 1984, significantly more universalist, complete with free education and health care, generous housing programs, and universal employment policies. The distance traveled pre- to postreform was therefore consider-ably greater in Aotearoa/New Zealand than in the United States. Thus Aotearoa/New Zealand "arguably presents the extreme case of policy reform and public sector reorganization among the developed countries in terms of the extent and speed of policy and institutional changes" (Schwartz 1997: 405–6). It was thus the dramatic, comprehensive, and high-speed nature of the shifts in Aotearoa/New Zealand in particular that produced a "worldwide following" (*Calgary Herald*, 29 May 1994) for its model. Indeed, of twenty-eight newspaper articles on international influences on the Alberta reforms published between 1993 and 1995, twenty focus primarily on Douglas—indicating not only media and public interest in a seemingly more exotic figure,[13] but also that of government officials (however contrived for public consumption). In the end, Douglas arrived on the scene at precisely the right moment to give legitimacy and fuel to a building cultural, discursive, and material trend. He provided external, "expert" justification for an already-conceived agenda, lending a strong air of credibility to a controversial and hard-hitting set of policy changes.

The Gospel according to Sir Roger Douglas

Although books and articles may circulate to influence policy elites across jurisdictions, there is as yet no replacement for the public, face-to-face encounters recognized as crucial to processes of policy travel (Hass 1992; Newman 2006; Peck 2001, 2002; Peck and Theodore 2001; Stubbs 2005). Beyond text, such encounters provide opportunities for particular forms of persuasion: stories can be shared, narratives peppered with anecdotes, co-membership established. Face-to-face encounters, in other words, pro-vide opportunities for proselytizers to answer questions, quell doubts, vali-date, and reinforce.

Roger Douglas made two visits to Alberta: one in September 1993, when he "appeared on the scene only three months after the June elec-tion that gave Klein the mandate to cut the deficit" (*Edmonton Journal*, 6 March 1994b), and a second in April 1994. Interestingly, I have been unable to determine if Douglas was hired as a consultant by the Alberta government, or if his interactions with government officials were offi-cially unofficial.[14] On 1 October 1993, Treasurer Jim Dinning was quoted as stating, "We have a consulting contract for him to provide advisory services to us" (*Edmonton Journal*, 1 October 1993). Douglas was referred to as a consultant to the government again in an 8 January 1994 editorial in the *Calgary Herald*. A 9 February 1994 *Herald* report on the Liberals' opposition to Douglas's influence also pointed to Douglas's status as a consultant: "[Liberal Leader Laurence] Decore told a Calgary news conference that by taking on former New Zealand finance minister Roger Douglas as a paid consultant, Alberta has the same rebuilding strategy that led to massive increases in that country's unemployment, surgery waiting lists, university tuition and class sizes." In the same article, however, Rod Love, Klein's chief of staff, was quoted as stating that Douglas "is not a paid consultant by any stretch of the imagination. He was here on a speaking tour and Jim Dinning invited him to come and speak to caucus" (*Calgary Herald*, 9 February 1994). Douglas, for his part, "disclaim[ed] any direct consultative connection with the Klein government but he did allow as how he has met with the Tory caucus" (*Calgary Herald*, 13 April 1994).

Puzzled, I wrote to the government in 2002 asking for details about its relationship with Roger Douglas in the early 1990s. Halvar Jonson, then minister of international and intergovernmental relations, responded as follows in his letter of 3 October 2002:

> Concerning your interest in visits or consultations between Alberta and New Zealand officials on the restructuring of social services, any discussions would have been unofficial and we have no records of these matters. However, based on some news articles that you may already be aware of in your research, we note that Sir Roger Douglas, architect of New Zealand's reforms, did visit Alberta in 1993 and is reported to have been a guest speaker at a Canadian Taxpayer's Conference. In addition, there was also some officials'-level interaction between Alberta and New Zealand in the mid-1990s in the area of performance measurement for government entities. In developing our model for measuring performance, Alberta looked at the experience of a number of governments around the world, which had pioneered in the area of developing performance indicators for government, such as Florida, Oregon, Britain, Minnesota and New Zealand.

The "New Zealand–Alberta Relations Paper" that the minister attached to his letter notes that "Alberta's links to New Zealand are based on Commonwealth ties, a shared inheritance of British Parliamentary democracy, and similar approaches to government restructuring and performance measures."

Although details of the official/unofficial nature of Douglas's interactions with the Klein administration are opaque, it is a matter of record that his 1993 visit was (also?) sponsored by the Alberta Taxpayer's Association, a right-wing antitax group closely aligned with the Klein administration; and that his 1994 visit was sponsored by Athabasca University Educational Enterprises. I have been unable to find information on Douglas's address to caucus, or on any other interactions he had with members of the Klein administration, although the *Edmonton Journal* reported that his conversations with MLAs and heads of government departments focused on "the necessity of sudden rapid change" (1 March 1997). Along with newspaper articles, however, several other sources provide insight into the message Douglas was trying to convey in his travels: an interview with Douglas by Jean-Louis Maxim published in Athabasca University Educational Enterprises' newsletter, *Insight*, in 1994; a transcript of his 1993 presentation to the Alberta Taxpayer's Association Forum on Public Debt (repeated in both Calgary and Edmonton); and, finally, a transcript of his presentation to the Atlantic Institute for Market Studies in Halifax in 1995.

Following are the key points Douglas made in these talks and interviews. Although based on his experiences with reform processes in a particular time and place, Douglas disembedded the NZ Model from its original context to present his messages as if they were universally relevant and applicable.

Governments Are Less Efficient than Markets and Have Generated Unsustainable Levels of Debt

Douglas argued that skyrocketing debt made reform "inevitable": "People will try to put the cork back in the bottle, but in the end our governments simply can't afford to go on as they have in the past" (Douglas 1994: 4). In one talk, he individualized levels of debt (using Saskatchewan as an example, he cited federal and provincial debt levels of $172,000.00 plus $14,200.00 in interest for a family of four); and claimed that such astronomical levels of debt were in part the result of the inefficiencies of "churning" (taking money from taxpayers and then returning it in the form of services)—inefficiencies that a market system would not produce (Douglas 1993b: 2).

Governments Are an Affront to Individual Freedom

In addition to undermining efficiency, Douglas claimed, the lack of competition in government also results in a standardization of services that undercuts personal choice, and therefore freedom. At the end of his Alberta Taxpayer's Association talk, Douglas quoted Archibald McLeech as follows: "What is freedom? Freedom is the right to choose, the right to create for oneself the alternatives of choice. Without the possibility of choice and the exercise of choice, a man is not a man, but a member, an instrument, a thing" (Douglas 1993b: 9). Individual spending in a market system is thus better than pooling ("churning"), Douglas argued, because of the personal choice that it allows.

Restructuring Must Be Total and Across the Board

"It is the interaction of policies that matters," Douglas (1995) said, "rather than any particular policy." Policies therefore should not be addressed one by one, in isolation, but all at once; and nothing should be left out of the reform process. He lamented in this regard that adequate reforms had yet to be made to New Zealand's health, education, and welfare systems.

Restructuring Must Be Swift

"One doesn't really know how long the lag will be between introducing a policy and seeing the benefits. So it's important to go fast. Otherwise, you can lose the consensus that might exist in a country to undertake reforms" (Douglas 1994: 2). Moving quickly would also give less time for special interest groups "to mobilize and drag you down" (Douglas 1995).

Politicians Must Not Blink

"People's confidence rests on whether they believe that the people responsible for implementing a policy believe in it and are going to ensure that they stay the course. ... So it's really important that politicians, when they come under pressure, don't blink" (Douglas 1994: 3). This "not blinking" would contribute to the credibility of the government, thus increasing the willingness of the populace to go along with reform. "[I]f you haven't got credibility," Douglas said, "the public and the interest groups will devote their time to getting you to change your mind and go back to the status quo. Only when they understand that you're not going to change do they get on with making the new arrangement work. So it is important for politicians not to blink in those circumstances" (Douglas 1995).

Restructuring Entails Removing the Privileges of Special Interest Groups

The point of reform, in Douglas's view, was to create a level playing field: "The program we went through here in New Zealand was essentially a removal of privilege. Those who are doing better now are those who stopped lobbying government, decided where they wanted to be in five years, and got on with the job. ... At the very heart of structural reform," then, "is the removal of this kind of privilege that a few people have gained at the expense of the community or the consumer overall" (Douglas 1994: 5).

Restructuring Will Help the Disadvantaged in the Long Run, Although They May Suffer in the Short Run

Douglas argued that restructuring would help the disadvantaged by increasing the efficiency of services, decreasing the power of special interests, and enhancing the power of the individual consumer—all by means of a reduction in taxes and the increased competition generated by privatization. This could, however, take some time: "The unfortunate thing is that some disadvantaged people can be the worst affected in the early stages in terms of employment" (Douglas 1994: 5).

In sum, Douglas's focus was on reducing (and eventually eliminating) debt, and on (he claimed) increasing the level of individual freedom. Since increases in taxation were untenable due to the effects of churning, "[t]he best approach to ridding the economy of deficits is a combined program of asset sales and *reduced government program spending. The latter is the most lasting in its effect*" (Douglas 1993b: 3; emphasis added).

Douglas placed overriding emphasis on two entities: the market and the consumer. In discussing his program of privatizing state-owned enterprises and eliminating what he referred to as "industry assistance" (e.g., subsidies and tax breaks), Douglas told his audiences that "if there is one lesson that I would draw from the New Zealand experience overall, it is that it is [market] competition that is important, not government regulations or handouts" (Douglas 1995). With regard to the consumer, he claimed that: "[i]n politics, you have to remember one thing. You are there, not for the vested interest groups, you are there to serve the public, the taxpayer and the consumer and you should look at every policy from that perspective. What is good for the consumer? What does the consumer need?" (applause noted in transcript) (1995). Douglas's focus, in other words, was on a consumer citizenship that flourishes best in the context of a free market.

There was a kind of snake-oil cure-all element to Douglas's pronouncements. As he put it to the Alberta Taxpayer's Association:

> If we stop this process [of increasing government expenditure and debt] it would be possible in Canada and New Zealand to balance the government budget inside three years, to cut government debt in half within ten years and eliminate it within twenty, to reduce personal taxation to below 15 cents on the dollar (flat within 15 years) and totally eliminate it and corporate tax within 20 years, to slash government expenditure by 70 percent

inside 30 years, to improve, and this is the important thing, to improve the quality of health care and education in the process for everyone, to ensure real security in retirement and high benefit levels and to improve security of low income families. (Douglas 1993b: 6)

Once personal and corporate taxes had been eliminated, he continued, the few remaining government expenditures necessary would be funded through a Goods and Services Tax (Douglas 1995).

Don't Blink

Douglas's message regarding how to best operationalize his vision of a market-based, debt-free society conducive to individual freedom and prosperity was consistent across his visits: do things quickly and do them sweepingly. This is precisely what the Klein administration did. Between 1993 and 1995, public spending was reduced by $1.9 million, entailing the elimination of more than 4,500 civil service jobs (Taft 1997: 28). Every sector was hit: education, health care, housing assistance, programs for seniors and children, cultural programs, the arts, human rights, and, as I outlined above, assistance for the poor (Harrison and Laxer 1995; Lisac 1995; Taft 1997). "Under Ralph Klein's government," Taft (1997: 29) argues, "public programs in Alberta became the most poorly supported in Canada." The only sector that benefited from the Klein Revolution (Lisac 1995) was the business sector.

In keeping with Czarniawska and Sevón's (2005: 10) point that names and slogans travel easily and fast, *don't blink*—a simple message that is precisely about speed—was the piece of Douglas's gospel that had the greatest resonance in Alberta. In its story on Douglas's meeting with the Conservative caucus at Government House in Edmonton, the *Edmonton Journal* summarized Douglas's key point as, "don't blink when making tough budget cuts" (1 October 1993). Blinking, Douglas reportedly told the *Journal*, was precisely what led to the defeat of David Lange's Labour government in 1990. Jim Dau, Klein's communications chief, reiterated this assessment in an interview with the *Journal*: "They [the New Zealand government] blinked. They backed down on one of their reforms and lost credibility" (*Edmonton Journal*, 1 October 1993). A year later, the *Journal* confirmed that *don't blink* had become Klein's new mantra: "'Don't blink' has come to symbolize the Alberta government's resolve to stay on track and cut its now $1.55 billion deficit by 1996–97, regardless of protests" (*Edmonton Journal*, 6 March 1994). Shortly thereafter, the *Herald* noted: "[Treasurer Jim] Dinning admits to being a student of Sir Roger Douglas, the former New Zealand finance minister whose 'do it fast and don't blink' approach to implementing government reform has won a worldwide following. Douglas's philosophy fits nicely into Alberta's attempt to kill its so-called 'deficit monster.' 'You can't jump a chasm in two small leaps, and we've got a huge chasm to get across,' Dinning says" (29 May 1994).

As adopted into the Klein administration's lexicon, *Don't blink* took on a double valence, referring, on the one hand, to doing something quickly, in the time between blinks; and, on the other hand, to staring down one's opponents—here, presumably, the various "special interests" opposed to the dramatic and drastic cuts. (Indeed, attacks against "special interests" became a keystone of Klein's political rhetoric; Harrison, Johnston, and Krahn 2005.) *Don't blink* resonated to such an extent that it was also incorporated into the discourse of media and other nongovernmental analysts. Reporting on the flagging opposition to the 1994 budget, for instance, Sheldon Alberts of the *Herald* wrote, "While the government doesn't like to admit to blinking, some protests have succeeded in getting changes made" (*Calgary Herald*, 29 May 1994). Earlier, in March, David Richards, a chartered accountant and taxation partner with Arthur Andersen & Company, wrote in a business analysis column that the Klein government recognizes that "if they blink at any point in the process, they will be eaten alive by special interest groups" (*Calgary Herald*, 8 March 1994). *Don't blink*, then, became part of local parlance, a key feature of the political and cultural terrain.

Temporal Disjunctures and Disregards

Local opposition to Roger Douglas and the NZ Model serves as one indicator of their influence on the Klein administration. In 1994, when the Klein Revolution was well underway, then Liberal leader Laurence Decore told a reporter, "When some evidence became apparent that Roger Douglas had been invited from New Zealand, our party starting doing a lot more work on the New Zealand model and paying attention to that model. … The conclusion of all that we've discovered is that it's a much harsher, a much more difficult society in New Zealand than it ever was before" (*Calgary Herald*, 9 February 1994). Other groups concerned about the administration's turn to the NZ Model brought in speakers from Aotearoa/New Zealand who presented views that challenged Douglas's message, underscoring the increased destitution, violence, and crime that accompanied Rogernomics and Ruthanasia. In May 1994, for instance, the University of Calgary and Mount Royal College brought in former New Zealand government economist Timothy Sinclair, who highlighted the negative social impacts of the NZ Model (*Calgary Herald*, 7 May 1994). Later, in 1997, Marilyn Waring, a feminist economist and former member of the New Zealand Parliament, was sponsored by the Edmonton Chamber of Commerce; she similarly focused her talk on the downsides of the NZ Model. In the *Edmonton Journal* report on her visit, reporter Linda Goyette commented: "You don't hear the Tories quoting Douglas much these days. Perhaps they've heard news from New Zealand that contradicts their abundant certainties" (1 March 1997). Opposition groups in Alberta would also have had available to them the results of other efforts in Canada to document the effects of restructuring in Aotearoa/New Zealand. The National Union of Public and General Employees in Ottawa, for instance, put out a publication entitled *If Pigs Could Fly: The Hard Truth about the "Economic Miracle" that Ruined New Zealand* (1994). If Douglas was welcomed by some in Calgary, Edmonton, Toronto, and Halifax, then, others viewed his appearance on the scene in Canada with alarm.

Opposition voices in Alberta—united in attending to both the fallouts of Rogernomics and Ruthanasia in Aotearoa/New Zealand and the results of the draconian cuts to social services that the Klein administration was undertaking in 1993 and 1994—were correct in pointing to the short sightedness of Alberta's infatuation with the NZ Model. Indeed, the Klein administration not only "unselected" all the data coming out of Aotearoa/New Zealand in the mid-1990s regarding the negative repercussions of restructuring; it also failed to attend to the changes brought in by the Labour-Coalition government of Helen Clark, voted into power in 1999. As I describe in more detail in chapter 3, these changes entailed a retreat from neoliberal approaches to financial assistance for the poor almost as radical as the restructuring launched by Rogernomics and brought to full fruition by Ruthanasia. The Klein administration was uninterested in these developments, however, and focused instead on what Douglas marketed, which was, after all, what they were looking for: a fast and across-the-board *don't blink* approach framed in terms of history- and culture-free universals. There was no need to monitor how things unfolded in Aotearoa/New Zealand, because that was irrelevant to an administration single-mindedly concerned with eliminating debt and creating a friendly business environment. Nor were the specific (and considerably softer) approaches to workfare in the NZ Model relevant, or wanted, since they would have undercut the Klein administration's harsher approach. This selectivity on the part of the Klein government indicates that "the policy transfer process should be seen as one of continuous transformation, negotiation, and enactment on the one hand and as a politically informed process of dislocation and displacement ('unfit to fit'), on the other hand"

(Lendvai and Stubbs 2006: 5). Klein made it clear in this regard that he was not copying, but, rather, carefully choosing and appropriating for his own purposes: noting that the Klein Revolution is really the "people's revolution," he said, "I don't see my agenda and the agenda of my government as being the Reagan agenda, or the (New Zealand's) Sir Roger Douglas agenda or the Thatcher agenda, but of this government" (*Calgary Herald*, 15 March 1995).

Cultural Articulations/Assemblages

The available evidence indicates that the Klein administration used the NZ Model as an external justification for its actions, harnessing (to use an Albertan prairie metaphor) the NZ Model to its own agenda. The so-called successes of the NZ Model—actual or potential—as outlined by Roger Douglas during his visits to Alberta and in his publications served to underscore its broad applicability and to bolster confidence in the Klein administration's approaches (at least among its architects and champions). The NZ Model was, in other words, "exportable in terms of its hortatory and heuristic functions. For the faint of heart—particularly politicians—it demonstrates that change is possible, and it provides them with a set of useful slogans, principles, and ideas" (Schwartz 1997: 416). Thus Douglas's gospel became fashionable among members of the Alberta government, representing "a collective choice among tastes, things and ideas ... oriented toward finding but also toward creating what is typical of a given time" (Czarniawska and Sevón 2005: 9). The travel of the NZ Model to Alberta was, in other words, an orchestrated event, on both sides, that entailed new and specific forms of assemblage.

Neoliberalism—in this case, neoliberalism as expressed in the NZ Model—clearly did not unfold in a vacuum, but by means of its articulation with what was already there (Kingfisher 2002a, 2007a; Kingfisher and Maskovsky 2008; Maskovsky and Kingfisher 2001). Hall (1986b: 23) argues in this regard that culture is "the historically-shaped terrain on which all 'new' philosophical and theoretical currents work and with which they must come to terms." The success of the NZ Model in Alberta must accordingly be situated not in the context of a generalized success or victory of neoliberalization per se, but in relation to its articulation with received and emerging Albertan cultural formations. This articulation, and the convergences and divergences that it engendered, is my focus in the remainder of this chapter.

At the most general level of cultural characterization is "Albertans' historic endorsement of American-style individualism, their post-war animosity toward organized labour and opposition political parties ... [their] fiscal and social conservativism ... and their general dislike of politics" (Helmer 1995: 71). Although the notion of Alberta as a province uniformly comprised of "self-satisfied rednecks, militant Bible-thumpers, and mouth-breathing rural bigots" belies a "much more diverse, complex, and contradictory social space than is often acknowledged" (Soron 2005: 67), the stereotypical "Martha and Henry," pull-yourself-up-by-your-own-bootstraps Albertans nevertheless served as the discursive reference and propaganda point of the Klein regime (see, e.g., Harrison, Johnston, and Krahn 2005). Thus the broad brushstrokes of the NZ Model were indigenized in Alberta via dialogue with already-present valorizations of prairie notions of rugged individualism and industriousness. The construct of the self-motivated, self-reliant individual who "is not only self-sufficient as a matter of fact but ... must strive toward it as a militant ideal" (Hsu 1993: 4), is, in this prairie context, articulated in relation to local reliance on cattle and agriculture, and to the spirit of cutthroat entrepreneurialism that marks the oil and gas industries in Alberta. Thus Robert Mansell, a University of Calgary economist and advisor to Treasurer Jim Dinning, stated, "Alberta is ruled by 'cowboy capitalism,' which is respect for small business, a belief in self-reliance, risk taking and co-operation" (*Edmonton Journal*, 6 March 1994a). Similarly, at the height of the reforms, Klein claimed that "the Old Alberta is gone forever" (*Edmonton Journal*, 6 March 1994b). Here, the "Old Alberta" was the welfare state Alberta, while the changes instituted by the Klein administration would allow the *original* Alberta—as it was before the state undermined citizens' resolve, determination, and "cowboy capitalist" orientation—to reemerge.

The need for adjustment between the general frame of the NZ Model and dominant Alberta culture and political economy was, in some ways, minimal, as the ideologies of the nature and proper interrelations of state, market, and person embedded in the NZ Model were congruent, not only with those of Ralph Klein and members of his administration, but also with both long-standing and emerging popular models of person, economy, and society in Alberta. These congruencies, in turn, contributed to an emerging convergence between the two sites—at least at a general level—which can be conjectured as contributory to larger, global convergences regarding neoliberal approaches to policy.

Several generic features of neoliberalism are relevant here. The first is economic reductionism: the claim, or assumption, that the economic determines "in an immediate way, in the first, middle and last instances" (Hall 1986b: 10)—in other words, that the economic determines in a "mechanical fashion" (1986b: 10). In economic reductionism, or fundamentalism, the economy, and the global economy in particular, is constructed as an omnipotent external force, one that is not built by men (pronoun usage deliberate) but that has to be responded to by them so that the outcomes might be the most favorable possible. State and substate governing bodies are accordingly enjoined to restructure how they do business (including how they look after those who for whatever reason are not actively participating in recognized economic activity), so that they may benefit rather than suffer from the machinations of this awesome global force, seemingly natural and eternal. The economic discourses embedded in the NZ Model and in the Klein reforms clearly evince economic determinism. This is not to claim that economic determinism originated with Rogernomics or Ruthanasia, or that Alberta drew exclusively on the NZ Model in developing its own version of economic determinism; rather, it is to claim that the New Zealand–Alberta connection served to reinforce economic fundamentalism, thereby contributing to an assertion, or acceptance, of its universal and commonsensical nature.

Economic determinism feeds, in turn, into a form of policy universalism. This idea that particular policy frameworks, designs, and approaches to implementation can be abstracted from their contexts of emergence and transported intact to new sites, where they can be replicated *in toto* regardless of local contingencies, parallels efforts in liberal economic philosophy to disembed the economic from the social (Polanyi 2001). The notion that the economy is autonomous from society and that it can, and should, provide the organizing mechanism for society, is, as Polanyi indicates, quite peculiar historically and cross-culturally; and moves to give primacy of place to the so-called self-regulating free market mean "no less than the running of society as an adjunct to the market" (Polanyi 2001: 60). The attempted development of a global neoliberal social policy regime reflects similar kinds of thinking. Like free market philosophy, which posits a natural *homo economicus*, the idea here is that social policy can be unmoored from place because it, too, is supposedly responding to the same natural condition and disposition of the species. Thus just as liberal economic thinkers work to disembed the economy from society, so transnational policy experts work to disembed policy from society. Indeed, policy elites seem to hold on with some intensity to the idea that policies developed in one site can address similar situations in other places regardless of cultural exigencies. Adaptations and tailorings to specific contexts may be called for, but these are just tweakings, and the fundamentals can—indeed, must, if what we are talking about is how to best organize a panhuman social system—remain the same.

The New Zealand–Alberta connection also contributed to a convergence regarding the neoliberal models of active welfare states and citizenship that I outlined in the introduction. In both cases, previous systems of relief were reclassified as "passive"—debilitating to individuals, society, and the economy—and replaced with systems designed to inculcate "activity," taking the forms of "responsibility" and "independence" from the state. Despite differences in the relative weight placed on various mechanisms for producing active persons and societies, "policy reform in New Zealand and Alberta had remarkable similarities, particularly in terms of the central aspect of the New Zealand model: the reengineering of institutions and thus individual behavior" (Schwartz 1997: 409).

Finally, Alberta's adoption of Douglas's high-speed, comprehensive, *don't blink* approach manifested and served to reinforce the commonsensical nature of both Milton Friedmanesque and Jeffrey Sachs-like shock policy/therapy approaches deployed in various locations across the globe, including in former Soviet bloc countries and countries in the global south subjected to IMF/IBRD structural adjustment programs. If a global neoliberal policy regime was in fact emergent, moving fast and across-the-board were among its key defining features.

There were, however, divergences. Given Roger Douglas's focus on general, supposedly universal ideas and ideals, and on general, supposedly universal strategies for operationalizing them, it is not surprising that the convergences produced via the travel of the NZ Model to Alberta also remained general. Nor is it surprising that these convergences would sit alongside divergences reflective of the particularities of each context. One of the key divergences in this regard was marked by the disjuncture between workfare discourses and workfare requirements in the two systems. This disjuncture reflected, in turn, differences in conceptualizations of individualism and motherhood. I have already referred to the kind of rugged individualism said to be characteristic of Alberta. In extreme caricatures, the focus is exclusively on white men: "The world, according to prevalent Alberta mythology, is like the famous Marlboro Man commercial. A simple, bold place with boundless horizons. One rugged, tanned, white man with a pack of smokes and a horse. No-one to stand in his way. And no-one to pick him up if he falls" (Murphy 1997: 109). (Interestingly, Ralph Klein's brother once described him as "almost the epitome of Alberta ... the persona ... the rough-neck, kick ass, in-my-face mentality;" *Calgary Herald*, 15 March 1995). The situation is, of course, more complicated than this. Harder (2003: x), for instance, claims, "It turns out that the rugged individualist will give you the shirt off his back while muttering about the need for welfare recipients to stand up on their own two feet." The stereotype nevertheless has considerable purchase in Albertan popular culture, certainly with respect to the role of the state, if not in relation to face-to-face interaction.

In terms of Indigenous populations, negative stereotypes that focus on laziness, alcohol or other drug addictions, and unregulated sexuality seem to have remained relatively constant through Alberta history. There are differences regarding the purported etiology of these characteristics—claimed to be, at one extreme, inherent, or, at the other, social and historical productions, artifacts of either cultural genocide or overly generous welfare programs—as well as differing ideas about how to mitigate their worst effects (Kingfisher 2007a, 2007b), but it is worth keeping in mind that the idealized model of the person in Alberta—the rugged cowboy capitalist—has been constructed in opposition to constructions of non-industrious, parasitic Aboriginality (Kingfisher 2007a, 2007b).

The tensions around gender are different. There is, on the one hand, an element of rugged individualism in Alberta that builds on historical valorizations of pioneering women's heavy work (Palmer and Palmer 1990). On the other hand, there is also a strong valorization of the domestic running through Alberta's history, tied, in many cases, to religious and political conservatism. Prior to the mid-twentieth century, popular and political support for nuclear family formation was evident in women's patterns of labor force participation. In the early part of the century, "[w]omen's work outside the home was carefully circumscribed" (Palmer and Palmer 1990: 234). During this period, "[w]omen's freedom from the homemaker role was widely feared" (Langford 2011: 18)—not only in Alberta, but throughout Canada (Little 1998)—representing concerns about women's sexuality as well as about juvenile delinquency. Figures on married women's labor force participation rates in Alberta prior to World War II are accordingly low, ranging from 2 to 3 percent (Langford 2011; see also Palmer and Palmer 1990). Married women's labor force participation skyrocketed, however, in the second half of the century. Between 1951 and 1971, women's labor force participation rates more than doubled, "led by the rapid increase in the participation of married women" (Langford 2011: 291). By 1985, "a higher percentage of Alberta women (60 percent) were employed than anywhere else in the country, and over half of women with preschool children worked outside the home" (Palmer and Palmer 1990: 363). Married women's labor force participation rates hit 69 percent in 1991 (Langford 2011: 291). These changes in women's work, which heightened tensions between feminists and traditionalists, were played out in policy debates related to equal pay, maternity leave, and kindergarten and daycare policies, among others (Harder 2003; Langford 2011).

In addition to tensions between family traditionalists and feminists, struggles around policies related to women's labor force participation must also be situated in the context of Albertan free enterprise culture, to which I alluded earlier. As Langford (2011: 221) puts it: "Alberta's political culture is defined by ... dominant beliefs about the role of individuals, families, private enterprise, and governments. ... One such belief celebrates private responsibility in all matters (including child care) and condemns government programs as 'interference' in people's lives. ... It is important to realize that the belief in private responsibility is widely and passionately held in Alberta society, which is why pro-family and free enterprise groups have found fertile ground in the province."

Alberta gender regimes thus reflect a confluence of forces: a prairie rugged individualism that includes women as well as men, a conservative valorization of domesticity and motherhood, the reality of married women's increasing labor force participation occurring alongside the emergence of feminism, and a free enterprise/cowboy capitalism approach to the role of government in private life—which, of course, relates back to rugged individualism. Two threads running through this confluence may help to situate workfare policies in Alberta. First, as women participate in the labor force in increasing numbers, so women's labor force participation is increasingly normalized. The idea of women returning to work shortly after giving birth loses its exceptionality, with the result that workfare requirements come to appear as no different from the generalized requirement to work to which increasing numbers of women are subject. Second, as a conservative cultural and political system suffers the assault of challenges to male breadwinner nuclear family formation, conservative governments can put policy to the task of buttressing traditional social arrangements. Harder (2003: 132) makes precisely this argument in relation to the Klein administration's cuts to kindergarten programs, which, she claims, presumed stay-at-home mothers or parents with sufficient economic resources to pay for child care. Harder and Trimble (2005: 303) argue further that "the obligation of single mothers on social assistance to pursue maintenance from their former partners, the inadequacy of child care, and the disproportionate tax benefits meted out to single earner, two-parent families all underscore the Klein government's reinforcement of the traditional gender order in which women's financial needs are met primarily through access to the wages of a spouse or partner." Thus rugged individualism and traditional familialism can work together (Harder, personal communication), with rigid workfare requirements simultaneously reflecting neoliberal transformations of women "into genderless and self-sufficient market actors" (Brodie 2008: 165; see also Brodie 2002), and working to push women into traditional family forms.

These patterns differ markedly from those in Aotearoa/New Zealand. While debates about women's roles as mothers versus workers permeate the history of Aotearoa/New Zealand as well as Alberta, the cultural valorization of motherhood in Aotearoa/New Zealand has been significantly stronger than in Alberta, cutting across class lines and becoming entrenched in state institutions and policies. Nolan (2000) points to a number of "contradictory tendencies" in New Zealand governing structures that work to simultaneously support and undermine domesticity: the wage-earner's welfare state on the side of domesticity, and educational policies, equal pay legislation, and government hiring practices on the side of women's independence. Although these contradictions have existed in Alberta as well, sometimes manifesting themselves in acrimonious policy debates (Harder 2003; Langford 2011), domesticity has held sway in Aotearoa/New Zealand to a much greater degree. As in Alberta, the historical tendency in Aotearoa/New Zealand was for married women to not engage in paid labor. However, although women's rates of participation in the labor force increased dramatically in the second half of the twentieth century, again mirroring patterns in Alberta, *married* women's labor force participation rates in Aotearoa/New Zealand remained among the lowest in the OECD (OECD 2005), in stark contrast to the pattern in Alberta. There has also been significantly more state support for motherhood in Aotearoa/New Zealand, taking the form not only of a much more generous welfare system for poor single mothers, but also of universal programs in specific support of mothering. The Plunket Society, for instance, focused on the care of babies, has well-baby clinics, provides home visits to new mothers, and runs "Plunket houses" to which new mothers can bring their babies during daytime hours to work on a range of problems with the assistance Plunket staff. Although Plunket was historically very much involved in the inculcation of particular values and practices, it has always provided across-the-board, free services in support of mothering to women in all social classes; it was never restricted to the poor. In addition to Plunket, Kingston, where I conducted fieldwork, also has a Mothercraft unit, a separate house on the hospital grounds in which mothers with problem babies (ranging from those with feeding or sleeping problems to those with spina bifida), or who are themselves suffering from postnatal depression, reside for a week at a time to get guidance and support from staff. Again, this service is free and available to all mothers, regardless of income. The valorization of motherhood in Aotearoa/New Zealand can of course be read as pronatalist and restrictive to women; and there is also historical evidence that the state actively encouraged high birth rates among Pakeha to address the racial threat represented by Maori (Belgrave 2004). Nevertheless, the support for mothering is real, and its loss would no doubt be bemoaned by feminists as well as conservatives.

Aotearoa/New Zealand's more culturally and institutionally entrenched valorization of mothering contributed, I would argue, to the relative lenience and short shelf life of its workfare programs. Thus, while in Alberta, motherhood has been more discursively than materially supported, in Aotearoa/New Zealand workfare has been more discursively than materially supported. As Brodie (2008: 167) explains: "Social policies can embody any number of representations of an appropriate gender order. For example, policies may assume and enforce male authority and agency (patriarchalization), or the primary role of families in ensuring individual well-being (familialization), or they may altogether disregard the importance of gender and the gendered division of labour (invisibilization and individualization)." In Aotearoa/New Zealand, invisibilization and individualization have been subsumed by familialization, while in Alberta the reverse has been the case. The sharing of frameworks for thinking about state, market, and society that occurred in that hybrid space (Lendvai and Stubbs 2007, 2009) of interaction between Roger Douglas and the Alberta policy elite thus did not lead to parallel workfare programs. It is, perhaps, ironic that the ideology of rugged, self-sufficient individualism embedded in the NZ Model found more fertile practical ground in Alberta than at home.

Discussion

There is no doubt that neoliberalism was circulating "in the air" across the globe in the 1980s and 1990s. My goal in this chapter has not been to explain it all, as there is no final explanation, no one origin, no complete package that can be delineated comprehensively. Rather, I have followed one thread of this assemblage of "global neoliberalism" to explore some aspects of how unique yet related constellations were put together, in both markedly similar and astonishingly different ways, in Aotearoa/New Zealand and Alberta, Canada.

Policy movement across jurisdictions has been said to be more likely—both more attractive and more feasible—when governing bodies share historical and/or emerging structural and political orientations, perhaps in response to shared language and/or shared social problems (Peck and Theodore 2001: 430–32; see also Evans 2004c). This was certainly the case with Aotearoa/New Zealand and Alberta, both English-speaking settler societies, both part of the Commonwealth, both parliamentary democracies, both suffering fiscal crises in the 1980s and 1990s, and both undergoing shifts in government of the kind that "can provide an opportunity structure for policy change to occur" (Evans 2004c: 216). Given these similarities, policy sharing would seem to make good sense.

It would be a mistake, however, to see shared governing structures, political orientations, and social problems as primarily the *beginning* point for policy collaboration, as if already-existing alignments are only the conditions of possibility for fruitful exchange. It may be just as much the case that the processes involved in sharing policy knowledge also serve to produce the very alignments that supposedly make policy sharing possible and attractive in the first place (see, e.g., Callon 1986 and Hall 1986b for discussion of the formation of alignments). Thus, where Evans (2004c: 216) hypothesizes that "[m]acro-level commitment to competition state principles … provides opportunity structures for policy transfer to occur"—a situation that most definitely held in both New Zealand and Alberta—this commitment itself was a production, at least partially an artifact of policy travels.

Disembedding—the lifting of policies from their contexts of occurrence in order to render them portable and ostensibly universally applicable—is one mechanism for producing such shared commitments. In his analysis of the travel of workfare programs, for instance, Peck (2001) describes how the needs of policy transfer can inform the very architecture of what are, in fact, pilot programs. This is facilitated by the use of particular discursive forms—Peck refers to Schram's (1995) model of economistic-therapeutic-managerial discourse (ETM) and to Fraser's (1989) hegemonic "means of interpretation and communication" (MIC)—that, on the basis of constructions of humans and of the societies they inhabit as profoundly generic, strip policies of their particular contexts and contingencies of development. This stripping also serves to erase the translation work involved in policy travels, disguising, in turn, the power relations in operation. Indeed, framing policy in scientific, technological terms is itself a form of translation that serves to erase both the social embeddedness of policy and, equally important, the volition of agents of transfer (Hass 1992; Newman 2006; Peck 2001, 2002; Peck and Theodore 2001; Stubbs 2005): those persons who facilitate policy travels, and who are, perhaps, best thought of as proselytizers, or global activists (Sklair 1998), carrying their products with enthusiasm, zeal, and conviction, and asserting, above all, their generalizability and universal relevance. As I indicated earlier, this includes those on the receiving end of policy travels as well, who "seek out, mobilize and transform ideas rather than … respond or … adapt them" (Newman 2006: 3, 13), and who may use policy ideas from elsewhere to "legitimate conclusions already reached" (Evans 2004c: 217).

Clearly, those involved in the New Zealand–Alberta exchange were highly selective in what they paid attention to with regard to both the architecture and temporal unfolding of the NZ Model. The New Zealand–Alberta story thus illustrates how policy frames can be disarticulated from their association with particular programs, becoming, in some cases, almost free-floating sets of signifiers that can be arranged and rearranged in Lévi-Straussian bricolage-like fashion—*if* the context and conditions are right, as I have argued was the case with aspects of the NZ Model in Alberta. The result in Alberta was a disjunctive constellation of bits and pieces from the here and the elsewhere. While certain aspects of the NZ Model—e.g., the speed of implementation and, perhaps, its vision of a golden past of enterprising colonial rugged individualism—were completely suited to the Alberta context, seemingly requiring little translation, others—most notably certain aspects of the Aotearoa/New Zealand gender regime, the negative impacts of Rogernomics and Ruthanasia, and the Clark reforms—were not, and so were elided. Neither neutrality nor complete policy packages were involved here. Policy transfer erases (at both the departure and arrival ends) as much as it includes (Stubbs 2002: 322). Some (e.g., Dolowitz and Marsh 2000: 17) may see this as "uninformed" or "incomplete" transfer, but this would be to assume that there is such a thing as straightforward, rational, total transfer.

Policy travels, never neutral, never automatic, and never pure or complete, always entail design and intentionality on all sides. The processes that comprise such travels are, accordingly, fundamentally about becoming, about translation, about erasure, and, above all, about interaction, which completely opens up the terrain to both intentions and accidents of assemblage. Rather than traveling *in toto*, then, policies often form themselves during the very course of travel (Freeman 2012; Johnson and Hagström 2005; Lendvai and Bainton forthcoming; Lendvai and Stubbs 2006, 2007, 2009; Peck 2001, 2002, 2011; Peck and Theodore 2001, 2010, 2012). If policies are first disembedded so as to be rendered portable, once they set off on their travels they may be subject to further disarticulations, so that pieces of what has already been decontextualized are further abstracted for use in new settings. From start to finish, policy travel involves translation and articulation with received cultural formations, engendering possibilities of assemblage that may reflect both convergence and divergence.

Notes

1. The Ordinance for the Support of Destitute Families and Illegitimate Children (1846), and the Destitute Persons Act (1877), the Hospital and Charitable Institutions Act (1885), and the Old Age Pensions Act (1898).
2. Family Allowance/Benefit and Mothers Allowance place this hierarchy in stark relief. The Family Allowance Act of 1926 provided a small benefit for children to

wage-earning households. Renamed the Family Benefit with the passage of the Social Security Act in 1938, the children of never-married mothers were excluded until 1946, when the benefit was made universal; and it was only in 1964 that the Social Security Act was amended to include "illegitimate" children in the benefit (Goodger 1998). Likewise, Mothers Allowance, introduced in 1946, targeted widows with children rather than all single mothers. It is worth noting that, even when universalized, these income supplements were very small (in 1946, the Family Benefit paid $1.00 per week per child, a fraction of male wages; Goodger 1998: 126), and were meant as supplements rather than as key sources of income. Poor single mothers, in other words, could not have survived on them even had they had regular access.

3. Indeed, in the 1950s and 1960s, women's rates of pay sat at around 50 percent of men's rates, and it was not until the Equal Pay Act of 1972 that efforts were made to equalize women's and men's rates of pay (Shirley and St. John 1997: 42).

4. When, in the lead up to the 1938 Social Security Act, the prime minister requested information on Maori rates of state support, statistics indicated that the Pensions Department "still held in nearly all cases to an arbitrary level for Maori which was one-fifth lower than Pakeha pensions" (McClure 1998: 79). During debates leading up to the passage of the Act, some members of government argued that Maori needed less because their standard of living was lower than the Pakeha standard. This view was written into the Act in section 72(7), which, although not referring directly to Maori, allowed for reductions in benefit levels if the full benefit was deemed unnecessary in the circumstances—a stipulation that was often applied to Maori (McClure 1998: 85–86).

5. Once the DPB was institutionalized, various groups of poor single mothers were combined, so that the distinction between never-married and divorced (formerly "deserted") was eliminated. (Men could also receive the DPB.) Despite the historical distinction in policy, however, both groups were always tainted, with divorced/deserted women often held to blame for marital breakdown.

6. The controversies related to state support of single mothers led to the striking of a Domestic Purposes Benefit Review Committee in 1976, which was charged with exploring, among other things, the causes of bourgeoning welfare rolls, the impact of the DPB on marriages and children, and the need to avoid letting fathers off the hook for support (Nolan 2000: 284–85). Responding to the committee's fears that "women would be attracted to the benefit in large numbers … [and] would prefer the benefit to the alternatives of adoption, marriage, or remarriage" (McClure 1998: 185), the benefit was reduced for the first six months after marital separation, and, in the case of unmarried women, until such time as maintenance from the father had been legally settled (McClure 1998: 288). Both measures were designed to undercut the "incentive" aspects of the DPB.

7. According to Esping-Andersen (1990:68), the strong labor movement in Aotearoa/New Zealand served to limit the universalism of its welfare state; specifically, it favored means-tested programs because they were more redistributional, and because the need for social protection was seen as best met via wage negotiations.

8. Boychuk (1998) argues, in contrast, that Alberta was less harsh than some other provinces, most notably Ontario and British Columbia.

9. Funds allotted to maintenance were to decrease from 792.9 to 669.5 million over the course of four years, while those allotted to employment initiatives would increase from 29.8 to 35.4 million over the same period (Alberta Family and Social Services 1994:6).

10. Later, in looking back on his experiences as finance minister in a 2003 interview with the editor of *Policy*, Douglas was even more pointed: "[F]ixing the cause of poor educational, health and crime outcomes involves not only finding ways to improve the health and education system *per se*, but also finding much more effective ways of dealing with welfare, particularly sole parents. ... So, up front, I would do something to try and fix the welfare system. ... We've got 190,000 children in single parent families. Some 20 percent of those families are dysfunctional. That's the problem. The solution is to make it less attractive to become a single mother by choice" (Windybank 2003: 23–25).

11. It is ironic, given recognition of the limits of "tightening eligibility and restricting and reducing benefits," that this is precisely what the Klein administration proceeded to do.

12. Interestingly, while Douglas's ideas traveled to Alberta, Alberta's ideas and programs also traveled. A 1995 article in the *Calgary Herald* told the story of how Klein's restructuring program made the agenda of an Americans for Tax Reform meeting via an article written in the *Wall Street Journal*. "Alberta is fast becoming a model of change," the reporter noted. The article ended with a quotation from *Wall Street Journal* reporter John Fund, who said that Ralph Klein "could be the next Roger Douglas" (*Calgary Herald*, 11 March 1995). The article also reported that Klein himself bragged to audiences about coverage of Alberta in the *New York Times* and the *London Financial Times*. Closer to home, an editorial in the *Calgary Herald* (19 July 1995) discussed the influence of the Klein Revolution on Mike Harris's Ontario. Finally, in mid-1996, the *Calgary Herald* (21 November 1996) reported on a segment of *60 Minutes* (broadcast in Australia, Aoteaora/New Zealand, and southeast Asia) called "Cruel to be Kind," which focused on the Klein Revolution, with an emphasis on the restructuring of the welfare system. Alberta, then, was one stop on the travels of Rogernomics. Rogernomics touched down here, was transformed into the Klein Revolution, and then repackaged for further export.

13. Douglas's visits to Alberta prompted discussion of the historical links between Alberta and Aotearoa/New Zealand as well as between Alberta and another Douglas. At the height of the debates around the 1994 budgets, two editorials published in the *Calgary Herald* (29 March and 13 April) provided background on historical links, noting with irony the importance of two Douglases: Major C. H. Douglas, who brought Social Credit to the province from the United Kingdom (social credit is an approach to political economy designed to eliminate poverty and debt by issuing "social dividends" to the population); and Roger Douglas, who offered the NZ Model as an approach to debt and poverty reduction. One of the editorials (29 March) also pointed to a long history of farm visits and agricultural exchanges between Alberta and Aotearoa/New Zealand; it concluded by pointing out that "[b]oth governments maintain sophisticated and professional communications and public relations skills and employ many people adept at sending the message that their political masters seek to send."

14. Evans (2004b) points out that it can be difficult to establish that policy transfer has actually occurred, given limitations on access to key players in the policy process. I certainly suffered such limitations.

Chapter 2

PRODUCING POLICY IN WELFARE OFFICES

∞

> ... the spread in time and space of anything—claims, or-
> ders, artifacts, goods—is in the hands of people; each of
> these people may act in many different ways, letting the to-
> ken drop, or modifying it, or deflecting it, or betraying it, or
> adding to it, or appropriating it (Latour 1986: 267).

The tensions between convergence and divergence that I described at the
end of the previous chapter signal that processes of policy development
and travel are always about assemblage—of the new with the old, the
close with the distant—and therefore always about selection and translation: they entail constructing, building on, extracting, and tailoring what
works, or fits, and excising or simply "not seeing" the rest. Official policy
makers, however, are not the only participants in this endeavor. Government elites cannot simply sit down, assemble particular policy frameworks, assert that their visions reflect what is natural and inevitable, and
have those ways of thinking and doing take on the valence of commonsense, materializing as if by magic. New approaches, especially, have to
be framed in ways that are convincing—perhaps because they somehow
resonate with received cultural formations, or tap into (and thus help
to build) emerging sentiments. More to the point, new policy mandates
have to be operationalized, taken up and put into practice, just as existing frameworks have to be continually reproduced in order to maintain
their currency. In this business of taking up and *doing* social policy, those
who administer and deliver services—in this case, welfare providers—are

key: they are the means by which policy practices and the ideas informing them are materialized and sustained. Insight into the emergence, travel, establishment, and continuance or interruption of policy frames remains partial, then, if analysis is restricted to official levels of policy formation. Rather, in order to generate holistic insight into "policy worlds" (Shore, Wright, and Però 2011), analysis must also explore how policy frames and programs are produced as they move through the points of "implementation" inhabited by providers. The translation and assemblage work of welfare providers is, accordingly, the second "stop" in my travelogue.

As I described in chapter 1, translation and assemblage associated with policy movement across jurisdictions unfold in contexts of political expediency related to large-scale governmental agendas and struggles. They also reflect the articulation of policy frames from "elsewhere"—in time and/or space—with contemporary and localized cultural formations. Translation and assemblage among welfare providers similarly reflect political and cultural production, articulation, and struggle, but they are situated in very different contexts of occurrence: street-level bureaucracies that are not at arm's length from the "street," but, on the contrary, sit precisely at the boundary between governments and the populations they ostensibly serve and govern. These bureaucracies are characterized by their own enablements, constraints, and enticements, and create their own conditions of possibility for forms of production.

Street-level bureaucrats are difficult to typify. Meyers and Vorsanger (2007: 153) point out in this regard, "In some studies these workers are portrayed as occupying a powerless position downstream of political and bureaucratic decisions; in others they emerge as loyal public servants who pursue the public good even when it means bending agency regulations; in still others they are described as self-interested bureaucrats whose coping mechanisms frustrate the will of elected officials." This variation reflects the basic tension between constraint and improvisation that marks all street-level bureaucratic work. This tension, in turn, is an artifact of the particular institutional location that street-level bureaucrats occupy. Janus-faced, welfare providers must be simultaneously oriented outwards and inwards in order to serve two groups—policy elites and clients—that often have competing interests. The tensions between the needs of the institution (e.g., reducing funds spent, meeting particular quotas regarding job placement) and of clients (getting access to assistance) are compounded by contradictions between rhetoric and ideology, on the one hand, and on-the-ground realities, on the other. In their analysis of welfare reform in Oregon, for instance, Morgen, Acker, and Weigt (2011: 84) note that providers needed to mediate a wide-ranging set of contradictions between "self-sufficiency versus low-wage work, choice versus coercion, helping versus enabling, work versus family and unpaid care work, diversity versus inequity, and empowerment versus regulation." Providers are thus betwixt and between both ideologically and in relation to the structure of their everyday practice.

Providers' practical mediation work entails, first of all, the transformation of human beings—complex creatures with often convoluted and contradictory biographies—into institutionally recognized categories; that is, one-dimensional characters that fit into particular institutional slots and agendas. This kind of transformational work requires a double translation: the translation of the bureaucracy's categories into something living—that is, applicable to human beings—and the translation of human beings into types or needs that are then administrable. It is worth noting here Jenkins's (2007: 31–32) argument that "informality, non-rule-governed discretion and even subversion" are not holdovers from prebureaucratic days, but are, rather, intrinsic to modernity and bureaucracy, the very structures of which bring into being their opposites, a kind of counterdiscourse. A similar insight has been provided by critics of Weber's focus on the formal aspects of bureaucracy. Blau (1970: 144), for example, claims that "departures from official procedures are not idiosyncratic but become socially organized. The social patterns that are informally organized by the participants themselves complement those formally organized for them by management. Furthermore, the informal organizations that always arise in formal organizations ... are essential for operations." Unofficial yet systematic and often widely shared categorizations of clients as deserving or undeserving, for instance, can help to manage otherwise overwhelming case loads. Welfare providers thus operate in a social structure that itself incites forms of translation that complement, and sometimes counter, its official structures and *modi operandi*. The double translation between institutional categories and real live clients is mediated, then, by providers' own frameworks of operation, produced in relation to, although not completely determined by, their institutional locations and work requirements. These official and unofficial frameworks of operation draw on the larger cultural contexts within which welfare institutions are situated, including the sometimes contradictory ideologies regarding work, personhood, gender, public assistance, and so on, that inform them and that provide the parameters of thought and action.

Management responses to this state of affairs have tended to take one of two basic forms. Representing a particular translation of the standardization and impersonalization that Weber saw as characteristic of bureaucratic rationality—efforts designed, ideally, to level the playing field among applicants/supplicants by eliminating arbitrary discrimination—"control" approaches (Yeatman 1990) to service delivery are marked by attempts to "people-proof" policy implementation, that is, to remove policy delivery from the realm of messy human interaction and place it instead in the domain of the technical and the routinized. In such frameworks, management outlines in precise detail how providers are to operate, instituting neo-Taylorian mechanisms (Pollitt 1993) that dictate the information to be gathered, the forms to be filled out, and the exact decisions to be made on the basis of those steps taken; often computer programs themselves become the "decision makers." As I describe later in this chapter, welfare policy delivery in Alberta was organized in terms of a control approach; providers, accordingly, had little or no say in official policy formation and very limited official discretionary power.

"Service" orientations, in contrast—in effect in Aotearoa/New Zealand at the time of my fieldwork—take as their starting point the observation that people processing (Prottas 1979) involves *people,* and that therefore it will inevitably entail a certain amount of discretion (Yeatman 1990). Positioning welfare providers as knowledgeable insiders who have something substantive to offer both clients and official policy makers, service approaches augment rather than reduce providers' discretionary power. The goal is to foster the ability of providers to develop rich and textured relationships with clients that in turn provide the basis for joint decision making and action. Not incidentally, service approaches also position clients as knowledgeable and competent.

Regardless of how service oriented an organization may be, however, providers are always more or less constrained by policy mandates and administrative structures (Brodkin 1997; Morgen, Acker, and Weigt 2011). Similarly, control approaches cannot eliminate improvisation, as Jenkins's (2007) and Blau's (1970) references to informal bureaucratic organization suggest. As Lipsky, whose *Street-level Bureaucracy: Dilemmas of the Individual in Public Services* (1980: xii) continues to provide the benchmark for discussions of street-level work, put it, "The decisions of street-level bureaucrats, the routines they establish and the devices they invent to cope with uncertainties and work pressures, effectively become the public policies they carry out." Given that they are human, cultural agents, then, and that they are engaged in the "messy, emotion-laden practical work of dealing with relationships and contingency" (to borrow from an observation about international aid professionals; Mosse 2011: 56), street-level bureaucrats' efforts to implement policy will at least to a certain degree actually serve to construct it (in addition to Lipsky 1980, see, e.g., Freeman 2006; Hudson 1993; Prottas 1979; Wirth 1991; for more ethnographic analyses, see, e.g., Brodkin 1997; Dunér and Nordström 2006; Kingfisher 1996a, 2001; Morgen, Acker, and Weigt 2011; Riccucci 2005). "In the process of implementation," Freeman (2006: 377) notes, "administrators and professionals alike discover not only how to put policy into practice but what a policy really means or entails. Their learning is reactive but ingenious." The official boundary between policy formation and implementation is accordingly troubled, rendered fuzzy. Nevertheless, constraints remain. Street-level bureaucratic work thus becomes a balancing act between limitation and improvisation.

Given their unique locations and requirements, street-level bureaucrats produce and have access to a range of knowledges that include not only formal policy directives and procedures, but also knowledge of the system's strengths and weaknesses and of where and how it can or cannot be manipulated, of categories of person and need built up by virtue of experience, and of local bureaucratic and community cultural systems, both tacit and explicit. These knowledges differ significantly from those held by official policy makers, who do not have daily interactions with and therefore generally lack insight into the actual needs and situations of recipients or into the limits of policy in application. This is not to say that welfare providers have direct, unmediated access to the realities of their clients' lives; just that they have *more* access to perhaps more bits and pieces of these realities—to situated, nuanced stories of poverty and of the impacts of policy, rather than only to the abstracted anecdotes deployed by politicians for rhetorical purposes. It is in the context of these specific kinds of everyday knowledge and practice that providers, as institutional and yet personal go-betweens, translate and assemble policy. Situated in a different location in the circuit of decision making, and cutting-and-pasting different entities and bodies of knowledge in particular sites of productive practice, policy providers are translators of a different sort than those engaged in official policy formation and "transfer."

In this chapter, then, I shift attention from the travel of policy across jurisdictions to the travel of policy within jurisdictions, focusing in particular on providers' engagements with the key guiding assumptions and claims informing the policy mandates they are charged to administer.[1] As I noted at the end of chapter 1, the New Zealand Labor-Coalition government, elected in 1999, back-pedaled on the reforms of the 1980s and 1990s by introducing major reforms in 2002 that raised benefit levels and eliminated workfare requirements. I accordingly worked with providers in Kingston in 2004 and 2005 in order to get a sense of how they were translating and articulating the frameworks of the new government in the context of their everyday knowledge and practice—including their understandings of the previous, more neoliberal regime—at a time when these new approaches had been in place for only a short time. My focus was thus not so much on the neoliberalism of the NZ Model as on the "after" neoliberalism (Larner, Le Heron, and Lewis 2007) of the Clark government. In Riverview, Alberta, in contrast, I explored providers' translations of the neoliberalism of the Klein administration in the period between 2001 and 2006, roughly a decade after the 1993 reforms, which were well entrenched at the time of my research. These temporal differences in the two sites allow for an exploration of providers' productive engagements with policy in the context of both recent policy change, in the one case, and policy duration, in the other.

While my analysis in chapter 1 focused on a range of governmental, nongovernmental, academic, and media sources—all textual—here I base my analysis on face-to-face encounters with providers in Kingston and Riverview. Riverview has one welfare office only; in Kingston, where there are several satellite offices as well as a main branch located downtown, I worked with providers in the main branch. In both sites, I was given access to providers through managers, and in neither location was I permitted unlimited access to all providers. Nevertheless, I was able to interact informally (although more so in Kingston than Riverview; see below) with a number of providers as well as to formally interview a subset of them. Although I was not permitted to be present in meetings between providers and clients, in Riverview I was able to participate in a mandatory orientation session for all applicants. I was able to do the same in Kingston, where several providers were also generous enough to walk me through a mock application process.

My interactions with providers in the two sites felt very different. Providers in Kingston—along with politicians and official policy makers in both Kingston and Wellington—seemed relatively open, freely making themselves available to me and giving lengthy interviews consisting not only of discussions of substantive issues, but also chit-chat, laughter, personal stories, and various asides. This was the case with all of the providers I interacted with in Kingston; and I was also able to meet with several of them on multiple occasions, allowing us to engage in extended conversations, if not develop close relationships. In Riverview, in contrast, access to providers was more tightly circumscribed—our meetings took place in a separate meeting room according to schedules arranged by supervisors, rather than in their own working spaces at times I arranged with them directly, as in Kingston; and providers themselves struck me as considerably more reticent: they often gave short, unelaborated answers to my questions and only occasionally offered information or views that I hadn't solicited. Nor was I able to meet with any providers more than once. As I describe in more detail below, these differences may have been artifacts, at least in part, of the control orientation to service delivery in Alberta versus the service model in place in Aotearoa/New Zealand when I was doing my fieldwork.[2]

Social Development in Aotearoa/New Zealand: The Reforms

In 2002, Helen Clark's Labour-Coalition government dramatically reversed the reforms of the previous regime by raising benefit levels and eliminating work tests for beneficiaries until their youngest child turned eighteen years old. An Enhanced Case Management (ECM) system, focused on attending to the needs of the "entire person," was also instituted. This new approach, as explained to me by a group of six analysts at the Ministry of Social Development and four ministers/members of Parliament,[3] is best summed up as a move from "obligation" to "encouragement," or "social development" (New Zealand Government 2001). According to internal government data, I was told, the work tests of the 1990s had been shown to be ineffective: they had produced no decrease in welfare caseloads, beneficiaries had been shown to engage in paid labor whenever possible, and when workfare was eliminated the numbers of people on the Domestic Purposes Benefit (DPB) actually dropped. My interlocutors' readings of these data marked a dramatic shift from the previous government's view of human nature: work tests were now considered ineffective because people were no longer seen as lazy and parasitic, but, rather, as actively desirous of engagement with the wider world, including the world of employment. Thus Liz Jones, then deputy national commissioner for Work and Income (the welfare department), wrote that "on the whole, DPB clients ... were motivated to work" (2004: 121). As one interviewee put it, "the previous government had a very miserable view of human existence ... a dismal view of the motives of women who ... wound up on the DPB." In particular, the previous regime was built on the assumption that beneficiaries had made a "lifestyle choice," and that, "they spent lots of money drinking booze, lots of money feeding their kids McDonalds, KFC [and] fish and chips ... that they had continuous wild parties and they had dumped ... the care of the children [on others]." The result, my interlocutor continued, was a tendency on the part of the previous government to tell people what to do—to impose decisions upon them concerning where to live, where and how much to work, who to have relationships with, and so on—to the point that "they had almost no decisions in their lives to make." The "partnership" or "social development" approach of the new government, in contrast, claimed that, as one interviewee put it, "there's no problem with their [beneficiaries'] *attitude*." Rather, based on the assumption that "most people want to be in the paid work force or have some kind of career, or some interest outside the home," emphasis was placed on "invitation" rather than coercion. This was not to assert that no one would ever abuse the system; rather, everyone I spoke with claimed that abusers comprised a very small minority, rather than the majority, of the welfare population—a reversal of the previous government's orientation.

Emphasizing both market principles and a restrengthened welfare state, the government rolled out measures designed to buttress social welfare. The elimination of work tests took effect in March 2003, and by 2004/ 2005, when I was doing fieldwork, the government was in the process of introducing a Working for Families package that would contribute to the development of a minimum basic income by providing increased assistance for housing and child care costs. The government was also endeavoring to put into place a child care scheme that would provide all mothers in Aotearoa/New Zealand—on the benefit or not, in the workforce or not—with twenty hours of free child care per week, beginning in 2007. These changes were part and parcel of a reconceptualization of poverty that focused not only on the personal problems of the poor, such as lack of training, but also on the larger structural issues that generated poverty. Individual deficits were certainly not eclipsed in the new approach of the Clark government: their 2001 *Pathways to Opportunity: From Social Welfare to Social Development* emphasizes a "capacity building" for individuals, families, and communities that is almost singularly concerned with encouraging people to be entrepreneurial. But the report also makes reference to the cost and availability of child care, health problems and health care accessibility, housing costs, access to tertiary education, and wage and benefit rates. *Pathways to Opportunity* accordingly outlines government pledges to raise minimum wage and benefit rates, invest in affordable housing and child care, work to create jobs, and make health care and tertiary education more widely available. Thus the focus on getting people into employment did not download all the responsibility for this onto beneficiaries; rather, the emphasis on employment was coupled with both an explicit recognition of structural issues that may help or hinder beneficiaries' efforts to find and keep jobs, and, crucially, government promises to address these structural issues.

Within this frame of the state's expanded responsibilities regarding social and economic well-being, the new Enhanced Case Management (ECM) system was designed to improve the quality of beneficiaries' lives by improving their skills and connections in the community. With ECM, beneficiaries would have one key contact at the welfare office (rather than numerous and frequently changing ones), who would serve as a hub for information and support related to every relevant aspect of their lives, including "training and education, accommodation, finance, work ability, health and wellbeing (both parent and child), personal needs, social participation, and other" (New Zealand Government 2007: 12). The idea was to address the specific and varied needs of each person, rather than slot them into predetermined programs: "We will work with people to identify their strengths and needs, [and] tailor services such as job placements and courses to the individual" (New Zealand Government 2001: 4). Accordingly, in addition to working jointly with beneficiaries to construct Personal Development and Employment Plans (PDEP)—sets of goals and aspirations accompanied by an outline of what was needed in order to reach those goals and aspirations—case managers would provide referrals to agencies that could help with issues not addressed directly by the welfare department, in order to meet its mandate to focus broadly on human development (New Zealand Government 2001, 2007). "Transparency," "outcomes," and "trust" were considered key to this highly service-oriented system that would ideally be "client driven."

As I noted in chapter 1, the Douglas-inspired Richardson reforms, while strongly workfarist in rhetoric, were limited in practice by an entrenched maternalist cultural orientation. Thus, at their peak, the reforms required women to seek full time work only when their youngest child reached fourteen years of age. Maternalist and work-focused tendencies continued to sit side by side in the 2002 reforms, only in reverse order: instead of combining a strong rhetoric of work with a quieter practice of maternalism, the government combined a strong rhetoric of "the family" with a quieter emphasis on employment. On the one hand, the Ministry of Social Development claimed that "the intent of the 2002 reform … was to allow parents to decide for themselves how to balance work and parental responsibilities" (New Zealand Government 2007: 5). Indeed, the government underscored the importance of the family and of women's roles as caregivers by giving official acknowledgement to the results of a 2005 survey in which 61 percent of DPB respondents indicated that they preferred to look after their children themselves rather than use child care (New Zealand Government 2007: 8). At the same time, however, the government claimed that "[t]he reform retained a focus on paid employment as the key to improving social and economic outcomes," even while it "shifted to a more facilitative approach" (2007: 13). In the government's view, a key deficiency of the previous regime had been the tendency among providers, overwhelmed by high caseloads, to focus their work-related interventions narrowly on those clients who had to meet the requirement for full-time work. Since most beneficiaries had children under fourteen years old, this meant that the majority of beneficiaries did not receive work-related interventions, leaving them unprepared to enter the workforce when the time came. The 2002 reforms responded to this lacuna by requiring that all clients begin working on their PDEPs within six weeks of signing up for welfare and by reducing caseloads to enable case managers to work with *all* their clients on the important project, however temporally distant, of preparing for participation in paid labor.

Welfare Providers'[4] Productions

With this context in mind, I now turn to explore how welfare providers translated these shifts in policy. I focus in particular on how providers translated the human development approach underlying the reforms, including its claims and assumptions about human nature, about beneficiaries as experts on themselves, and about the causes of poverty. I also explore how providers translated and assembled their own roles as facilitators in an ECM approach, with specific attention to how they made sense of the contradictory messages regarding employment and parenting embedded in the reforms.

Human Development

All the welfare providers with whom I interacted expressed support for the human development approach of the Clark regime. They translated its terms directly into their speech, making frequent references to "holism," to the importance of attending to "the whole picture"—to entire, complex persons and situations, rather than just parts of them—and to a system that "clients steer ... themselves"; that is, one in which clients take on key decision-making roles. This adoption of a human development model entailed the rejection of certain aspects of the previous regime, including its general ethos as well as some of its particular stipulations. Beryl, for instance, who had been a welfare provider since just before the 1996-legislated work tests, and who had also been on the DPB herself when the 1991 cuts were introduced, noted a significant change in what she referred to as the "atmosphere" of the welfare department since the election of the Clark government. Beneficiaries were no longer "made to feel there's a big hand out and that ... they have to beg for their money type of thing," she said; "so it kinda went from an atmosphere of 'Don't give them money unless you have to,' to 'They're entitled ... and see what you can do to help out.'" In Beryl's reading, the human development approach was both more sympathetic and generous, and less moralistic and punitive, than what had come before.

Other providers focused on more specific aspects of regime change, such as the labeling of beneficiaries. I was once given the opportunity to participate in a mock interview process (during which my fictitious self would be screened for eligibility and then interviewed to determine what benefits and programs I would have access to), with three providers: John, an intake worker, and Patti and Marilyn, both case managers. The process took the better part of a morning. After John had established that I (now a newly single mother of two girls under the age of five, with one year of nursing school completed before the birth of my daughters) was eligible for the DPB, Marilyn and Patti took over. As we walked through the application process the two women moved back and forth between role-play and commentary, periodically stepping out of the DPB interview frame and into a research interview frame to explain to me why they were following a particular procedure or to comment on what they thought about it. One aspect of the application process they were both enthusiastic about was the new categorization of beneficiaries that would place them into one of three slots: *early response* (when people first arrived at the welfare office and needed immediate assistance), *work-focused case management* (which entailed actively working with beneficiaries on training, education, and job searches), and *work unlikely* (which was, nevertheless, not meant to indicate a *permanent* state). While I read this new system of categorization as overwhelmingly employment-focused (see discussion below), Patti and Marilyn read it as providing a much-needed intervention into a system that had formerly encouraged stagnation: "It's gonna be much, much better," Patti said, "because you're not a 'DPB beneficiary.'" Marilyn explained: "I have worked for a long time with people that are receiving DPB, so, and that's part of people's blockage. ... They see themselves as a 'DPB person.'" *DPB beneficiary*, then, was a label that kept people fixed in place, while the new categorization would signal to beneficiaries that they were in transition—not stuck, but *going someplace*. When clients arrive in the welfare office now, Marilyn said, "we're not saying 'You've gotta work,' we're saying 'What's [your] situation? Where do you wanna go? What's your motive?'—rather than 'You must work'—and 'How ... can [we] help you along the way to achieve your goals in life?'" What Patti and Marilyn were underscoring here was the wider scope of attention afforded by the new categorization relative to the one-slot "DPB beneficiary" of the previous regime.

In addition to translating the new category system into something that indexed holism and flexibility, some providers also eagerly adopted the reconfiguration, embedded in the 2002 reforms, of beneficiaries as best situated to decide how to balance parenting with paid labor. Marilyn's questions—"What's your situation?" and "Where do you wanna go?"—mark this relocation of expertise from agents of the state to clients themselves. Providers spoke in this regard of helping beneficiaries develop "their full potential" in a way that broadened "potential" beyond finding and keeping a job. Assessments of what beneficiaries needed in order to reach this full potential and of how to go about meeting those needs emerged, providers explained, during the course of constructing Personal Development and Employment Plans (PDEPs). The accent here was on "development" rather than "employment;" the former could include the latter, but even if the latter was considered necessary, it was no longer considered sufficient to personal development and fulfillment. In other words, these were not Personal Employment Plans, or even Personal Employment and Development Plans, but *Personal Development* and Employment Plans. In keeping with the new frame of beneficiary-as-expert, providers accordingly constructed the PDEP as a completely transparent and "client-driven process" that addressed a range of areas in beneficiaries' lives; and many reported that they had clients who came in to discuss the plans more frequently than once a year, as required.

Combining the beneficiary-as-expert frame with a pastoral, paternalistic approach to guidance and encouragement, some providers stressed not only the empowering, but also the *responsibilizing* aspects of this new client-driven process. As Phillip, for instance, put it, "The policy is more about when the client is ready. ... This is good because then they feel that they have the responsibility, rather than [me] telling them what to do." He claimed that both he and his clients benefited from this "philosophical change": clients because the system was now "giving [them] back their power," and providers because they no longer felt that clients' lives were *their* responsibility. When clients attempt to get him to make decisions for them, Phillip told me, he lays out the options and tries to "put it back on them": "At the end of the day it is their life. They need to establish their own goals."

Work

As providers took up the new regime, they rejected what they now, in retrospect, saw as the narrowness of a previous system that focused on parts of rather than entire persons, and that located expertise and decision making in the system rather than in beneficiaries—who, in the current frame, now had the right as well as the responsibility to make decisions about their own lives. As my discussion above indicates, this emphasis of the new government on whole and knowledgeable beneficiaries was easily embraced by providers; it was almost transparently translatable. A more detailed exploration of how providers approached the issue of paid work, however, indicates that they struggled with the contradictions embedded in the reforms, and that some aspects of the reforms were lost in translation, deemed "unfit to fit" (Lendvai and Stubbs 2007, 2009), either inappropriate or simply irrelevant to their agendas.

I begin by returning to my mock assessment interview with Patti and Marilyn, who told me that an important part of their job was to correct the ill-advised approaches to work that they had imposed on beneficiaries before 2002; viz., that they needed to accept any job that became available, regardless of how appropriate it was in terms of remuneration or their abilities. Typically, Patti explained, when she asks beneficiaries what they want to do, they tell her that they want a job. Once she scratches the surface, however, she finds that they only say that "because there's been institutions telling them … [they] have to work." Moreover, in the context of this new, more expansive system, Patti has come to realize that many of the jobs beneficiaries were willing to take would not in fact pay them enough to cover child care costs, let alone suit their temperaments or goals—things the previous regime had placed no value on whatsoever. Instead of pushing work for work's sake, then, her new focus was on: "let's find some skills that … makes it affordable for you to work and that you can develop up. … Just because you're [on the] DPB doesn't mean you have to be a cleaner. You have a potential for whatever you want to do, okay, and it's about tapping into that potential and helping it to develop." In "tapping into that potential," Marilyn and Patti explored with their clients not only how to pursue their life goals, but also what was getting in the way of this pursuit, whether that included child care issues, psychological distress, relationship breakdown, housing costs, addictions, access to education, and so on. Their role in these explorations was to provide assistance in teasing out goals and blockages—much as facilitators or counselors might operate—as well as specific information that beneficiaries might not have on how to access particular forms of assistance or support. The most important knowledge was thus held by clients; the case manager's role was limited to assisting in its articulation and to supplementing it with information on additional available resources.

Clearly, the move away from forcing people to take whatever jobs are available to thinking about jobs in the larger contexts of beneficiaries' lives represents a significant shift. However, while explicitly arguing against narrow constructions of beneficiaries as potential workers, Patti and Marilyn nevertheless remained focused precisely on employment, as did all the providers with whom I interacted. As they translated it, the government's emphasis on "paid employment as the key to improving social and economic outcomes" (New Zealand Government 2007: 13) morphed into the view that most people wanted to have the material means to enjoy life, and that the only way to acquire these was to get a job, rather than stay on the benefit. Much as "Let's find some skills that … makes it affordable for you to work" avoids work for work's sake, it remains oriented to paid labor. "Most people," Patti said, "want to have more money for their families, so they can enjoy life, do things they want to, but [if] you come in here and you go on this benefit … then you're not [going] to develop." *Development* here is inextricably tied (and, in the final instance, reduced) to employment. Similarly, Beryl, focused on helping beneficiaries develop their "full potential," also expressed expectations of some level of engagement in paid work: "[Case management is] about building that person's self-esteem and so then to be rich in their goals that they set … whatever they might be, their own personal goals, and it might not necessarily be work.… They might want to work part-time or just ten hours a week and volunteer five hours a week and bring up their children, and I think those things are far more important than money." Beryl moves seamlessly here from "rich … goals" to working "part-time or just ten hours a week and volunteer[ing] five hours a week." Work, then, is normalized as part and parcel of any set of "rich goals." Indeed, when she listed the areas covered in PDEPs, Beryl slightly shifted the order of items from the official "training and education, accommodation, finance, work ability, health and wellbeing (both parent and child), personal needs, social participation, and other," to "employment, education, accommodation, financial, health, personal needs, social participation, [and] other issues." Employment was now at the top of the list, prior to the training and education that provide the grounds for accessing sustainable and fulfilling jobs. In addition, in Beryl's rendition, children have fallen off the list altogether, which raises the question of what happens to the identity of beneficiaries as *parents* (a point to which I return in chapter 3).

I also encountered providers who were not at all interested in rejecting the previous regime's singular focus on employment, but, rather, carried it with them, as it were, into the terrain of the new regime. Maria, a provider for over twenty years, was representative of this group. Although never officially coercing beneficiaries to work, since policy no longer permitted that, Maria told me that she routinely pressured them to accept whatever jobs were available: "We're not getting them jobs for job's [sake] but some of them don't even know what they wanna do, so we're saying 'Well, there's a job here.… this doesn't mean to say you have to stay there forever, this is a stepping-stone for you [to] get you started, [and] while you're in your job … you can start looking outside instead of coming begging to us all the time.'" Whether available jobs fit beneficiaries' (full) needs or desires was irrelevant; Maria wanted them to get work experience and to move beyond dependence on the state. She took this approach, she explained, because she had seen welfare become a "lifestyle" in too many cases: she had encountered too many women who "use their babies to get a hand out." Maria, who like Beryl had also been on the DPB as a young single mother, was adamant that dependency on the system was a bad thing and that only hard work—by which she meant work looking for and keeping jobs, even when they were poorly paid, demeaning, or otherwise taxing—with no crutches to lean on, would get you anywhere you wanted to be.

In some ways, the contradictions of the 2002 reforms—"allow parents to decide for themselves how to balance work and parental responsibilities" (New Zealand Government 2007: 5), versus "paid employment ... [is] the key to improving social and economic outcomes" (2007: 13)—created the space within which the view of the previous regime that all beneficiaries must be enjoined to undertake paid labor for their own good as well as for the good of society could endure. This was no doubt buttressed by the new requirement that beneficiaries begin constructing PDEPs within six weeks of signing up for the DPB, a requirement that may have balanced out, or even eclipsed, the message behind the elimination of work tests—namely, to allow parents to decide for themselves whether and when to enter the labor force—since it required continual encouragement and monitoring of work plans, work readiness activities, and so forth. Official deference to parents' knowledge and expertise thus becomes empty rhetoric when the focus of joint activity is repeatedly oriented to and framed by PDEPs that require attention to employment, even if its official place in the sequence is *after* "development."

Beneficiaries and Case Management

Encouraged in part by the contradictions of the new policy discourse as well as by the discourses and practices of PDEPs, enduring emphasis on employment among providers also indexed their translations of policy in the light of their everyday knowledges of beneficiaries. The government's construction of persons as naturally oriented to being-out-in-the world did not, in providers' view, fit every applicant that they encountered across the desk, as Maria's reading of women using their babies "to get a hand out" indicates. While some saw potential in their clients that only needed some gentle facilitation and support in order to be realized, others feared the potential to *not* engage, to choose welfare as a "lifestyle." In providers' view, "client-driven" human development approaches would not work with beneficiaries who did not have sufficient knowledge of themselves to know that they really should take any job that came along, or who had no idea whatsoever of what they wanted to do with their lives. The movement of a human development approach from policy-making centers to welfare offices thus met its limits in what providers referred to as "the dependency thing"—a phenomenon, according to many providers, that challenged the model of beneficiaries as engaged and motivated people who simply needed some guidance and encouragement. As Phillip put it: "We've had this benefit for thirty years and it's turned into a lifestyle thing.... People feel they can't live without it. People have no understanding of why you would have to go to work." A part of him, he said, wanted to follow the US model, particularly with regard to lifetime limits on the receipt of the benefit.

All of the providers I met had developed unofficial systems for categorizing clients. Phillip's binary approach, which placed clients in one of two opposed camps, provides a representative example. In one camp were beneficiaries who "know where they are going, they know that this is a temporary thing, they know where they want to get, they have a clear path." Such clients were easy to work with: they wanted to understand their "bad choices," to make something of their lives, to participate in their PDEPs, and to get off of welfare as soon as possible—and they often succeeded, he said, within two years. In the opposing camp were those beneficiaries who had no motivation—the "no commitment" people who often stayed on welfare for years. These clients never agree to anything, and "are quite happy staying at home looking after their babies.... Some of it is just that they think they can just sit there on the DPB till the day they die." In exasperation, Phillip asked, "What are we gonna *do* with these people?" "*Would you just get a life!?*" he feigned confronting them. Once in poverty, then, some people chose to diagnose where they had gone wrong and "to make some changes in their life and then things can get better rather than going into the victim pile which goes nowhere," while others clearly chose the latter route. These tended to be the "no commitment" people who "live for the day ... [and] don't think past next week." Although Phillip noted that some beneficiaries fell somewhere between these two extremes, and that some moved through both categories at different points in their lives depending on context and circumstance, the two extremes capture both the range of and the most typical patterns he encountered in his day-to-day work.

Phillip approached the would-you-just-get-a-life people by means of the same tactic that Patti and Marilyn had described to me during our mock assessment interview:

> Sometimes I ask them what they will do when their child turns eighteen and you've not done anything and you are not prepared. It's about giving them a reality check, challenging the nonresponsibility.... Sometimes I ask, "Wouldn't you like to go on a holiday or to be able to buy new clothes?" [It's about] trying to find out what they like and then working with that and saying, "You can't do that and stay on the benefit. This is not a good idea in the long run, you just get poorer and poorer. When your child is a teenager and wants the flash gear and you only have five dollars to spare, what are you going to do about it? Is it a good thing to sit and wait for ... [that] to happen?"

This represents a particular take on the "facilitative" approach informing Enhanced Case Management. Here, ECM articulates with the more "pushy" provider approach of the previous regime, producing a hybrid, pastoral type of "tough love." As with the human development model of the new regime, the idealized "facilitative" ECM model was thus only partially adopted by providers. From where they sat, *not* all clients were actively engaged knowledgeable insiders with expertise on their own lives; therefore providers could not always interact with them in accordance with the ECM model. While certain practices and ideologies of the new regime fit with providers' knowledge and experience, then, others did not, because they failed to address what providers actually encountered in their daily lives: not just people who were excited about embracing their own expertise and moving out into the world, but also the "no commitment" people, who saw welfare as a "lifestyle" choice.

Social Structure

What fit providers' knowledge the least—and was thus completely lost in translation—was the new regime's effort to reposition poverty as a property not only of individuals but also of social and economic systems. For instance, although eager and motivated clients were worlds apart in temperament from the "no commitment" people Phillip encountered, he felt that in most cases poverty had the same basic cause:

> I think a lot of it is about bad choices. . . . You know, either they've chosen the wrong type of person to have a relationship with or, or they've got themselves in bad situations through, you know, they've bought this or they got this on HP [hire purchase, or rent-to-own] ... [and] then they end up in this big mess and then they don't know what to do and all the stress from that creates the friction and then they end up separating from, in their relationships [splitting up with their partners], so I mean it's not always like that but a lot of it is ... not just one thing that's gone wrong, it's six or seven things that have gone wrong and that all happened sort of in a short space of time, you know, and ... people just can't cope with it, you know, and you get a lot of that sort of stuff happening.

Phillip moves here from individual "bad choices," such as choosing the wrong partner, to a conglomeration of "bad choices" that take on a life of their own, becoming overwhelming and impossible to "cope with." The emphasis remains on the choices themselves, with little attention given to the contexts of those choices—the impetus for making them, or the cultural and socioeconomic structures and processes framing the kinds of "choices" people make concerning where to live, what to buy, or even who to partner up with or call on for support. This assumption of poverty as a property of individuals who somehow fail to reflect the valued neoliberal attributes of autonomy, responsibility, and risk management, so forcefully articulated by the previous regime, was shared by all the providers with whom I interacted, none of whom made any reference to possible structural causes of poverty. Such destructured, decontextualized formulations are, of course, no news; and in one sense, there is really nothing remarkable about people whose job it is to work with individuals having individualistic as opposed to structural explanations of social phenomena.[5] What is particularly interesting here, however, is that this construction of the causes of poverty is being asserted in a context in which the state had been taking explicit measures to move away from neoliberal formulations of poverty as the exclusive artifact of individual failings to explore not only other individualized phenomena, such as physical and mental health, but also specifically structural phenomena related to housing costs, wage rates, access to health care and tertiary education, and so on (New Zealand Government 2001, 2007). This part of the government's framing had no imaginary or practical purpose for providers, and was simply left behind.

Discussion

The 2002 reforms contained contradictory messages. On the one hand, work tests were eliminated in favor of a more "facilitative" approach that validated single parents who preferred to stay at home until their children were fully grown. On the other hand, a discourse of work was injected early (within six weeks of signing up for the benefit) and repeated at regular intervals (in the form of PDEP meetings) in order to reinforce the need for "personal development," which, in the end, really meant employment—perhaps in the government's intention as well as in providers' translation. (Indeed, I found it ironic that in one of the section headings in the government's 2007 evaluation report on the 2002 reforms, Personal Development and Employment Plans is reversed, reading Personal Employment and Development Plans; New Zealand Government 2007: 17.) Engagement in paid labor thus remained the marker of citizenship and was constructed as the best route to personal growth and fulfillment. Larner, Le Heron, and Lewis (2007: 228) correctly point out in this regard that the post/after-neoliberal policies of the Clark government "continue to draw on highly economistic language and are tied to increasing participation in the globalizing economy for both men and women."

This double valence was translated by welfare providers in a way that was commensurate with the ideologies of the previous regime. In chapter 4, I discuss how beneficiaries in Kingston felt enormous pressure to look for jobs, even when caring for very young children, such that they did not personally experience the validation of mothering written into the 2002 reforms. Here, suffice it to point out that the welfare providers with whom I spoke, all of whom had adopted the language of "holism" and "social development" with some zeal, also all reported pressuring clients to take jobs in the face of legislation that had done away with workfare—although some did this more gently than others. The Ministry of Social Development's 2007 evaluation report on the 2002 reforms indicates that the pattern I encountered in Kingston was not atypical. Evaluating PDEPs constructed in 2003 and 2005, the ministry found that fully 57 percent focused on education, training, and employment. Beneficiaries' financial concerns were foregrounded in only 7 and 5 percent of PDEPS in 2003 and 2005, respectively; accommodation was the focus in only 4 percent of PDEPs in each year; and social participation was the emphasis in only 2 percent of PDEPs in 2003 and in only 1 percent in 2005 (2007: 17).

One way of reading this is that the emphasis on employment was, in fact, the intention of policy makers in the first place: pay lip service to the family and parenting, but really focus on employment. The requirement to begin work on PDEPs very early on in the welfare "careers" of beneficiaries supports this interpretation. This practical orientation to employment, in turn, buttresses—or is buttressed by—the ideologies of the previous regime. All of the providers I encountered had worked in the previous system, and during the course of some fifteen years of neoliberal governance in society at large as well as in the welfare office, they had been encouraged to develop readings of beneficiaries and of welfare commensurate with neoliberal frameworks. It should thus come as no surprise that some providers drew on the rhetoric of the old regime (which was, after all, present in their ideological tool kits) in their face-to-face encounters with beneficiaries, some of whom seemingly did not give any indication that they knew what they wanted to do with their lives, or that they were motivated to find out. Having been "raised" in the previous regime, then, and in the face of policy that continued to stress the importance of employment, some providers' views of lazy beneficiaries and of the need for responsibilization and self-sufficiency in the form of engagement with paid work remained viable, even as they sat alongside valorizations of "social development."

Thus while providers fully embraced an ECM approach that encouraged them to interact with whole persons and that positioned them as facilitators, they were mixed when it came to actually treating beneficiaries as knowledgeable insiders. Phillip, as mentioned above, was happy to give beneficiaries back "their own power" by recognizing that they needed to set their own goals, for example, but this did not apply to his "no-commitment" beneficiaries, who required pressure more than "facilitation." Maria also felt that clients needed to be pushed, a sentiment expressed in less draconian form by Beryl, Patti, and Marilyn. They did not translate the beneficiaries-as-expert-on-their-own-lives framework of the 2002 reforms into a practice of validating clients who chose to be stay-at-home mothers, for example. They were also mixed in their constructions of their roles as ECMs. They certainly took up the new, more detailed approach to assessment and referral focused on in the government's adoption of ECM; but they also went beyond this to construct themselves as therapists, life coaches, or personal trainers who sometimes have to exert pressure and impose direction, in spite of government acknowledgement that case managers are not trained to deal with sensitive psychological issues (New Zealand Government 2007: 22).

This departure from the government's "facilitative" approach in favor of more direct and intrusive pressure on beneficiaries may be read as an inchoate critique of the one-size-fits-all frame of the current regime; namely, the view that all persons had not only a tendency but also an active desire to be engaged in the world at large. Providers did not encounter such a homogenous population. This is not to argue that the previous regime was more accurate in *its* portrayal of beneficiaries. Indeed, the argument could be flipped to claim that in emphasizing exclusively negative personality characteristics (laziness, dependency, parasitic tendencies), the previous government failed to take into account beneficiaries who were both hard working and interested in being engaged in the world. In other words, both the previous and current regimes based policy on a homogenous, one-dimensional view of "the beneficiary" (however surprising this may be in an ECM model that emphasizes "whole persons"), in the process leaving out and therefore failing to respond adequately to persons who, in providers' view, did not fit the template. Interacting on a daily basis with a range of persons, providers felt this narrowness keenly.

Finally, as noted, two key features of the reforms—the situating of poverty (at least in part) in structural context, and the assertion that dependency on the state is acceptable in some situations, particularly those related to parenting—were completely elided. In the end, case managers assembled policies that consisted of bits and pieces of the old regime—individualism and personal responsibility, the need to force people to look after themselves, and the idea that dependency on the state is inherently negative—with the more holistic and gentler approaches of the new. Their assemblages were comprised of selective translations articulated with their new roles as ECMs (which widened their discretionary power), their everyday knowledges of a range of beneficiaries (some of which was built during the course of the previous, more neoliberal regime), and their positions as go-betweens in the context of vague and contradictory policy directives. In their interactions within the terrain produced by the "delegation down" (Mosse 2011: 59) approach of ECM, providers in Kingston adopted certain pieces of the new policy frame intact (the language of human development), transformed others (the model of the person, the approach to work, their roles as facilitators) into something they could work with, and jettisoned yet others (structural analyses). Translation was partial, piecemeal, and firmly situated in the context of providers' institutional location, agendas, and knowledges.

Tough Love on the Alberta Prairie: The Reforms

As I indicated in chapter 1, the 1993/94 reforms in Alberta focused on making welfare unattractive and work mandatory. In an ethos of cowboy capitalism—comprised of long-standing visions of rugged individualism and contemporary practices of cutthroat competition among industries of resource extraction—and in a political climate in which government debt and "special interests" were construed as the greatest detriments to society, welfare rolls were slashed and workfare requirements tightened. Reducing the number of people on the welfare rolls was one of the government's key goals. In *A Better Way*, government "strategies" regarding Supports for Independence (SFI) included decreasing caseloads by 3,000 in 1994/95, and by an additional 3,000 in 1995/96 (Government of Alberta 1994: 5). In *A Better Way II*, SFI "strategies" included, for 1995/96, that the "average caseload will be 54,500 compared to the original budget of 65,100"; for 1996/97, a "further reduction of 3,000 cases"; and finally, for 1997/98 yet a "further reduction of 2,800 cases" (Government of Alberta 1995: 7). These decreases were to be accompanied by increases in support for employment initiatives in the context of a business plan that was overwhelmingly oriented to the province's fiscal health and economic growth, both to be accomplished in part by the creation of an environment friendly to business interests.

Over the course of the 1990s and into the new millennium, the government of Alberta continued to refine its approach, repeatedly stating in both public pronouncements and policy requirements that welfare was meant to be a last resort and that independence from all forms of state support was the ideal. In 2004, on the recommendation of the Low-Income Programs Review (Government of Alberta 2001), SFI was replaced with Alberta Works, which consolidated social assistance and employment programs. With the launching of Alberta Works, even recipients with children under six months old were officially categorized as "expected to work," since their inability to work was considered only temporary (Al-

berta Human Resources and Employment 2004). Despite periodic alterations in the arbitrary time period during which mothers of young children
would be excused from work requirements—at one point during my research it was expanded to one year after the birth of the youngest child—
the Klein government never wavered in its stance that poor mothers, if
not dependent on a male breadwinner, needed to be in paid labor.

Under Alberta Works, welfare recipients were required to collaborate
with Career and Employment Consultants (CECs) to create Client Investment Plans (CIPs). CIPs resembled New Zealand's PDEPs only insofar as they were forms jointly filled out by providers and recipients. In
contrast to PDEPs (in structure, if not in practice), CIPs were narrowly
employment focused. Representing a "contract" between recipients and
the welfare department, CIPs obliged recipients, at the risk of cuts to their
benefits, to submit monthly reports detailing all aspects of their financial
situation and to undertake any or all of the following:

- looking for work every day,
- keeping a record of where you looked for work, your applications
  and interviews,
- going to any appointment that may help you find work,
- going to workshops or programs,
- telling your financial benefits worker when you get a job,
- trying to increase your hours if you are working part-time, and
- actively seek other work with higher pay. (Alberta Human Resources
  and Employment 2004: 4)

I got a sense of the Alberta Works approach to the poor when I partici-
pated in the half-day "orientation" that welfare applicants were obliged
to attend prior to meeting with a benefits worker to determine eligibility. During this orientation, applicants were told that they were expected
to make looking for work their full-time job. They were given forms on
which they had to indicate, on a daily basis, precisely what actions they
took to secure employment (hand in resume, interview, talk to manager,
phone call, etc.). The form, which had boxes for indicating the names and
phone numbers of persons contacted at each potential place of employment, was to be handed in at the welfare office at the end of each week.
The following was printed at the bottom of the form: *** I am aware that
random contacts may be made to verify the above. *** At the end of the
session, applicants were given a certificate verifying their participation,

with the following printed at the bottom: *Please note that you are expected to follow through on all referrals identified in your employment plan at the time of intake, or at a future date by any department staff.* When a prospective client at the session I attended asked what she should do if the funds provided to cover child care while she looked for a job were insufficient, or if the only job she could find paid the same as what she would have to pay for child care, the session facilitator responded, "Working is better than not working." The reforms in Alberta were explicit about the need to move people off the welfare rolls and into employment, and on the placement of responsibility for that move onto recipients themselves. The orientation facilitator was equally explicit in conveying this message to orientation participants.

This orientation session differed dramatically from that I attended in Kingston, similarly scheduled in advance of the intake interview. The session in Kingston focused on two themes: first, the goals of the welfare department, which included not only moving beneficiaries into employment but also providing assistance in meeting a range of needs related to housing, health care, child care, psychological counseling, and so on; and second, the specific programs and referral services available through the department. Beneficiaries' obligations—to work on PDEPs and to be honest in their interactions with the welfare department—were mentioned, but they were not the primary focus of the presentation. In Riverview, in contrast, the entire orientation session was devoted to the topic of department expectations and client obligations regarding employment, and I walked away with a strong sense that, given the government goal of reducing case loads, the orientation session was at least partially meant to serve as a deterrent to potential applications, a kind of prophylactic designed to reduce demands on both department staff and state coffers.

In addition to work requirements, ongoing benefit cuts, as outlined in chapter 1, continued to take their toll. To briefly refresh the reader's memory: by 2005, following repeated cuts, welfare rates for a single parent with one child were lower in Alberta than in any other province in the country, sitting at 48 percent of Statistics Canada's before-tax low income cut-off (the Canadian version of the poverty line; National Council of Welfare 2006: 32). The Klein Revolution also entailed cuts to public service employment. Again, a refresher: between January 1993 and December 1994, the public service lost approximately 7,000 jobs, and the government announced plans to cut an additional 8,000 positions, reducing the public service by 22 percent (Taylor 1995: 105; see also Dacks, Green, and Trimble 1995). In both *A Better Way* and *A Better Way II*, "staff reduction through attrition and redeployment" was listed as a key "strategy" for SFI for each year from 1994 to 1997 (Government of Alberta 1994, 1995). This was in keeping with the key questions the new

Klein administration used to frame its approach to government, as outlined in *A Better Way* (1994: 2): "What are the core responsibilities of government? What businesses should government be in? And, how can we do the job better, achieve better results and spend less money?" The metanarrative was one of efficiency, economic growth, and a shrinking state—in short, of a reorganization of society to meet the needs of the market (rather than vice versa). Cuts to both the welfare rolls and public service provided means to achieve these ends.

Reductions in the numbers of providers were accompanied by the placement of increased pressures on those who managed to hold on to their jobs, who were themselves now subject to surveillance of the heightened surveillance they were required to exercise vis-à-vis their clients. Far from the human development–based Enhanced Case Management put in place by the Clark government in Aotearoa/New Zealand, then, the approach to welfare in Alberta post-1993 represents a control approach to social service delivery: both clients and providers were subjected to minute, exacting, and persistent forms of surveillance, and neither was authorized as a knowledgeable insider capable of making informed decisions. The welfare providers I encountered in Riverview were thus operating in a climate that contrasted sharply with that in effect when I worked with providers in Kingston. The emphasis on moving "from a passive system to an active re-employment program" (Government of Alberta 1994: 8), did not activate providers' or clients' motivational and entrepreneurial possibilities, but instead fixed both in a passive state, as recipients and conduits of *government* action.

Nevertheless, despite being situated as mere conduits for the implementation of government programs in an environment in which their discretionary power was severely curtailed, welfare providers in Riverview did not mechanically translate, intact, the policy frames of the Klein regime. As I describe below, they certainly did adopt as sensible, reasonable, appropriate, and even commonsensical certain aspects of the new regime's approach; but their unique angle on issues related to poverty and financial assistance led them to question other aspects of policy mandates, producing in the process policy assemblages that were considerably more complicated and nuanced than the more direct translation of the orientation facilitator I described above.

Welfare Providers' Productions

Helping Clients

Like their colleagues in Kingston, welfare providers in Riverview took the opportunity provided by reform to retrospectively reevaluate the previous system; and, also like their colleagues in Kingston, they found it wanting. However, whereas Kingston providers constructed the old regime as too harsh—inappropriately drumming home the message that beneficiaries had to accept any job they could find, regardless of its financial or personal suitability—providers in Riverview, looking back in time, felt that the system had not been demanding enough, that it had, in effect, taught recipients how *not* to work, how *not* to be motivated.

A story told to me by veteran provider Margaret captures this negative reconstruction of the old system. Margaret's client, Bertha, had been on welfare for over a decade, since the birth of the youngest of her five children. Prior to the reforms, and with Margaret's oversight, the welfare bureaucracy had poured seemingly endless resources into Bertha's household, not only in the form of direct financial assistance, but also in the form of hours of effort expended by an array of counselors, including youth workers involved with the children. Given Bertha's myriad problems—"The family home was in chaos," as Margaret put it—it was the considered opinion of the various staff involved that Bertha would have to stay on welfare until her children were grown up and out of the house. When the reforms came in, however, this became impossible: welfare providers were now required to increase their expectations of clients, who were in turn expected to cooperate in their state-directed remediation and reconstruction as persons capable of independence. Margaret accordingly pressured Bertha to undertake training to be a personal care assistant, and then to get a job, which Bertha succeeded in doing. The result, Margaret felt, was "phenomenal": "Here we'd been so passive and not doing anything, not encouraging her to do anything else 'cause 'Oh, it's just too crazy at home,' whereas she actually took some training … and got a job and … her going out and working, suddenly she had a routine, she had more self-respect, she had all these wonderful things, yes, and you know what?—the impact on the kids at home was phenomenal!"

In retrospect, then, it turned out that doing Bertha the "favor" of supporting her to stay at home with her children was in fact harming her. Every provider I met in Riverview shared this reading of the previous regime. Postreform, they constructed what existed before as neglect: a tendency to throw money at clients, only to abandon them to "fester," as several put it (indicating a shared imagery of suppurating wounds), in whatever unhappy situation had brought them to the welfare office in the first place. The old regime, in other words, was disempowering, demotivating, and destructive of self-esteem. As Mark—who, like all the providers I met in Riverview, had been working in the welfare office since before the reforms—put it, it was unconscionable "to relegate somebody to fifteen, twenty, or thirty years of welfare," since the inevitable outcome was stagnation, a fixing of recipients in an always bad place. In contrast, in providers' translation of the new policy framework, actually *caring* for clients meant moving away from this kind of benign—but in reality highly injurious—neglect and towards something more proactive and engaged. Thus the "love" side of "tough love."

Rather than leaving recipients to fester in their own misery, then, the reforms, which produced a system significantly leaner in terms of eligibility (thus the reduction of the rolls by almost 50 percent in little over two years), and meaner in terms of workfare requirements, forced recipients onto what Mark called a "fast track towards ... independence." No longer were clients permitted to "sit and get comfortable." Instead, he said, "you're in there and before you have a chance to look left or right you're ... committed to a plan and off you're going."

However "fabulous" or "wonderful" the results, providers concurred that the "tough" side of "tough love" emerged when it came to getting clients to actually *be* proactive and engaged. Margaret's exuberance at Bertha's success, for instance, was in direct proportion to the struggles involved in getting Bertha on track. And listening to Mark, who said more than once in the course of our discussion that "it's very painful" for clients to deal with the department's expectations, I couldn't help but think of the wisdom on pulling band-aids off quickly rather than slowly. It was as if Roger Douglas's *don't blink* approach, imported by the Klein administration, applied in the welfare office as well as to processes of restructuring: "Before you have a chance to look left or right you're ... committed to a plan and off you're going." As providers framed it, high-speed fast tracking and discomfort were key characteristics of the new regime. The dangers of letting recipients "get comfortable" and the need to instead "make them uncomfortable" were, accordingly, ubiquitous topics in our conversations. Richard, the longest serving provider in the office, framed this need to make clients uncomfortable as follows: "It doesn't seem to me that ... change happens often for the folks that we're working with, particularly on SFI, without some crisis or something that makes people uncomfortable." The before-you-know-it-you're-off-and-running shock-and-awe approach described by Mark—or, as Margaret put it more directly, the insistence that "you gotta do *something* towards independence"—produced just such a crisis: recipients were told, immediately upon applying for welfare, that they had no choice but to look for work, persistently, while someone looked over their shoulder to make sure they did so. This was, in providers' view, a healthy and productive crisis—much-needed medicine. Indeed, they argued that no one *wanted* to be on welfare; and in this sense, they considered the reforms to be an appropriate response to the authentic desires and aspirations of recipients themselves.

In keeping with this frame, providers agreed unanimously that recipients needed to: (1) exhaust all other resources before applying for welfare; (2) take responsibility for how they ended up in poverty; (3) put effort into being as independent as possible; and (4) accept that decisions have consequences and that the welfare office was not in the business of covering up, or compensating for, those consequences. This no-pain-no-gain orientation reveals both continuities and disjunctures vis-à-vis reform legislation. Exhausting all resources and putting effort into being as independent as possible were explicit in the reforms: the first was an initial eligibility requirement, while the second was the basis of the workfare system. Taking responsibility for how one ended up in a particular situation (as opposed to taking responsibility for becoming independent) and not covering up the natural consequences of peoples' decisions, however, were not explicitly in the legislation, but, rather, were written in—produced—by providers themselves. Legislation, in translation, engendered an orientation to the role of provider that was more therapeutic—even parent-like—than the straightforward requirements of the state.

Given that the increased pressure on clients in the new system was constructed as to their benefit in the long run, providers considered the increased pressure to which they themselves were subject in the new regime to be also generally useful, albeit somewhat burdensome. As I noted earlier, the post-1993 "active" welfare system entailed not only increased workloads for providers, but also increases in the steps and documentation that they had to produce to justify their actions and decision making. In particular, providers were now closely monitored to make sure that they did not fall outside the norm in their assessments of clients' potential employability, most notably with regard to the "unemployable" category. When discussing this aspect of their jobs, Mark feigned being asked by a supervisor, "How come you've got ... seventeen or eighteen 'unemployables' this week when normally you should have six or seven?" There were targets, under this new regime, that providers had to meet, and whereas the previous tendency with respect to clients who were on the borderline between "employable" and "unemployable" had been to put them in the latter category, this pattern was now reversed—when in doubt, employ. Providers were accordingly questioned by their supervisors if they stepped outside of the "norm."

This "norm," however, was not related in any direct way to the actual circumstances or characteristics of clients, but was, rather, an arbitrarily set number that met *departmental* needs. Government of Alberta business plans accordingly included specific performance indicators relating to both "outputs" and "efficiency" in all government agencies, including welfare offices; for example, "percentage of error-free files," "ratio of training placements to total welfare caseload," "cost per case," "administration and program costs per capita," and "department expenditures as a percentage of provincial expenditures and GDP" (Alberta Family and Social Services 1995: 19). *These* represented the official field of orientation, not client circumstances. Thus, in addition to being pressured to stay within a preset norm of categorization patterns, justificatory supports for providers' placements of clients into the "unemployable" category were now more narrowly delimited, necessitating a note from an MD or PhD where previously a note from a registered social worker would have sufficed. The tighter requirements initiated by the reforms thus diminished not only clients' room to move, but also providers' discretionary powers.

Again, however, the providers with whom I spoke did not translate the bureaucracy's surveillance of their own work into something demeaning or limiting, but, rather, situated it in relation to a larger, and overwhelmingly positive, program that would provide the best possible outcomes for recipients. They did not even translate it as "surveillance" or "monitoring," but, rather, as "reporting"—and useful reporting at that, since it would in the end help clients to move off the welfare rolls and into employment. In the language of business management, these providers were "stakeholders" who had "bought into" a "win-win" system.

Complicating Factors: Circumstance and Social Structure

The therapeutic orientation of providers contributed not only to a benign reading of surveillance, but also to particular constructions of clients. In providers' view, most people on welfare were poor for one of two reasons: they had been disempowered by the previous welfare regime (although this was increasingly less the case, since the reforms had been in place for over a decade and most pre-reform clients had long moved on), or they had somehow been "incapacitated" by something in their social environment. Sharon, who, like her co-workers, was completely supportive of the "greater expectations" put on clients by the reforms, was the most detailed in her descriptions of "incapacitation": "The finances is a huge struggle," she said, but, "it's not the only struggle that people face as single parents. … The things that people have lived through, I think … how do you keep going? Never mind trying to balance all this other stuff!" She enumerated both the "great traumas" that some recipients have suffered (e.g., child abuse, domestic violence), and the less dramatic but nevertheless pernicious family conditions that were not conducive to economic, psychological, or social "success": "I think what people don't realize is … you take [it] for granted if you grow up in a household where people are … run by a fairly tight schedule of going to work and managing life

... [but some people] don't even know to set their alarm to get up. ...
Some people don't have that basic information that they're bringing with
them here [to the welfare office]. ... So how could we give kids those resources ... [to] find some of those structures that help hold them together
when that's not there ... 'cause it really isn't just finance in my mind."
In order to be able to truly assist her clients, Sharon felt, she needed to
know more about what else was "immobilizing" them, and this knowledge
had to be taken into account in the operationalization of the reform's
"greater expectations." Not only that, but "we"—the state, or dominant
society—needed to also use this knowledge to create interventions (in
homes or schools) that would give children the tools they needed to grow
into successful (unpoor) adults. Putting aside for the moment that this
will to knowledge on the part of providers was often read as intrusive by
clients (as I discuss in chapter 4), as well as the problematic nature of culture-of-poverty views regarding "regular routines" (which I discuss further
in chapter 3), Sharon's talk expressed a critique of reductionist explanations of poverty and of one-size-fits-all policy prescriptions. In her view,
some people had just been, for whatever reason, "incapacitated," and so
the welfare bureaucracy should not apply its rules uniformly to everyone,
or expect that all recipients should be able to meet its stringent eligibility
and work requirements.

Providers also went beyond enumerating the kind of personal circumstances that might lead to poverty to highlight structural forces that were
even more out of the control of recipients. Mark, enthusiastic as he was
about the "wonderful" results of the reforms, argued that "an ineffective judicial system in regards to child maintenance" was one of the key
reasons why women ended up on welfare. In addition to this problem—
which he considered to be the single most important cause of poverty
among single mothers—Mark drew attention to "barriers" that he felt got
in the way of women getting off of welfare. Most notable here were, first,
the lack of available and affordable child care, especially for those women
whose work schedules fell outside the regular operating hours of daycare
facilities in Riverview; and, second, an unrealistically low minimum wage
"that doesn't help that much either," resulting, he claimed, in a situation
in which women could not afford to both work and pay their child care
costs. Poor self-esteem was not on his list. Nor did he reference the "lack
of skills" highlighted by members of the Klein administration when rolling out the reforms.

Others focused not only on particular features of the economic and
judicial systems, but also on widely held social attitudes and values. Richard, for instance, told me that "Riverview is a pretty redneck, at many
times racist, community." Non-Natives,[6] he claimed, often looked down

on Indigenous persons to such an extent that the latter had difficulties securing employment, or even finding apartments to rent. Although he was the only provider to mention racism, his views on the "redneck" aspects of Riverview were widely shared among his coworkers. As he put it, "There's a real sense that if you want to get off your butt and do something with your life you do it and you'd be just as successful as I would. ... The community generally thinks that success is available to all." These orientations to larger structural factors (daycare accessibility, child support legislation, the minimum wage) and social patterns (pull-yourself-up-by-your-own-bootstraps rugged individualism, and, in Richard's case, racism) foreground phenomena that are not under the control of individual poor persons, but that providers felt both contributed to the generation of poverty and hindered individuals' efforts to emerge from it. The idea that "individuals and families are responsible for meeting their basic needs, and for the safety and security of their children" (Government of Alberta 1995: 7) was thus rendered problematic, or, at the very least, as an incomplete view of reality. In taking into consideration material and ideological aspects of the wider socioeconomic contexts within which welfare recipients were embedded, these providers brought into the frame phenomena that were ignored by the architects of the Klein reforms.

The narrow focus of the Klein administration on the individual was thus not carried through by providers in Riverview. Even when providers discussed individualized issues, they translated the Klein administration's poverty-is-the-fault-of-poor-people stance into a broader, each-individual-case-is-different-and-must-be-dealt-with-accordingly frame, voicing a call for more information about each recipient's unique circumstances, and for more tailoring of policies to the needs of each specific person. They thus replaced the one-size-fits-all abstract individual of official policy with a more nuanced each-individual-is-unique approach. Richard was critical in this regard not so much of workfare per se as of the rigidity of the new workfare requirements, which he felt did not give providers sufficient latitude to decide whether particular clients were, in fact, employable. Over the years, he explained, he had come to the conclusion that it was not so much *what* the welfare office did (e.g., force someone into paid labor), but *when* it was done that mattered: "So much of success seems to be about timing, not about what we do but whether it was the right time to do those things." He expounded:

> I can think of lots of examples where we've done all that work and made all these plans and it's always resulted in failure, and so we say, "Ok, so here's someone that it's just not going to happen," and so we say, "Let's move that person ... into a place where there aren't those kinds of expectations and

they're gonna be with us for an extended period of time," and then out of the blue ... something will happen and ... suddenly they'll blossom and they're off and they're working and they're doing stuff you never even were asking—they're exceeding your expectations even when they fail, and I think it boils down to sort of "Was the time right?" And it doesn't seem to relate much to whether it's the right worker or the right program, it seems to be about something else that the stars are aligned. Sometimes I wonder about our ... very intrusive kind of way of saying, "Okay, you'll be doing the following." What would happen if we just sorta sat back and said, "We're open for business so when you're ready come talk to us?"

Richard's talk does not express a pure, direct translation of neoliberal individualism. He instead articulates an approach to the individual tempered by an understanding of local social and economic organization and of the details of those cases in which clients *were* able to exit the welfare system—occurrences, in his view, that depended not on coercion, but rather on an unpredictable confluence of the desires of the bureaucracy and the actions of clients, very little of which can be measured, surveilled, or mandated. In this frame the individual is not just in need of being responsibilized, but is, also, a complicated human being living in a complex social system to which a rigid and standardized welfare bureaucracy is often ill equipped to respond. Richard's talk, in addition, challenges the particular reading of the active society model of the person asserted in the reforms. In asking what would happen if the welfare office waited for recipients to initiate changes in their lives, he raised the possibility of a more service-oriented approach to delivery, such as that launched via the 2002 New Zealand reforms, in which clients are positioned as the ones to determine what actions to take and when, rather than the government.

This is where providers' departures from the framing of welfare mandates are most clear. Although they often *did* reduce poverty to the level of the individual, in keeping with the framing of the reforms, they rarely claimed it was the *fault* of those individuals. Thus, in contrast to what I encountered in my interactions with providers in Kingston, there was no discussion among providers in Riverview of the "bad choices" clients had made, or of the "no commitment" people. Rather, the focus was on disempowering circumstances—such as those engendered by the previous welfare system, or by the range of "incapacitating" situations that Sharon underscored—and on structural forces related to both ideology and political economy. It was in the context of these particular knowledges of poverty and of their clients that the responsibilization thrust of the reforms was articulated by providers—not as a form of punishment, and not as something that would help the government meet its fiscal goals, but as something that would be good for clients. The active society frame of the Alberta reforms did not attribute expertise to recipients, as did the 2002 New Zealand reforms. Instead, recipients' activities in Riverview were designed for them by the welfare department. Eventually, however, in providers' framing, these activities would lead to increased self-esteem, which would, in time, engender the motivation required for engaging in self-directed activity. *This* is what providers in Riverview were oriented to.

This orientation was only partially in keeping with that of the Klein administration. Providers were in complete agreement with the government's assertion that engagement in paid labor was the route not just to self-sufficiency, but also to a specifically dignified and self-respecting self-sufficiency. But they did not subsume this dignity and self-respect, as the government did, to the larger goal of a balanced budget. The latter, as I discuss in more detail below, was ignored by providers. Providers thus both "wrote-in" aspects of the reforms that were not in the reforms themselves (e.g., some of the therapeutic orientations outlined above), and left out, as "unfit to fit" (Lendvai and Bainton forthcoming; Lendvai and Stubbs 2007, 2009), others.

Discussion

The Alberta reforms did not contain the kind of overt contradiction embedded in the 2002 Clark reforms in Aotearoa/New Zealand. As I discuss in more detail in chapter 4, there were a number of latent ways in which the Klein administration pushed for traditional nuclear family formation alongside its degendering of the individual in the public sphere; but its official approach to welfare was clear and uniform: people should be in the workforce, not on assistance. In some ways, this stance did not represent an abrupt departure from the previous regime: as I outlined in chapter 1, Alberta welfare regimes were historically neither ideologically nor materially generous, and workfare measures had been in effect in the province for some years. In terms of actual cuts to benefit levels and to the rolls themselves, however, the shifts were radical. The government provided two justifications for these dramatic changes: a fiscal one, having to do with the need to balance the budget and reposition the province in a competitive global economy; and a philosophical one claiming that "individuals and families are responsible for meeting their basic needs and for the safety and security of their children" (Government of Alberta 1994: 9–10). Both were directly tied to the almost exclusively economic orientation of the government. Among the recommendations of the Financial Review Commission (Government of Alberta 1993: 6), for instance, were the following, all designed to "meet the challenge of radical changes to revenues and expenditures":

- Develop and adopt a workable and enforceable fiscal plan first to balance revenue and spending in a way that eliminates overspending on a sustainable basis, and second, in the longer term, to generate a surplus to eliminate the net debt.

- Downsize the entire government infrastructure, at the same time, considering the full impact of any action.

- Develop, with the help of external expertise, a management control structure for all department and government-owned, funded and controlled corporations, funds, boards and agencies.

Everything the government did stemmed from these economic priorities, and all other concerns—those related to education, health care, or welfare—were subsumed by them. This approach, however, was presented as the means for achieving prosperity for all: "… balancing the budget is not our goal. Our goal is to secure Alberta's future … to maintain essential programs and our quality of life … to build a strong Alberta with jobs for Albertans. We will not be able to reach our goal of a secure future unless we take steps now to balance the budget" (Government of Alberta 1994: 1). The Klein administration accordingly explicitly presented *A Better Way* (1994: ii) as a *business* plan: "For the first time in Alberta's history, the Klein government is presenting Albertans with a comprehensive business plan for government and individual business plans for every department and agency that is part of government's operations. … Preparing business plans is a new approach for the Alberta government and it's a first for Canada. Alberta is the only province that prepares detailed three-year plans complete with financial targets. By doing so, we will set the standard for effective government operations in Canada." Government, then, was to be run according to market principles. Its "business," in a fundamental sense, was internal rather than external to the market, since there was no outside-of-market—no issue related to a general societal good that could not be best addressed in business terms.

In translating welfare reform in their position as front-line workers, providers picked up and appropriated for their own purposes only some of this thinking. The first, and primary, economic justification for the reforms was irrelevant to them and so left behind. As members of a front-line provision office, providers were expected to meet government requirements, including targets for numbers of people in workfare programs or cut from the rolls, as well as various monitoring specifications. While balanced budgets and competitive workforces—discourses of which were in wide circulation in the province at the time—could have provided useful framing for these requirements, providers in Riverview chose to focus instead on the needs of clients and on the benefits they would reap from the reforms—however problematic these constructed "needs" and "benefits" may be in terms of a critical analysis of neoliberalism, and of neoliberal constructs of personhood in particular. In the process of translating policy mandates, then, providers abandoned one of the Klein administration's major framing devices. A key token, as Latour (1986) would put it, was dropped. Instead, the frame within which welfare reform was translated shifted from one in which the overriding concern was with fiscal issues— debt, inefficient use of taxpayers' money, the business climate (Government of Alberta 1994, 1995)—to one in which the focus was on the long-term well-being of the poor.

In addition, providers altered even that which they actively adopted. In particular, they produced a more complicated rhetoric of responsibility and self-sufficiency than that included in the reforms. Rather than an exclusively hardened *tough* love, there was a tendency to discern complexity, if not also an element of compassion, accompanying providers' positive assessments of welfare reform. The translation of the welfare-is-bad-and-so-we-need-to-get-everyone-off-it-no-matter-what approach underlying the Klein reforms was interrupted, only partially carried over into providers' discourse. Rather, there was a strong sense of "This is great, *but* …"—of "It's both great *and* limited." What could be read as contradictory—Mark's claim, for instance, that the reforms are "wonderful" because they force people out of places of "comfort" and into something new that puts them on a "fast track" towards independence, juxtaposed against his recognition of the limitations of an inadequate minimum wage and absent child care services—is perhaps better read as reflective of situated, cut-and-paste interpretations and productions of welfare mandates in the face of everyday experiences and realities. Welfare recipients may have needed to be pushed out of their comfort zone, but, from the perspective of providers, that was only one piece of a larger puzzle that included problematic wage rates, inadequate judicial systems, and insufficient or inaccessible child care facilities, not just recipients' "motivation." Providers also considered certain aspects of local Riverview culture—such as its "redneck" and racist tendencies—to be relevant to the situations in which their clients found themselves. Their everyday knowledges, then, provided them with a wider context of understanding, and they concluded on this basis that the individuals they were dealing with lived in some kind of *social and economic context*. If poverty was individualized by the reforms—situated as a property of persons who must then be held responsible for getting themselves out of the bad circumstances they themselves created—providers in Riverview reinserted poor persons back into the social. And so, a decade and more after the Klein reforms, providers gave no indication that they were totally convinced, without reservation, of the utility of the reforms, or of government claims about what is best for human beings. Their considerable enthusiasm for the more "active" system institutionalized by the reforms thus met its limits in what they encountered in their everyday practice, influencing, in turn, what and how much they translated of policy mandates, and in what tone.

Welfare providers in Riverview were considerably more constrained than those in Kingston: they had fewer official discretionary powers, and they were subject to forms of surveillance that closely mirrored those that they practiced vis-à-vis their clients. They thus had limited opportunities to directly contravene policy mandates, and they certainly did not report doing so in their conversations with me (which, of course, does not mean that they did not do so in practice). Nevertheless, they voiced concerns about official policy makers' failure to take into account the real-life situations of clients, including the structural, material, and ideological constraints that characterized those situations. In reflecting on their work, then, even in the context of the relatively constrained nature of our interactions that I described earlier, providers assembled approaches that coupled coercive and punitive policy approaches with both a for-their-own-good rhetoric and a rejection of the bureaucracy's one-size-fits-all model of the person in favor of attention to nuance and complexity. Neither of these is particularly surprising: the first mirrors and complements part of the government's justification for reform; while the second is in keeping with the characteristics of street-level bureaucratic work I outlined at the beginning of this chapter, and to which I return below.

Perhaps more surprising is Riverview providers' invocation of structural forces in the face of deeply reductionist policies that drew on the marked individualization characteristic of dominant Albertan political discourse. There was nothing in policy mandates that encouraged attention to structural issues—quite the opposite. Nor was there necessarily anything in the nature of providers' everyday work, focused as it was on face-to-face interactions with and assessments of individual circumstances and dilemmas, which invited structural analysis. But structure is where providers ended up—for, as I discuss in the following section, very good reasons.

It is worth noting that even though providers transformed what they adopted, they *did* adopt it, waxing lyrical about what they saw as the "fantastic" and "self-esteem"–inducing results of forcing clients to "take responsibility for themselves," and lauding the increased expectations placed on clients postreform—even to the point of supporting the shock-and-awe crises that fast tracking would invoke because they would push their clients out of their comfort zones and into productive spaces of personal improvement. Interestingly, given that the reforms had been in place for almost a decade when I began my research, the providers I encountered—all of whom had worked pre- as well as postreform—spoke about the reforms as if they were new and fresh. They rarely referred to the 2004 policy shifts, perhaps because they only tweaked what was already there. Instead, they took the 1993 reforms as their before/after benchmark, as a significant and generally positive turning point in how the government and they themselves approached welfare provisioning. Their enthusiasm about a system that no longer "abandoned" clients, but that instead took an active role in their lives, in turn encouraging (or forcing) them to similarly become more actively engaged, was, nevertheless, tempered by their criticisms of one-size-fits-all models and their insights into complexity, and, in particular, structural complexity.

Translation, Assemblage, Convergence, and Divergence

From the point of view of the state, welfare providers are simultaneously targets and conduits. They are targets because they need to learn policy mandates in order to implement them, and because, to a certain extent—since even the most control-oriented welfare bureaucracies do not engage with their employees on the basis of coercion alone—they need to be at least minimally convinced of the appropriateness of policy directives. Welfare providers are, in addition, conduits insofar as they are the mechanisms by means of which—or through which—policy is operationalized: they are the gatekeepers to the benefit system, and they are the ones who persuade, or coerce, clients to abide by policy approaches.

In the same way that the travel of policy across jurisdictions is about translation—about emergence, assemblage, disassemblage, and reassemblage, rather than about the mechanical movement of intact items from one setting to another—so policy implementation is about interpretation, translation, more or less partial or complete appropriation, and, above all, about situated production and application. Freeman (2006: 379) argues with regard to policy travels that "[p]olicy does not exist somewhere else in finished form, ready to be looked at and learned from, but is finished or produced in the act of looking and learning." The same point holds at the level of "implementation," where policy is "generated rather than disseminated" (2006: 379). Policy providers, in other words, working in specific institutional contexts with particular structures and cultural histories, do not apply government mandates in robot-like fashion, but, rather, translate them into practice. Such translations will always articulate in some way with what is already there: with past regimes, received institutional arrangements and systems of meaning, and with the range of knowledges providers have developed over time through the practice of their trade. The result may in some ways fit with, and in others modify, or even pervert, what policy elite had in mind.

What was "fit to fit" from the perspective of welfare providers in Kingston and Riverview—what they translated well—was the active society approach to welfare and the neoliberal model of the person on which it is based. All the providers I interacted with saw this approach as not only reasonable, but also to a certain degree as natural and self-evident. The forms that "activity" took varied, but providers agreed that welfare recipients needed to claim responsibility for their lives and that their role, as providers, was to assist and/or pressure their clients in this endeavor. Similarly, employment was *the* route that clients needed to take, whether the end result was self-sufficiency, fulfillment, or a combination of the two—indeed, a key marker of the neoliberal active society model is precisely the confluence of employment and fulfillment, and welfare providers in both Riverview and Kingston took such confluence more or less for granted. Although they may not have agreed with the active society move away from a conception of society in which the market has its place and towards one in which everything has to be put into market space (Walters 1997), they uniformly (re)produced arguments that employment was the path to liberation from dependency and therefore towards fulfillment and satisfaction. This was the case in both the harsher workfare context of Alberta and the softer, more pastoral and "facilitative" context of post-2002 Aotearoa/New Zealand, which was, as I discussed above, nevertheless very oriented to the engagement of beneficiaries in paid labor. Providers' translations of the active society were, indeed, "good" ones, carrying equivalences of meaning from central state offices to offices located on the border between states and citizens. This was a convergence, then, not only between welfare providers and official policy frames in each site, but also between providers working in welfare bureaucracies across the Alberta–New Zealand divide.

Welfare providers in Kingston and Riverview also converged in rejections, as well as acceptances, of policy frameworks. One-size-fits-all models, and the abstract individual on which they are based (Douglas and Ney 1998), did not translate well in either site. What providers produced instead mirrored the critique of standardization made from an academic standpoint, namely, that "[k]eeping things simple works against attending to a plethora of differences which would cast doubt on 'one size fits all' policies. It favors attributing to apparently similar verbal or physical acts a standard meaning, and similar intent and affect" (Bobrow 2006: 578). Thus all single mothers are the same in background, intentionality, and personality, and all are best treated in similar fashion. Such simplification is, in a way, built into the official policy production process itself, as "[a] determined effort to think and act otherwise would compound the work involved in public policy formation, implementation, and evaluation" (Bobrow 2006: 579). Providers, however, cannot get around these confounding variables—the complex biographies of the persons they encounter on the other side of the desk—at least not completely, or at least not to the same degree as official policy makers. While states deal with populations, welfare providers interact with people. No unitary and homogenous accounting of "human nature," as embedded in particular policy frameworks, can possibly address the range of personalities and situations that welfare providers encounter; they will inevitably note variations, while at the same time, when faced with trying to put people into categories that fit the administrative needs of the bureaucracy, they often also tend to construct "types," shorthands for efficiently dealing with otherwise complicated characters. Policy providers are thus constantly dealing with ambiguity—they operate in a complex social terrain in which events can be read in a range of possible ways, and in which policy directives are subject to change—yet they are forced to provide some kind of stability, to arrive at some place of "knowing," however temporary, that allows them to proceed (Hajer and Laws 2006; Laws and Hajer 2006).

Providers' rejections of abstract, one-size-fits-all models index the gap between official policy formation in spaces removed from practice, on the one hand, and implementation in real-life encounters with applicants/supplicants, on the other. However ethnographically problematic the distinction between policy production and policy implementation may be, it is certainly the case that official policy production happens in rarified spaces. This is not to say that providers are always more reasonable, balanced, realistic, or friendly because they are in face-to-face contact with clients, as opposed to their superiors who are able to take a more distanced stance; there is ample evidence (some of which I have provided above, and more of which I provide in chapter 4) that providers can be hostile, mean-spirited, and punitive (e.g., Davis 2004, 2006; Herzfeld 1993; Kingfisher 1996a, 2001). But it does mean that providers occupy a different space vis-à-vis clients than do official policy makers. This is a space in which policy mandates and official administrative procedures come into contact with the messy realities of providers' and recipients' circumstances, and with the contingencies of local economic and cultural contexts. That this space is occupied by another set of participants—welfare recipients (even if they have considerably less power than their interlocutors)—indicates that translation in this context will be even more about improvisation and composition and less about harmonious "equiva-

lences of meaning" than is the case in instances of "transfer" across jurisdictions among cooperating, similarly invested parties. Policy providers'
inability or unwillingness to translate abstract, one-size-fits-all models of
the person and of policy provision in the context of their work with actual recipients signals a recognition of these characteristics of the spaces
they occupy, and of the unique knowledge they have generated by virtue
of their engagements in those spaces.

Providers in Riverview and Kingston, however, did not just recognize
complexity unrecognized by official policy makers; they also converged
in specifically highlighting the *exact opposite* of what current mandates
emphasized. Thus in Riverview, where policy underscored individual responsibility—period, with no mention whatsoever of the structural forces
that might enable or inhibit people from taking responsibility for their
own lives—providers highlighted precisely such forces, and used them as
a basis for arguing that they needed to take into consideration all aspects
of recipients' lives, not just their relationships to paid labor. In contrast,
in Kingston, where both Enhanced Case Management and the tenor of
the 2002 reforms invited providers to attend to complex lives and structural forces beyond the control of individuals, providers underscored
individualized causes of poverty and offered up employment as the sole
remedy. Again, the 2002 New Zealand reforms were vague and contradictory about parenting versus paid labor, and individual versus structural
forces; but this very vagueness and contradiction provided space in which
providers could move, and they chose to emphasize individualism and responsibility. As I argued earlier, the latter may be partly an artifact of the
ideological power of the previous, more neoliberal regime; and it is also
likely an artifact of the very individualized resources that providers have
at their disposal (after all, they have no resources or powers with which to
promote institutional structural change, for instance). Significantly, however, providers in Riverview also had limited—perhaps even fewer—resources, and they had markedly less officially sanctioned decision-making
power than their counterparts in Kingston; yet this did not prevent them
from engaging in discourses of structural causation and remedy. There was
thus an element of reversal happening in both Riverview and Kingston—
of an antistructure recognition of the arbitrariness of whatever regime
was in place, and of its concomitant inability to take into account the
full picture. In consistently pointing to what the current regime failed
to take into account, providers in Kingston and Riverview converged in
diverging from official policy mandates, and in producing narratives (and
sometimes practices, at least as reported to me in some interviews) that
countered official story lines. Significantly, this occurred in the control
organizational structure in operation in Riverview, and not just in the

more open, service-oriented structure operant in Kingston. While both control and service approaches are designed to somehow channel providers' translation work—to remove "translation" from the process altogether, to channel it in particular directions, or to tailor it to specific contexts—neither approach precludes opposition, and neither guarantees particular kinds of service provision.

Policy providers are thus not conduits, but transformers. In neither Kingston nor Riverview were policy mandates translated unimpeded; rather, in both sites, providers assembled policy knowledges comprised of bits and pieces of current policy mandates and bits and pieces of previous mandates, articulated with aspects of wider cultural systems of meaning and structures of sentiment, understandings (albeit partial and incomplete) of the exigencies of clients' lives, and adaptations to (and simultaneous constructions of) the parameters of their own institutional lives and identities. Even on this most official first "stop" in the travel of policy from state policy-making centers to policy "targets," some things can shift at the same time as others move more or less easily.

Structure and limitation nevertheless remain present. As I pointed out in my introduction to this chapter, welfare providers are not freewheeling policy producers; their agency is more or less limited by policy mandates as well as by institutional structures and administrative guidelines and oversight. These limits may in turn serve to channel providers' productions in particular directions; their agency may, to a certain extent, then, be structurally directed to note what is absent in policy mandates: the complex, real people they encounter across their desks, and the power of individual choice (in the case of Aotearoa/New Zealand), or of structure (in the case of Alberta). This does not mean that welfare providers are predictable automatons; rather, it is to indicate that their translation and assemblage work occurs in particular contexts, in relation to situated constraints, possibilities, and agendas.

There are thus elements of both structure and agency at work here. In her discussion of student fee policies in Denmark, Nielsen (2011) challenges the move, in some interpretive policy analysis circles, from "implementation" to "appropriation," with the latter focusing on translation and transformation. Although intended to trouble simplistic models of mechanical implementation, Nielsen nevertheless finds the construct of "appropriation" problematic insofar as it keeps intact the notion that policy is "a somehow objectified essence that can be followed as it moves in different settings" (2011: 82). She continues: "A dichotomy is assumed between 'policy force' and 'local responses' in that 'the policy' (objectified as, for example, words or technologies) is defined as a substance, entity or 'text' that meets a 'context' which it appropriates (i.e., a process of 'implementation') or in which it is appropriated by particular intentional people (i.e., a process of 'appropriation')" (2011: 82). Rather than reading providers' engagements with policy in Kingston and Riverview as instances of the "appropriation," "adoption," or "rejection" of policy, then, it might be more appropriate to theorize them—in a literal, fundamentalist reading of Lipsky (1980)—as *productions*. Even when in agreement with policy frames—such as those concerning models of the person—these productions were not identical to those of policy makers; the context was different, the lens was different, the valence was different. Thus while some aspects of policy mandates were translated directly, some were dropped, some were changed, and some were added, all were written anew.

Notes

1. While a fully adequate understanding of everyday policy translation and assemblage would obviously require participant-observation in welfare offices, focusing simultaneously on providers' interactions with clients, each other, their supervisors, and policy mandates—as embodied in policy manuals, forms, and computer programs—stringent privacy regulations in both sites made this impossible. I was, however, able to interact with and interview a number of providers, and my discussions with them provide an entry point into an initial and provisional understanding of how they translate and assemble policy.

2. In some ways, this situation mirrored the experiences I had in the late 1980s and early 1990s when I shared the results of my dissertation research on recipients and providers with policy officials in Michigan, where I had conducted my research, and in Wellington, where I conjecturally applied my findings to the New Zealand policy context. I found that policy analysts in Aotearoa/New Zealand were considerably more receptive to my work than either the head of social services or the state governor in Michigan (who had a large clock on his desk to keep track of my allotted time, which was less than 10 minutes). I have reflected elsewhere on these events (Kingfisher 2009), speculating whether the difference had to do with my method of presentation, or with the relative distance (in Aotearoa/New Zealand) or closeness (in Michigan) of the data—which could easily have meant the difference between interpretations of my work as indictment versus interesting information.

3. I do not name the ministers/MPs, or identify their ministries or constituencies, since they were given the same rights to confidentiality awarded other interviewees. Although I am well aware of the problems associated with not situating speakers, in what follows I group the six analysts and four ministers/MPs together, and refer to them anonymously as "interviewees" or "persons," or provide quotes without any identifying information whatsoever. It is worth noting that access to people at these levels of government in Aotearoa/New Zealand was not awarded to me in Alberta. In keeping with the greater reticence I encountered among providers in Riverview relative to Kingston, this perhaps reflects general differences in styles in organizational and political cultures.

4. In what follows, I focus on the subgroup of providers with whom I had the most detailed discussions, and whose views are representative of the group as a whole. I follow this practice with all of the providers discussed in this and the following chapter.

5. Some of the preceding analysis is taken from Kingfisher 2006.

6. In Riverview, Indigenous persons were referred to as *First Nations*, *Native*, or *Indian*, with *Native* being the most common appellation. Non-Indigenous persons were most commonly referred to as *Non-Native*. Throughout this book, I alternate among terms for Indigenous persons, with some preference for *Native*, in keeping with local usage among both Natives and Non-Natives.

Chapter 3

READING THROUGH WELFARE POLICY IN COMMUNITY SERVICE AGENCIES

∞

The views of welfare providers indicate that while the state may have desired *transmission*, what it got was *translation*: welfare providers making sense of policy in the context of particular institutional arrangements, specific kinds of face-to-face interactions with clients, and their situated understandings of poverty and of the effects of policy generated by means of those arrangements and activities. Providers' sense-making in some ways drew on and reproduced the dominant ideologies informing welfare mandates, particularly those regarding the nature of the ideal person; but in other ways it challenged current regimes by both rejecting the abstract individual of policy and pointing to exactly what the regime in place tended to miss, or ignore. Even those aspects of official policy makers' frames that were most robustly viable in the context of the welfare office were given life in specific ways by providers who articulated what they adopted with other ideas and practices that were meaningful to them. These patterns reveal something about the policy process: namely, that it is, in fact, a *process*, that it cannot be orchestrated in a top-down manner, and that welfare providers operate in their own—not autonomous, but nevertheless unique and distinctive—environments, regardless of the more or less politically progressive or regressive nature of the policy regimes within which they are located. In tracing the movement of policy and the work that it does in making cultural meaning and enacting power, then, the orientations and actions of welfare providers are as crucial to follow as are those of policy elites.

The story does not end here, though. There is a second group of providers that also plays a pivotal role in the social life of policy. Accordingly, in this chapter I expand out from official sites of policy making and implementation to explore the engagements of community service providers, those who dispense policy information and proffer support in their capacity as employees or volunteers in nongovernmental organizations (NGOs). Although the role of NGOs in formal policy formation and travels has been noted (e.g., Stone 2000), the literature on welfare for poor single mothers rarely explores the place of community service providers in either the interpretation of policy or the provision of essential nonstate services. Instead, the literature tends to focus almost exclusively on street-level bureaucrats and/or recipients. This is an unfortunate gap, since community service providers may be as relevant as welfare providers to the lives of women on welfare, as well as to government projects of regulating the poor. The centrality of NGOs is revealed by the actions of welfare mothers themselves, who frequently seek advice and service from such agencies—as was the case with all welfare mothers I met in Kingston and Riverview, most of whom availed themselves of the assistance of several agencies. The network of policy travel and translation thus comprises not only government elites and official providers, but also a range of unofficial providers, situated in an amorphous constellation of community service organizations that play a crucial mediating role between poor people, the state, and society at large. A policy travelogue, accordingly, cannot restrict itself to following policy "downstream" through official lines of dissemination, but also needs to explore its branches and eddies.

A Note on NGOs

My work with welfare mothers centered on and radiated out from one key site each in Kingston and Riverview. In Kingston, this primary site was Parent Connection, a community house for low-income single parents; while in Riverview, it was Aboriginal Alternatives, a homeless shelter for primarily, albeit not exclusively, First Nations women. Parent Connection and Aboriginal Alternatives offered an array of services: food, counseling, training and education programs, legal assistance, advocacy, social gatherings, and, in the case of Aboriginal Alternatives, a place to live. It was through my interactions with the women at Parent Connection and Aboriginal Alternatives that I encountered a number of other organizations that the women turned to in their efforts to cope with poverty. My method was to go where they went, to follow the women. In Riverview this led me to three food banks, a soup kitchen, a second women's shelter, a women's advocacy group, two organizations working with teenage mothers/high school drop-outs, and a Native community outreach organization; the women's advocacy group led me, in turn, to a local antipoverty group whose members included social workers, public health nurses, city employees, and educators. In Kingston, poor single mothers pointed me in the direction of a food bank; two family services organizations providing everything from child care referral and support to food, clothing, and household goods; an organization supporting teenage mothers; and two organizations serving the needs of Maori, in one case, and Pacific Island women, in the other.

NGOs are not easy to categorize: they can be secular or faith based, left-wing or right-wing; they can serve (in this case) poor populations in general or particular age groups, ethnicities, or genders among the poor; and they can be connected to international networks or be more narrowly local. The label "NGO" is thus somewhat problematic, insofar as it "lumps a broad and contradictory array of diverse organizations together in a single category" (Leve and Karim 2001: 53)—what Ferguson and Gupta (2002: 991) refer to as "a disparate hodgepodge of social groups and institutions that have in common only that they exist in some way outside of or beyond the state" (see also Fisher 1997: 447). This qualification of existing "in some way outside of or beyond the state," however, must itself be qualified, insofar as NGOs rarely operate completely outside the ambit of state control (Ferguson and Gupta 2002: 993; Li 2005: 386; see also Fisher 1997). The histories of relief in both Aotearoa/New Zealand and Alberta are typical of this often-complicated relationship between NGOs and states. In both places, poor relief was first organized by charitable aid organizations rather than by the government. Emerging welfare states built on these organizations, sometimes incorporating them, sometimes erecting their own institutions alongside them, but always working in some kind of relationship to them. More recently, in the course of widespread retrenchment, governments have actively encouraged the proliferation of NGOs, inciting the "community" to step in where the state has been stepping back. (It is worth noting in this regard that the Clark government in Aotearoa/New Zealand fostered the development of a number of government-community "partnerships.") In many instances, both historically as well as in the context of neoliberal state "retreat," governments have at least partially financed the work of NGOs, directly via grants, or indirectly by means of, for example, tax exemptions. All of the community service providers I encountered worked in organizations that were dependent on money from the state to one degree or another, without which none, regardless of other sources of funding, could have survived.

As a result of their complex engagements with the state, many NGOs find themselves caught in a double bind (Mertz and Timmer 2010: 174): on the one hand, they may operate as agents of democracy, empowerment, and grassroots mobilization; while, on the other hand, they may be co-opted by sources of funding that either overtly or more gently lead them to mute their criticism of government and/or received social arrangements (Fisher 1997; Leve and Karim 2001; Lister 2003; Mertz and Timmer 2010).[1] Ferguson and Gupta (2002: 989) further point to the role of NGOs in neoliberal forms of government-at-a-distance, particularly with regard to the dissemination of forms of enterprise culture. There is no reason, however, to assume that NGOs are by definition caught in a double bind, as some may be actively interested in buttressing certain aspects of the state's ideological agenda. The double bind, then, may apply only to those organizations whose agendas in some way challenge the state or dominant society. In any case, either/or categorizations remain problematic: simplistic, dualistic approaches that refer to "either the idealistic claim that NGOs work to protect vulnerable and oppressed groups against the tyranny of the state and global capital, or the opposite, that NGOS are the instruments of an emergent neocolonialism" (Leve and Karim 2001: 55), fail to capture the spaces "in between," where progressive NGOs have "carved out some room for marginalized voices to be heard despite the many compromises they've had to make," and where there is room for "talking back to mainstream culture" (Mertz and Timmer 2010: 175). Nor do such either/or categorizations capture the complexities of organizations that support some state agendas while functioning, intentionally or unwittingly, to undermine others. NGOs, in other words, can operate in contradictory ways, working simultaneously, for example, as "stimulants of a critical, justice-oriented politics *and* as the educators of deficient subjects in need of improvement" (Li 2007: 176; emphasis in original). Thus a number of the community service providers I worked with were invested in altering clients' characters as well as the operations of the welfare system.

As an antidote to simplistic and abstract categorizations, Fisher (1997: 449) calls for ethnographic insight into "what happens in specific places and specific times." What I am concerned with in the specific places of Riverview and Kingston in the specific times of the early to mid-2000s is the work of community service providers in mediating between welfare institutions and welfare recipients. Although I attend to the lens through which this work was refracted (e.g., feminist, faith-based, Indigenous), I do not foreground the NGOs themselves, but instead organize my discussion around patterns in providers' views that correlated loosely with the kinds of organizations in which they worked, recognizing, even as I do so, the danger of assuming that community service providers blindly reproduce their institutions' agendas. First, however, I turn to a brief overview of the relationship between NGO and street-level bureaucratic work.

NGOs and/versus Welfare Bureaucracies

As agencies that respond to particular constructed needs, NGOs strongly resemble welfare bureaucracies. In many ways, however, they are fundamentally different. They are, first of all, part of civil society rather than of the state. As such, they do not need to appear to be apolitical, as state bureaucracies often attempt to do by framing policy as technical and transparently self-evident in nature (Li 2007; Shore and Wright 1997). Thus, as I already mentioned, while NGOs may align themselves with state interests in some ways (by, for example, encouraging the development of enterprising selves), they can also more or less (depending on limits imposed by funders) unabashedly and overtly promote particular agendas not explicitly endorsed by the state, such as, in the case of some organizations in Kingston and Riverview, the revival of Indigenous culture as the solution to poverty, the empowerment of women, or the enhancement of specifically Christian "family values." Nor are NGO practices subject to the same kinds or degrees of standardization and depersonalization required of state agencies, although NGOs often institute their own administrative procedures and mechanisms for accomplishing what they consider to be a fair and equitable distribution of services. Perhaps most importantly for my purposes, NGOs occupy a unique location, simultaneously alongside state agencies and in between those agencies and the populations they ostensibly serve and regulate.

These overlaps and contrasts mean that NGO workers function as street-level bureaucrats and *more*. Like frontline workers in welfare offices, community service providers sit at the boundary between institution and population: mandated to pursue particular agendas, constrained by the resources available to them and the regulations they must follow, and allotted the task of transforming needs, and the persons they inhabit, into administrable form. In thus serving as intermediaries between the philosophical orientations and resources of their institutions and the needs of their clients, community service providers are no different from welfare providers.

Community service providers sit betwixt and between in somewhat more complicated ways than do their colleagues in the welfare office, however. They mediate in a double sense, operating as liaisons not only between their clients and the organization for which they work, but also between their clients and a different organization—the welfare office. In this capacity they provide information about welfare policy to clients who are often ill equipped to understand it (by virtue of the limited information available to them, or because they are in crisis situations), help them fill out forms, and sometimes accompany them to the welfare office as supports or advocates. Given that their raison d'être is often to fill in the gaps left by inadequate state provisioning, they are also in the business of providing material support—an activity that serves to simultaneously critique and buttress the welfare state by doing some of what *it* is supposed to be (and is not) doing. If welfare providers have to be bilingual, as it were, mediating between the state and welfare recipients, community service providers have to be trilingual, at the least.

A Note on Relationships

With the exception of two welfare providers (both in Aotearoa/New Zealand) with whom I was able to establish ongoing relationships, my interactions with street-level bureaucrats were restricted to formal interviews, all of which occurred in welfare offices. At the other end of the continuum were my engagements with welfare mothers, which were significantly more informal and sustained, spanning event types (one-on-one interviews, discussion groups, hanging out) and spaces (community service organizations, homes, restaurants, the street). My relationships with community service providers fell somewhere in the middle of these two extremes, ranging from those cases, about half, when I met community service providers only once or twice, in the context of formal interviews in their places of work; to those cases, about half, in which I developed ongoing relationships with them. In several exceptional cases, in both Riverview and Kingston, I was able to establish relationships with community service providers that were as deep—and even more enduring, since community service providers tended to stay in place across the years—as those I established with welfare mothers.

Reading through Welfare Policy in Riverview

One of the differences between my interviews with welfare providers and community service providers in Riverview concerned the relative emphasis each group placed on macro versus micro issues. I started all interviews with the same general preamble—something along the lines of, "I'd like to learn more about the kind of work you do, the kinds of people you work with, and your views about welfare more generally"—and left it up to my interlocutors to decide how they wanted to proceed. The result was a clear divergence in the weighting, and to some degree also in the sequencing, of topics in interviews. Welfare providers tended to focus on welfare mandates with reference to their specific roles as providers and to interactions with their clients; this is what was most salient to them, and this is what they spent the most time discussing. They did voice concerns about problems in the state's approach to provisioning as well as about wider social issues, as I outlined in chapter 2, but these topics tended to emerge later in interviews, and providers devoted less time and attention to them. In contrast, community service providers tended to start with their views about what was wrong with society at large and with Riverview culture in particular, situating their ensuing readings of the welfare system and of their work with their clients within these larger frames. Although this pattern held for interviews only, the differences index the divergent lenses through which welfare and community service providers translated policy.

Society

I begin, accordingly, with the diagnoses of society (as opposed to the poor) that took precedence among community service providers. Here providers across the political spectrum agreed that the key problem with Canadian society was its overvaluation of money. Denise, for example, the director of a feminist activist organization, argued, "We're valuing the dollar, the almighty dollar, at the expense of everything else: 'Go make an income, go pay your own way.'" Bernadette, who ran a Christian organization providing assistance to pregnant women as an alternative to abortion, concurred: a preoccupation with money eclipsed all other concerns, including, in her view, what should be most important—the family. Because money and material acquisitions have become so central in our lives, she said, we now find ourselves working all the time, "like robots." She proposed, instead, a recalibration of our approaches to life, beginning with on-site day care in all institutions, work hours amended to accommodate employees' family responsibilities, and work responsibilities decreased so that they would no longer displace family as the locus of attention. Denise's reform agenda, even more comprehensive, called for an education system that leveled the playing field rather than reproducing an uneven one, an adequate system of social provisioning, and a reduced gap between the wealthy and the rest. She asked: "Could the tax system work better? Do we get nearly enough from the high-income families to help support the low-income families? … My suspicion is that no … we're not taking enough at the corporate and high income levels to help pay for the low-income levels." In Denise's view, the income gap, deeply rooted in history, had been in place for so long that people were no longer cognizant of it. From where she sat, it was only getting wider, feeding a social system in which people "begrudge somebody because they're poor." This critique, focused on a cluster of issues related to materialism, capitalism, and the distribution of wealth, provided key framing for how community service providers made sense of and engaged with their clients and with the welfare system. Despite their philosophical and political differences, they came to the same conclusion: money trumped people, the family, and community.

Riverview: Rugged Individualism, Cultures of Poverty, and Racism

Although converging in their views about the deleterious place of money and materialism in Canadian society in general, community service providers pinpointed as problematic different aspects of the cultural environment of southern Alberta in particular. At one end of the spectrum were those providers—primarily in feminist organizations and in the antipoverty group—who were highly critical of the local rugged-individualist, I-was-able-to-do-it attitude that they felt translated into an intolerance of the poor. This intolerance, as they saw it, manifested in a tendency to blame poverty on the poor themselves, a widespread fear of poor persons that engendered a desire to "hide them away" (as Cynthia, who worked for the woman's advocacy group, put it), and a sense of embarrassment or humiliation that the poor even existed in Riverview—as if that fact damaged the community's image and sense of self.

Other providers, mostly those who worked in organizations serving members of the Aboriginal community, focused on a different feature of dominant Riverview culture—racism—which they felt produced the very poverty that was then blamed on the poor themselves. Samantha and Diane, for instance, staff members at a homeless shelter, claimed in this regard that landlords in Riverview were often unwilling to rent to poor Indigenous mothers; as a result, the women were pushed into substandard and overcrowded situations, which, in turn, provided the basis for negative stereotypes—as if Native women deliberately chose to live in large groups in run-down housing. Their colleague Carla saw this discrimination as part and parcel of a general pattern in which Indigenous persons, regardless of effort, are not given the same opportunities as non-Natives:

"I don't understand non-Natives because I went to school, got my education and I tried to work, but I'm never given that chance. I don't work in a white organization, do you know what I'm saying?" (What she was saying, as I translated it, was that as an Indigenous person she could find a decent job *only* in an Indigenous organization.) First Nations persons are thus caught in a double bind: on the one hand, despite their effort, they are not given a chance to succeed; but then, on the other hand, as Carla put it, "When we don't work and, you know, we live on SFI, then we're … lazy, drunk bums." These racist structures and attitudes converged, in providers' view, in producing generations of people living on state provisioning, whether on or off reserve,[2] engendering an inclination to see living on the edge, on assistance, as "just the way things are." As Samantha put it, most of the women at the shelter "had no life skills whatsoever [before they came to the shelter], other than just trying to kill the pain by drinking."

At the other end of the spectrum were those providers who focused their critiques not on dominant society, and certainly not on racism, but, rather, on First Nations culture itself. Usually prefaced by the observation that the bulk of their clients were Native, these providers, mostly from faith-based organizations, described Indigenous culture as "backwards," and inadequate to the task of producing competent adults. Ruth, for instance, a food bank employee, claimed that many Indigenous persons were poor because they were not parented properly and therefore did not learn how to be in the world effectively: "You don't grow up to know that if you wanna hold a job you have to get up at nine o'clock, you can't be late, you must be showered, you must be clean, you must have clean clothes." When Ruth spoke of the need for education, she meant it in an expansive sense: "It's not just the job-marketable skills, it's all their other ones, like having to take care of their babies, how do you interact with other people." She told me, still astonished, of a recent incident in which a Native woman, just out of the hospital with her newborn baby, put it on the floor while she went to line up for her food hamper, "with people walkin' around!" When people are raised like *that*, she argued—implying that they were not really raised at all—they get so overwhelmed by the daily struggles of getting through their lives that "they aren't able to … focus their attention on how to get out of it [poverty]." Instead, she said, they get used to being poor, and "so it's acceptable." Others similarly argued that Indigenous children were not properly educated. Mary, for instance, a long-term volunteer at the soup kitchen, who referred to the basic coping tools required to emerge from poverty as "heritage," claimed that First Nations "aren't … as some families where their heritage goes on, we learn to cook and … we pass it on to our children. And it's a lot of them, they didn't have that, so I think they're like lost sheep. They don't know what to do with their time." It was as if Aboriginal culture was not, in fact, a culture; as if the only form of socialization among Aboriginals was socialization to not being socialized, an antisocialization. At the end of the day, she said, "They're just not fit."

Some providers with backgrounds in social work articulated similar views, albeit couched in more relativist terms. For example, Katie, a child and family services social worker, asserted that First Nations had *different*, rather than deficient, heritages and norms. On the reserve, she explained, people are not evicted for not paying their rent, and they don't lose their jobs if they fail to come to work for several days—a not uncommon occurrence, she said, since family or ceremonial matters often take precedence. Given these priorities, she continued, when First Nations persons come to town, they suffer "a rude awakening: 'What do you mean my landlord's gonna kick me out that I didn't pay my rent on time or my employer ... is ... firing me because I didn't show up to work today and I didn't phone?'" If Indigenous persons failed to learn dominant, non-Native norms, in other words, they could very easily end up living in poverty—which was, in fact, the case in Riverview, where, at the time of my research, fully half of the First Nations population was poor, relative to under one fifth of the non-Native population (City of Riverview 2005). While Mary and Ruth focused on basic bodily care and comportment—how to prepare food, take showers, and wear clean clothes, or even where to put a baby (not on the floor!), Katie focused on the routines required of work life—knowing how to set an alarm, or that it is important to get to work on time. In either case, Indigenous persons were unable to succeed.

Poverty and Welfare

Regardless of whether they constructed it as the artifact of cultural deficiency, racism, capitalism and consumerism run amok, or some combination of these, community service providers converged in locating poverty in social forces rather than in individual poor persons. There were a few exceptions to this. Janice, for instance, who worked as a youth education supporter, claimed that everything boiled down to "attitude": "I think it just starts in your worldview, which is how you see the world. ... If you see it's always been handed to you and it always has been handed to you or it's always been tough for you, never had money or ... you've got the attitude ... that you're never gonna find a job or you're never gonna do this, you're never [gonna] be a success then ... if you believe it you become it." Lorraine, a member of the antipoverty group, also argued that poverty was to a certain degree about "choice." And, finally, Linda, an education/outreach worker in an Indigenous organization who had herself been a welfare mother, claimed, "Once you realize any success has to come from within you, once you really want something … you're gonna go up the ladder." These voices, however, were stark in their exception to the general view of community service providers that one of the key problems was the welfare system itself, which, they claimed, both reflected and contributed to the negative patterns in society that produced poverty in the first place.

Providers who focused on racism, for instance, constructed welfare bureaucrats as conduits for this racism in their treatment of First Nations clients. Francis, a volunteer at a Native organization who often accompanied women to the welfare office, claimed that welfare providers "bring these ideas with them to work about why … [Indigenous people] are having a hard time and it is their own fault, right?" She frequently encountered welfare providers who expressed the view—sometimes directly, sometimes in more subtle ways—that First Nations people belonged on the reserve rather than in town, and that they should get help from their "own people," rather than from the welfare system. Riverview in general, she felt, and the street-level bureaucrats who worked in its welfare office, in particular, were "trying to not be responsible for the [First Nations] people in the community." Francis thus translated welfare providers' treatment of her clients as expressions of a larger social pattern of racism that trickled down through the welfare system and its agents to enter into, and further damage, the lives of the poor women she and her colleagues worked with. For their part, those community service providers who focused their critique on what they felt was a highly problematic ideology of blame-the-victim rugged individualism felt that this stance manifested in an institutional as well as personal meagerness and meanness that oppressed welfare recipients, misread the realities of their lives, and erected barriers to their economic and social well-being. Providers who espoused a culture-of-poverty approach produced a similar assessment of the welfare system, albeit within a markedly different frame of reference.

I begin with levels of provisioning, which community service providers uniformly considered to be woefully inadequate. Sylvia, for instance, knew from her own experiences as a welfare mother and from her current work with high school dropouts that welfare did not provide enough money for women to meet basic needs, let alone make progress in establishing a viable economic life. As a result, welfare mothers were forced to engage in deception in order to survive. (In Sylvia's time on welfare, this meant not reporting the extra funds she acquired by taking in a roommate and babysitting on the side.) She felt strongly that welfare should "give them enough money so that they don't have fear in their life," since only this would prevent recipients from being "debilitated," relegated to living in poverty for the rest of their lives.

The idea that welfare had to "give them something they can live on," as Denise put it, was an often-repeated refrain in my discussions with community service providers, who claimed that neither the system nor its agents understood the realities of poverty. As Bernadette explained, "When you are a single mother and you have to get up at six in the morning and get your child ready and get out and that kind of thing, there has to [be] … more give and take in welfare [and] society." "Too often," she said, "we think that support is breeding … dependency, and perhaps we should look at it differently." Extending a parental, therapeutic model to the care of the poor, she argued that people needed to be looked after and given time to "grow," and that, above all, "you have to give them enough freedom to be able to make mistakes but to make mistakes that are manageable." If what the system is trying to achieve with single mothers is independence, then "our society needs to realize that we need to have time for these types of things"—for growing, for making mistakes. While she was all in favor of self-sufficiency, if "there's not enough support for that girl," the results could be devastating.

However, providers complained, the welfare system did not attend to these realities, but instead made inappropriate, and, in the end, damaging, assumptions about what people were, or should be, like. Denise, herself a former single mother, made this point most succinctly when she argued that the "will and determination" so valued by the welfare system had to be *learned*; in other words, it did not come naturally to everyone. Drawing on a culture-of-poverty framework, she constructed a parallel between what she called "third generation" poverty and situations of domestic violence: if someone grows up knowing only domestic violence, then that is all they know; likewise, if someone grows up in poverty, with parents and relatives who are unemployed or on welfare, they never get the opportunity to learn the work ethic—"They've never seen anybody get up and go to work in the morning." She was adamant that those who did not display "will and determination" were not to blame, and she argued strongly against forcing people into work programs without recognizing that "there's a whole learning cycle that needs to happen." In addition, she claimed, not everyone was "career material": "You see women who … don't have educations and that are not … necessarily candidates for a university education, so for them it's particularly difficult because they're gonna be minimum wage workers." Accordingly, and in keeping with her design for a better society, Denise argued that the minimum wage had to be increased to a level that would enable people to actually *live*, not just survive.

The welfare system's misconstruals of persons and their needs were compounded, in community service providers' views, by the bureaucracy's (and society's) fundamental misunderstandings of the social networks in which recipients were embedded. Rita, a nurse who ran nutrition education programs for poor mothers, pointed in this regard to the contradiction between the state's treatment of recipients as isolated individuals capable of self-sufficiency, and its assumption that the poor had extended families to pick up the slack, particularly with regard to child care. She reprised, with contempt, statements made by Ralph Klein to the effect that (as she sarcastically paraphrased him), "Young moms with single children [on welfare] get paid enough with all the other resources that are available to them." "Well," she responded, "how does any young mom live on the money that they get? ... It's like there's absolutely no way." Most recipients, she knew, did not have "other resources" in the form of family or friends able or willing to make up for the difference between what welfare mothers received from the state and what they actually needed.

These misunderstandings of reality and of the nature of persons resulted in what community service providers read as "ridiculous" and completely "unrealistic" requirements for the receipt of welfare. Cynthia and Allison, for instance, members of a women's advocacy group, zeroed in on the rigidities—and ironies—of the requirement that potential clients exhaust all reserves before turning to welfare. Allison recounted the case of a woman escaping domestic violence who was refused support by the welfare department because she had moved out of her home and into a friend's apartment before approaching the welfare office for assistance: her reason for going on welfare—"leaving a situation of domestic violence"— was deemed to be no longer applicable by the intake worker because she was no longer living with her abusive partner! Never mind that she had tried to make ends meet on her own, using up all her resources (including her friend's good will) before applying for welfare—never mind, in other words, that she had done exactly what she was supposed to do. Cynthia, who had encountered similar cases, claimed that the welfare department failed, repeatedly, to attend to the exigencies of client's lives. Something as simple as transportation to child care could get in the way of a woman meeting workfare requirements, she explained, but this was read by welfare providers as a reflection of recalcitrance or laziness on the part of the client rather than as a reflection of a real, material constraint that was out of the client's control.

From the perspective of community service providers, the welfare department also neglected to take full account of the fact that recipients had dependents, even though they were eligible for state support precisely because they were *mothers*. Community service providers thus complained, frequently and bitterly, that in forcing recipients to find employment, the welfare department ignored both the parenting work in which the women were engaged and the needs of their children. I encountered the same lacuna in my own conversations with welfare providers in Riverview, who tended to refer to children only when discussing accessibility to child care services, never once raising the importance of mothering per se, or the nonlogistical difficulties women might encounter in juggling parenting and employment. In contrast, community service providers placed children front and center, speaking at length of the need for adequate nutrition so that children could learn properly, for a leveling of the playing field in school by discouraging displays of wealth (by means of, e.g., uniforms), and for equal access to leisure and sports activities. Susan, an antipoverty activist, was most adamant with regard to the latter, citing studies indicating that poor children who had opportunities to engage in recreational activities were more likely to "succeed" (emerge from poverty):

> I'm gonna tell you a story about a mom that came to see me and she was trying to find some activities for her children. ... She had just moved from the Maritimes looking for work, thinking that she was going to get work here. She ended up living in some housing on the west side, her children went to school ... downtown [and were able] to get a bus pass only for to and from school, right, so living on the west side they had no access to any free activities because she couldn't afford it, she was on [welfare], there was no opportunity for the kids to participate in any extracurricular activities. So here she was with two adolescent boys and no activities because she couldn't afford it, it was sick, and so we don't from a transportation perspective or from a mental health perspective and a benefits perspective [have] ... access to recreation, positive influence.

Sometimes, community service providers became so focused on children, and on the welfare system's failure to meet their needs so that they would not grow up to end up on welfare as adults, that the mothers of the children were eclipsed, positioned as conduits for the care of children rather than as worthy of state support in their own right. This became clear to me when I worked with the antipoverty coalition and served on the board of directors of one of the food banks. Both groups, at different points, discussed undertaking social marketing campaigns, consisting of strategically placed ads in busses and newspapers, along with TV clips, that would exclusively emphasize *children* as both needy and deserving. In both cases I raised objections, arguing that a focus on children, abstracted from the contexts in which they lived, permitted the ongoing vilification of their mothers; I also gave a talk for a local social interest group on the topic of "the last remaining deserving poor" that explicitly criticized campaigns against child poverty. Members of both groups countered that we needed to pull on people's heartstrings in order to increase contributions and sympathy. Children, they argued, provided more leverage in this endeavor than mothers, and also provided a "wedge" that would eventually expand out to include mothers and families more generally. Community service providers' focus on children, then, both indexed what they saw as an ironic gap in the welfare system, and served as a propaganda point in their own campaigns against poverty.

Adding Insult to Injury:
Welfare Providers' Mistreatment of Recipients

From where community service providers sat, the inadequacies, inaccuracies, and contradictory views and expectations of the welfare system all emerged in the attitudes of welfare providers toward their clients. I have already referred to the stories that Native community service providers told me about the racism their clients encountered in the welfare office. Francis was particularly distressed by this treatment. One day I met her for lunch shortly after she had "lost" one of her "ladies" to a drug overdose. She told me, tearfully, that this was the second client she had lost this way in recent years, and since both overdoses had occurred within days of humiliating episodes in the welfare office, she felt that welfare providers were partially to blame for the women's deaths. Battered down by years of hardship, mistreatment in the welfare office was the straw, Francis felt, that broke her clients' backs; they simply could not cope with it.

Sylvia, a non-Native who had to go on welfare shortly after the institutionalization of the Klein reforms, told a somewhat different story, one that underscored not a targeted racism, but what she saw as the impersonal, arbitrary, and disrespectful nature of welfare providers in general:

> I was a number.... [I] went in, filled out a form, they asked me five, six, seven questions, they wrote it down and then it's like, "Okay you'll hear from us." Totally impersonal.... I was sent a letter saying that I had to appear ... for a job search at such and such a day, such and such [a] ... time, "This place be there or bust," and ... so I tried to phone the lady that I was told to phone for two weeks, the whole two weeks [I] couldn't get a hold of her, and I never went because I was home with my child, I had no idea about how to find a babysitter, how to find [childcare] subsidy.... So I got a letter two weeks later saying I'd been cut off welfare and I just kinda went

"*What!?*" So then I phoned again and she said, "Well, you didn't comply," and I [said] like, "But with what? I mean, I was phoning you to find out what the hell am I supposed to do here and you didn't even phone me, you didn't phone me back".... So I wrote a letter to ... the minister at the time and I sent a copy to her [the provider] and her superior and then after they received that letter she called me back and asked for an appointment with me, and asked me to come down and I was reinstated on welfare.... So when I did talk to the woman my main thing with her was, "Don't treat me like a number. I am not twenty years old or eighteen or sixteen, I'm thirty-three, I've been in the work force."

Not only did the welfare office put everyone in the same category ("You fit in there, if you don't fit in you're out"); in Sylvia's experience, welfare was also "totally degrading" because "you're a number." Sylvia situated this poor treatment of recipients in the context of societal attitudes that stigmatized young pregnant women and welfare mothers as "partiers" who were "irresponsible" vis-à-vis their children—an attitude that she felt SFI providers channeled. "I believe that some women could get stuck in that," she added. "If you're treated like an animal, you're gonna act like an animal."

Discussion

Community service providers in Riverview produced knowledge that in some ways overlapped with but in many ways was more expansive than that produced by welfare providers. They tended to have access to more details about their clients' situations, and, as outsiders to the system who were at least partially in the business of compensating for its lacks, they tended to know more about the inadequacies of the welfare bureaucracy—or at least they attended to these in ways that welfare providers did not. While both welfare and community service providers recognized the larger social and economic contexts of poverty, community service providers placed these larger forces in the foreground rather than the background. This emphasis on societal contextualization manifested in a pattern of apportioning blame for poverty and responsibility for its remedies beyond the individual poor person, and of underscoring the inadequacies of government programs, the shortcomings of institutions such as schools and work places, and the damage produced by a range of what they saw as faulty and pernicious ideologies and cultural frameworks.

Attending to larger social forces and to aspects of their clients' lives other than employment status, community service providers placed into relief what welfare providers elided, or sidelined. Two issues are particu-

larly relevant. The first is the absence of attention among welfare providers (with the one exception of Richard) to Indigenous issues, whether
with respect to racism or, in contrast, to culture-of-poverty frameworks.
This is a remarkable lacuna, given that Riverview is adjacent to one of the
largest First Nations reserves in Canada. Similarly placed in relief by my
conversations with community service providers is a lack of attention on
the part of welfare providers to children, aside from the need for child care
associated with employment—an equally remarkable omission given the
centrality of children to the lives of welfare mothers. Community service
providers thus explicitly noted what welfare providers marginalized, given
the latter's almost exclusive attention to clients' work status. Although
welfare providers did move beyond the abstract individual of policy to the
actual individual on the other side of the desk, as I described in chapter
2, community service providers went much further in placing those actual
individuals in larger social contexts characterized by networks of relationship and affected by a range of ideological and structural forces.

Community service providers' knowledges in turn produced particular
translations of welfare policy and unique approaches to how they engaged
with it in their everyday work. Assessing the welfare system as informed
by blame-the-victim ideologies and built on misinformation and errone-
ous assumptions about the nature of people and the actual conditions in
which the poor live, community service providers assembled a view of the
welfare system as not only inadequate but also damaging. They rejected
the "tough love" approach to reform promulgated by welfare providers,
since this approach, from where they sat, was based on toughness alone,
with no love. Moreover, this toughness was not, in community service
providers' reading, an artifact of a desire to actually serve the interests of
recipients. Rather, focusing on congruencies rather than disjunctures between government mandates and welfare providers' actions, community
service providers read welfare providers' "tough love" as a mechanism used
by the government to fulfill its true agenda: the elimination of provincial debt and the creation of a business-friendly environment (buttressed
by the availability of a cheaply paid and poorly protected workforce).
Martha, for instance, a social worker and antipoverty activist, claimed
that the government's first priority was not the eradication of poverty,
but rather for "people not to be dependent on them." Her colleague, Katie, agreed, noting that, since the Klein reforms, welfare workers would
use "any excuse possible" to deny potential clients access to benefits. In
contrast to welfare providers, who left behind economic justifications for
welfare reform as "unfit to fit," community service providers zeroed in precisely on the economic interests of the government, rejecting outright
both government and welfare provider claims that what they were really

interested in was helping people achieve "independence" and "dignity." On the contrary, in community service providers' view, the government's focus on eliminating debt and creating a friendly business environment belied a complete lack of interest in the eradication of poverty. This is not about simply dropping a token (Latour 1986), but about directly challenging its legitimacy.

What was not actively rejected but instead radically reformulated was the model of the independent individual at the foundation of both policy mandates and "tough love" approaches. This is not to say that community service providers operated outside the parameters of dominant valorizations of self-sufficient individuality. There were, as I noted above, those community service providers (albeit few in number) who underscored the need for their clients to make good "choices." In addition, some community service providers indexed the value of developing "will and determination," while yet others lamented the (supposed) poor personal or work habits of Indigenous persons. And all told me that they counseled their clients to work on getting the kinds of credentials that would enhance their economic status. In some ways, then, community service providers willingly translated dominant models of "success" that were, at base, focused on employment. But their efforts were not focused primarily—or even to any significant degree—on employment, and they did not hold their clients in contempt for not valorizing paid labor above all else. Insofar as they translated dominant neoliberal ideologies, then, they translated them with a number of caveats and qualifications: people need to be treated as *people*, and society needs to take responsibility for how it organizes itself and how it approaches its most vulnerable members. Community service providers' "independent individual" thus sat alongside rather than jettisoned models of society as a collective—and ideally caring— entity. In this sense, rather than positing society (and taxpayers) as the victim of parasitic individuals, community service providers posited poor people as victims of a dysfunctional society—mean spirited, judgmental, unequal, racist, and in some cases exploitative. (It is worth noting, however, that while some community service providers called for a wholesale rethinking of society, none, even those most concerned about racism, explicitly called for a realignment of dominant society to better accommodate Indigenous culture, for example, rather than the other way around.)

This wider stance of community service providers had inevitable implications for their interactions with policy. On the one hand, they translated it accurately, insofar as they kept abreast of eligibility and work requirements, informed their clients of welfare rules and regulations, helped them fill out forms, and ran interference between welfare providers and recipients when necessary. However, while the mechanics of welfare requirements were translated directly and completely, they were not translated in the frame used by either welfare providers or the government. Instead, highly critical of the welfare system and of the larger society in which it was embedded, community service providers disarticulated policy frames regarding independence and dignity from administrative processes, reading the latter through a lens that constructed them as rigid and punitive, rather than supportive or empowering. Significantly, this critique was also expressed by those voicing culture-of-poverty approaches—all of whom, like their peers, were profoundly invested in situating individuals in social context and in not holding them personally accountable for whatever shortcomings they exhibited, even if their cultural backgrounds were "inadequate." Although adhering to specific rules and regulations—since that is what their clients had to do to get assistance—community service providers altered their meanings, and thereby their legitimacy.

These translations—or transmutations—of the justification and framing of welfare mandates as illegitimate contributed to the kinds of approaches that community service providers described taking in their work. First, they were open with their clients that the welfare system was inadequate; none, in other words—even those providers who were concerned about clients' "choice"-making behavior—told me that they conveyed to their clients that the welfare system gave them what they needed. Nor were they reticent about communicating their disagreement with many of the system's rules and regulations, even though clients had to abide by them in order to receive support. In community service providers' readings, welfare requirements were hoops clients had to jump through—a means to an end—rather than anything reasonable with a useful long-term purpose vis-à-vis clients' overall lives. Community service providers also routinely advised their clients to go to the welfare office armed with knowledge of what they were entitled to. Some encouraged their clients to stand up for their rights on their own, while others accompanied their clients to the welfare office to advocate on their behalf. Most community service providers also reported encouraging their clients to get off welfare as soon as possible—not only because dependency was bad for them, as some providers and dominant discourse claimed; but also, and more importantly, in their view, because the system was oppressive and mean spirited, subjecting clients to unwarranted and debilitating humiliation and debasement. Finally, a number of community service providers also reported engaging in activities—e.g., writing letters to ministers, producing community reports—designed to pressure the government to make the welfare system more supportive (particularly with regard to funding rates) and therefore more effective in actually working to eradicate poverty.

Positioned differently than welfare providers, having different kinds of access to aspects of clients' lives, and sometimes having had personal experiences with poverty and welfare themselves, community service providers in Riverview did not read policy mandates as policy elites intended; nor did they read policy in the same ways as welfare providers. They attended to and worked with SFI rules and regulations, but they adopted little of the supporting justification and philosophy that accompanied those rules and regulations. Instead, they stripped policy down to its bare requirements and provisions and dealt with these requirements and provisions as best they could, while complaining about and working to supplement the system's inadequacies. They translated welfare policy in terms of the larger social context within which it was embedded, constructing it as an expression of larger social forces that more often than not worked to the detriment of their clients. The claims making of the government was thus undercut, its justifications and approaches rejected outright or reframed in negative terms. Community service providers instead assembled alternative claims about the nature of our social system, about the realities of poor mothers on welfare, and about what the state should be doing with regard to welfare, as well as in other arenas.

Reading through Welfare Policy in Kingston

As in Riverview, community service providers in Kingston tended to situate the welfare system within the context of larger social formations and to point to erasures in the welfare system that they considered to be particularly damaging to the lives of their clients. As I highlight below, however, the substance of their orientations differed from those of their counterparts in Riverview, reflecting the historically more communitarian ethos of Aotearoa/New Zealand, its entrenched maternalism, and the politics of biculturalism.

Society: Racism, Consumerism, Individualism

Community service providers in Kingston did not distinguish between society at large and local culture, as did their colleagues in Riverview, but focused on negative aspects of culture in Aotearoa/New Zealand in general, with particular emphasis on racism and consumerism. Providers across the board (rather than just Indigenous providers, as in Riverview) saw racism as a significant cause of both poverty itself and the treatment to which the poor were subjected. They claimed that the "problem" was not Maori or Pacific Island culture, but Pakeha culture and Pakeha institutions. A welfare system based on a Pakeha nuclear family model, for instance, did not just fail to reflect cultural realities; it also structured provisioning in such a way that poor mothers who were active members of their *whanau*, or extended families, could not meet their basis needs. Thus Elena, a social worker in a family support organization, argued in favor of a bicultural welfare system, consisting of parallel Pakeha and Maori service delivery models. Maori beneficiaries would then have the choice to enroll in a system that took their embeddedness within their *whanau* into account in determining both eligibility requirements and levels of provisioning. In Elena's experience, *whanau* were significantly more beneficial than detrimental: they required input in terms of time and resources, but they provided more than they took. The failure to consider the *whanau* system in the official formation of welfare policy thus clearly disadvantaged Maori clientele; it was, in Elena's view, racist.

From the perspective of community service providers, not only the welfare system in particular, but also the state more generally took steps that served to undercut Maori culture in ways that exacerbated, rather than ameliorated, the long-standing disruptions of colonialism. Indeed, Sophie, Powhiri, and Kathleen, community service providers in organizations serving Maori and Pacific Islanders, specifically blamed Rogernomics for the increasing prevalence of single motherhood among their constituents. Maori and Pacific Island men, they argued, were not as well educated as Pakeha men, tending as a result to be employed as manual laborers. The various cuts ushered in by Rogernomics forced many of these men out of the workplace and onto the unemployment rolls; and many, having suffered a major assault against their sense of masculinity, subsequently abandoned their families. Restructuring thus had a "huge impact" on Maori *whanau*, according to Sophie. Kathleen put it in even stronger terms when she said that the 1980s restructurings served to "suck the heart out of the men." As a result, Powhiri said, "we've just left our men behind, basically." Something needed to be done, she argued, to "get our men back up to speed," because "the women actually want them involved."

A second social pattern of concern to community service providers was consumerism. This was also an issue among community service providers in Riverview, but in Kingston, in contrast to Riverview, providers rarely explicitly tied consumerism to a critique of capitalism or of the value of money over people; instead, their focus was on the *individualism* that consumerism gave rise to. In addition, and again in contrast to Riverview, where the critique of money as an overriding value was voiced by providers across the political spectrum, in Kingston concern with the close ties between consumerism and individualism was the exclusive purview of providers involved in faith-based organizations. Two examples serve to illustrate the pattern. Thomas, who worked for a family support agency, phrased his argument that consumerism was a key contributor to poverty as follows:

> In this day and age of the instant gratification ... they [the poor] get caught in this trap of, "Looks good on TV I need it or I want it or I'll have it" ... so all those pressures from society. ... And I think it's to the detriment of families who are on low income because they end up believing they need those things too, otherwise their life is not fulfilling. ... Life isn't just "I want, I can have." It's actually a bit more. I just think that there's a whole lot of issues in society now that kind of makes it "quick, quick, quick" ... that causes a lot of problems in society.

Although consumerism and individualism presented problems for society as a whole, Thomas said, those on low income suffered from them more than others; and he felt that "if we get back to being a community rather than being individualistic then life would be easier for some people." Herbert, who worked in an organization providing child care placement and support, took a related stance, arguing that consumerism and individualism had steered society "right away from Christian principle[s]" of care, dignity, and respect: absent fathers neglected their children, couples failed to honor each other, children did not receive unconditional love.

Dependency culture, in these providers' estimation, was one of the key negative repercussions of consumerism and individualism. Herbert waxed lyrical in this regard about life in pre-DPB days, when "people were a bit down with luck ... but people still support[ed] each other." When he was young, he told me by way of illustration, "we had a family down the road that had a bit of bad luck, the father got killed and ... the mother ... couldn't read or write but those kids were well looked after, you know, a loaf of bread was dropped off or someone mowed their lawns and picked the kids up and took them to the youth group." Then came the DPB, which "is one of the biggest cross[es] we are having to bear," because it has "lured" people into poverty with "a promise of an easy path": money for food, money for children's school uniforms and supplies, funds to help pay for children's Christmas gifts, dental work, relocation funds, and so forth. "Personal responsibility is taken out of the equation," he said. Claiming that fantasies of gaining access to everything one needed through the welfare system provided a form of escapism that served to "stock this big cesspool," Herbert thought that being on welfare was "like a drug addiction," because beneficiaries "become dependent upon the handout." For his part, Thomas wondered whether providing school lunches to poor children, most from welfare homes, was "helping or hindering": was it "just applying a band-aid" in cases where "mom and dad either have got a hangover from the weekend [or] they've run out of money because they spent it all?" Such parents, he said, were "abdicating responsibility," and school lunch programs were "enabling" them by supporting their reasoning that they did not have to pay rent on time because "'the landlord can wait, he's rich anyway,' or 'we'll catch up next week.'" Thomas hankered for a return to a "New Zealand before the rise of the social welfare system"—to a society in which people were both responsible for themselves and caring of others. In keeping with the views of the National government of the early 1990s, Herbert and Thomas invoked a golden past when "the state did less and individuals did more" (McClure 1998: 233). Community service providers in faith-based organizations all agreed that the current state of society was at the root of contemporary poverty, and that the welfare system, embedded as it was in this society, reflected rather than ameliorated the problems generated by it. Only a return to values of community and commitment would remedy the damage done by a welfare system that gave its so-called beneficiaries very few benefits indeed.

Although racism and consumerism/individualism were the key social patterns condemned by community service providers, several providers also gave voice to culture-of-poverty theories that blamed Maori culture in particular for high rates of both single motherhood and poverty. Claudia, who counseled poor single mothers in a family services organization, and Fiona, who worked in a program supporting teenage mothers, both claimed that Maori had not only higher rates of teenage pregnancy than Pakeha, but also higher rates of incest and other forms of sexual abuse. They both also claimed—along with Thomas—that *whanau* placed unreasonable demands on their clients, particularly with regard to housing and food. Thomas argued that the women he worked with "just can't afford ... to feed the people who come who don't have any money, who spent money getting here; they just have *whanau* drop in and it's quite expensive sometimes just to feed another four or six mouths over extra days." Claudia pointed out in this regard that she had a number of clients who had moved to Kingston, arriving with absolutely nothing, simply to get away from their obligations to *whanau*. As with those providers in Riverview who focused on individual "choice," however, these providers were in the minority. Moreover, when they referred to Maori culture in critical terms, they did so almost in passing rather than focusing on it as a key point of discussion. The different histories of segregation in each site—the Canadian reserve system, in which Indigenous populations are quarantined, never took hold in Aotearoa/New Zealand—and the fact that Aotearoa/New Zealand is officially (albeit often only nominally) bi-cultural and bilingual, in contrast to Canada, where recognition of In-digenous rights is at least partially eclipsed by Anglophone-Francophone debates and controversies regarding immigration, may help to partially explain the relatively poor purchase of culture-of-poverty frameworks in Kingston relative to Riverview.

Consistently Inadequate Provisioning, Consistently Poor Treatment

Although some community service providers, like their counterparts in the welfare office, despised what they referred to as "dependency culture," this did not mean that they thought the welfare system was too generous. On the contrary. Thomas, for instance, made a point of underscoring the "amazing job" that many single mothers were doing in the face of the "scant" resources provided by welfare. Herbert was even more critical, claiming that there was no way that anyone could survive on what the state provided. The 1991 cuts, he said, resulted in an overnight blossom-ing of his organization's case load, and even now, with the softer Clark regime, people on welfare are "just on poverty level ... so you can't even quite make ends meet no matter how frugal you are." He told me that he had confronted several members of Parliament who had come to visit his organization, asking them, "How would you like to survive on this amount of dollars?" Inadequate welfare rates, he said, resulted in two problems: they forced agencies such as his to "pick up the government load more than we should be doing," and they eroded recipients' dignity: "You start chipping away at a person's dignity," he said, and "you're in trouble." The allure of the poor's fantasy of getting everything they needed from the state was belied by the reality of bare bones provisioning; beneficiaries became hooked on a drug that provided little satisfaction. Like their col-leagues in Riverview, then, all the community service providers I worked with in Kingston lamented the inadequate resources provided by the wel-fare system—resources that were never enough to make ends meet, and that always had to be supplemented by the limited resources community service agencies had at their disposal. They were nevertheless extremely grateful that welfare existed. Fiona, for instance, felt that welfare pro-vided a source of "empowerment" for women in their dual roles as moth-ers and providers: "You get to be ... [a] parent and be there twenty-four hours [a day] and still get an income. It may not be enough but there's still an income"—one that was all the more crucial, she felt, when women were leaving abusive relationships. Although in her view still insufficient,

Fiona noted that the welfare system had improved markedly since the election of Helen Clark's coalition government; women could now pursue training or education knowing that their children would be looked after in quality daycare facilities.

What community service providers were unambiguously unhappy with was the treatment their clients received at the hands of even the most well-intentioned welfare providers. Samantha, a social worker and activist with whom I had numerous conversations both in the late 1990s and across two periods of ethnographic research in the mid-2000s, had observed and intervened in the daily workings of the welfare system for years. With few exceptions (who she listed by name), the welfare providers in the Kingston office did not, in her view, meet poor single mothers' need for someone to "stick with them." Instead, beneficiaries experienced one or both of two patterns. The first was a tendency among welfare providers to withhold information: "They don't tell you what you can have, [what] you're entitled to," she said; "It's all what you can't have." Given the ubiquity of this pattern, Samantha had constructed a checklist of entitlements that she gave clients to take with them when they went to the welfare office. The second pattern had to do with beneficiaries' lack of control over their relationships with welfare providers. Not only did they have no say regarding which case manager they were assigned to—no small matter, since some were supportive while others were not—but also, in Samantha's experience, there was so much turnover in case managers that beneficiaries never got the opportunity to really develop relationships with them. This was harmful, in her view, given her clients' need for stable relationships they could depend on; it undercut the very support that the welfare system was supposed to provide. Harriet, who worked for a food bank, felt that the high turnover rate among case managers, which meant that "there is no time to develop a relationship," could, in fact, "be part of their [the welfare system's] plans."

Community service providers claimed that this poor treatment was magnified for Maori and Pacific Island women. Harriet argued in this regard that racialized stereotypes of beneficiaries, based on the behavior of only a few Maori who abused the welfare system, tarred all Maori "with the same brush." Kathleen, a nurse in the Pacific Island organization, had no doubt that Maori and Pacific Island women were investigated for welfare fraud and "undeclared" relationships with men more frequently than were Pakeha beneficiaries. Kathleen, herself of Pacific Island descent, described her own experience of being on welfare in the mid-1990s as humiliating and demeaning: she was repeatedly questioned about the nature of her relationship with her ex-husband and regularly treated as if she were dishonest. She described the feeling of going into the welfare office as one of being "naked," her eyes filling with tears even a decade later as she recounted her story. Sala, one of Kathleen's co-workers, had sent her young son back to her home island to be raised by his grandparents specifically in order to avoid having this experience.

Given these patterns, many community service providers were concerned about welfare provider ethnicity. While some argued that having more case managers of the same ethnic background as beneficiaries would ease the stress of going to the welfare office, others felt that poor Maori and Pacific Island mothers would be hesitant to expose themselves to members of their relatively small communities; in other words, just because a welfare provider is of the same ethnic background as a beneficiary does not mean that they will treat that beneficiary with respect. All agreed, however, that Maori and Pacific Island women were subjected more frequently and with greater ill effect than Pakeha to negative stereotypes, repeated ad nauseam in the media, focused on high rates of crime, imprisonment, teenage motherhood, and benefit receipt among non-Pakeha. As Powhiri put it, when welfare was discussed as a public issue, the focus was "always on Maori single mothers, not [on] all single mothers." Accordingly, she said, Maori suffered the brunt of the stigma associated with welfare.

The difference in the treatment of racialized minorities versus Pakeha was a matter of degree, not kind, however. In addition, a number of community service providers claimed that the poor treatment of beneficiaries in general occurred irrespective of the regime in place. Again, Samantha was most articulate and critical in this regard. She was appalled, she told me, by the 1996 legislation that imposed part-time workfare requirements on welfare recipients once their youngest child turned seven, increasing to full-time when their youngest turned fourteen. Her clients at the time were "terrified" by these changes, and many did not know how they could possibly cope. "Let's face it," she said, "if you've got three, four little children … there's not much actual time you've got really to put into [education or work]." Despite her clients' terror, however, most were never in fact required to seek employment: Samantha discovered that if she phoned or paid a visit to welfare providers who had sent letters to her clients indicating that they were now expected to work, they usually backed off—the "heavy handedness of the letter," and she put it, was not often matched by heavy handedness in practice. The pressure, albeit keenly felt by beneficiaries, never really amounted to much.

But nor did the 2002 reforms have much impact. Despite the elimination of work tests (which, again, as Samantha explained, were never systematically enforced), beneficiaries continued to be feel pressure from their workers to find jobs. Although relieved that the even the idea of work tests had been officially put aside, in her view the difference between the welfare regime of the 1990s and the current system post-Clark was "not actually that much." While welfare legislation changed—work tests in, work tests out—the discourse of work and the stigma of being on welfare remained the same, as did the age-old reality that beneficiaries had to go to the welfare office equipped with knowledge of their entitlements, since it was unlikely that such information would be forthcoming from their case managers.

Persistent and intrusive surveillance of beneficiaries also seemed to remain constant in the face of regime change. Community service providers told me that their clients were deeply resentful of these intrusions, which, perhaps more than anything else, engendered a desperation to get off welfare. As Samantha put it, encapsulating beneficiaries' unique approach to individualism (discussed in detail in chapter 4): "I'll get a phone call from someone that I haven't seen for a while: 'Guess what, Samantha? I'm off the benefit right now, tell them where to stick it!' ... Recognizing that it was good at the time, but 'I'm not answerable to anyone. I can do what I like. I can have whoever I like in my home. I can have my boyfriend or whatever to stay every night if I want.'"

Fiona, mentioned above, was one of the few providers who noticed a big shift post-Clark. Most, in contrast, shared Samantha's view that the faults of the system—inadequate support, poor treatment by case managers, intrusive surveillance, and unrealistic and inappropriate expectations—remained the same. As I discuss in chapter 4, this assessment mirrored welfare mothers' experiences.

The Psychology of Stigma and Deprivation

As I noted earlier, some providers, particularly those working in Maori- and Pacific Island-focused agencies, claimed that increases in single motherhood were the artifact of state practices that undercut traditional Indigenous forms of social organization. Others also pointed to an increase in single motherhood, but with more of a sense of puzzlement rather than clarity regarding its causes. Elena, for instance, made the following observation: "Previously there was the mentality that ... men were providers, women the nurturers.... We've already almost done a three-sixty: we're at [a] point now where women are the providers *and* the nurturers, so almost self-sufficient and independent and so forth, to say, 'Hey I can do this on my own.' I sort of [feel that] no, women are not responsible for everything: 'You [the fathers] play a part in this.' So I mean, how did we get to that? I don't know, I just don't know." In community service providers' view, however, few beneficiaries really experienced the "Hey I can do this on my own" feeling. Thus Elena went on to point out that that her clients had developed a "psychological need" to stay on welfare that reflected both a fear of what was involved in moving off of welfare and the damage inflicted by the stigma associated with being a single mother, and a poor single mother in particular. Together, these produced a sense of being "stuck"—a kind of paralysis that sapped beneficiaries' motivation. In Elena's psychologically oriented view, this sense of being "stuck" represented a form of hiding, a refusal to accept the reality of one's situation. Accordingly, she reported working closely with her clients to get them to a point where they could say, "Hey, I am a single parent. ... This has happened, this is crap, how do we work together to get out of this?"

Other providers focused on longer-term sources of deprivation and disempowerment. Samantha, for instance, argued that most of her clients had led extremely difficult lives, let down by their families and society alike. Everything from their material survival to their self-esteem had been battered by years of abuse and neglect: "A lot of our clients have never had anyone that really would stick with them," she explained. "Some of my clients think they're dumb; often they've been told it often enough." As a result, clients needed considerable help in developing both basic life skills—reading, writing, budgeting—and a sense of confidence in themselves and trust in the world, so that they could be strong and nurturing mothers. A big part of Samantha's job was thus "to encourage," although she was quick to note that encouragement would only be useful if it was accompanied by adequate material support. Samantha's clients, in other words, were people who had had the rug pulled out from under them; citing Maslow's hierarchy of needs, she claimed that they needed it all: food, clothing, and housing, as well as legal assistance, training, and, last but not least, she told me repeatedly, someone to "stick with them." Moreover, she insisted, with the same frequency, welfare is "not a privilege, it's a right."

Discussion

The idea of welfare as a right rather than a privilege was emblematic of community service providers' distinctive frame on society in general and on financial assistance for the poor in particular. In contrast to their colleagues in the welfare office, community service providers were wedded to the communitarianism of pre-1984 Aotearoa/New Zealand (at least in its ideal, rather than real, forms; see chapter 1); specifically, they were uniformly in favor of state and community support for women as *mothers*.

As in Riverview, this focus on mothers can be read as at one level really a focus on *children*. Thomas, for instance, was adamant that women needed to be free to be mothers for the duration of their children's youth: "She [a mother] doesn't need to be harassed into thinking she has to get a job, that being a mom at home is not important. Being a mom at home, being there when the kids come home from school even when they're up to fourteen and fifteen, 'cause that's an important time as well, it's just as important as when the child is five or preschool." Melanie, a nurse who ran parenting courses for poor single mothers, had similar views. She felt that putting pressure on mothers to work was profoundly misguided, since the absence of mothers at home gave rise to a range of negative "social issues," including family dysfunction and increased crime. And Samantha, definite in her assertion that parenting is "the most important job in the world," was particularly concerned that welfare provide sufficient support to enable children to pursue their interests. The exact nature of their interests was irrelevant—sport, literature, music, science, art—anything. The point was the support and encouragement, not only because this might give children something to do other than become juvenile delinquents or teenage mothers, but also because they, like their mothers, deserved it—they had the right, simply by virtue of being members of society.

Unlike their counterparts in Riverview, however, community service providers in Kingston did not disarticulate mothers and children, but saw them as a unit. They never spoke of children separately from mothers. Nor did they separate mothering from "work"; on the contrary, mothering was women's primary work. This emphasis on women's roles as mothers placed community service providers in stark opposition to welfare providers. In this sense there was a kind of division of labor between welfare and community service providers in the translation of the 2002 reforms. As I described in chapter 2, welfare providers in Kingston adopted the employment-focused aspects of the reforms only, leaving behind those elements that focused on the support of parenting; the message they conveyed to beneficiaries was that they should be in paid labor. Community service providers did the reverse: they emphasized the importance of parenting, while sidelining employment, so that the message *they* gave beneficiaries was that they should be at home, looking after their children until they became adults. The two streams of the 2002 reforms were thus "implemented" separately by two different sets of providers, the one aligned with the deep currents of maternalism in Aotearoa/New Zealand culture, and the other with the post-1984 emphasis on self-sufficient, independent individuality. In other words, each group attended to, and thus translated, only a portion of the reforms.

Community service providers' conviction that mothering was what their clients needed to be up to contributed to their particular policy assemblages. Rather than encouraging clients to move off of welfare and into employment, their primary interest lay in helping their clients resist pressure from case managers to get off of welfare before they were "ready." They were adamant that beneficiaries should stay on the DPB as long as necessary, and that, above all, they avoid compromising their roles as mothers. It was with this particular agenda in mind that they assembled an approach to supporting their clients that focused on advising them to go to the welfare office armed with knowledge of their rights and to develop a willingness to "confront ... [case managers] and demand respectful service," as Harriet put it—or, failing that, to bring someone to the welfare office to advocate on their behalf. They also intervened directly, petitioning individual case managers to be more generous toward their clients.

This did not mean that community service providers did not applaud their clients who did get off welfare, especially given the intrusiveness of the system and the humiliations to which it subjected beneficiaries. But they would much rather have had the welfare system itself change so that it reflected *real* support for parenting (rather than racism, consumerism, individualism, mean-spiritedness, and coercion) than that beneficiaries take up employment to the detriment of both themselves and their children. Active society models of the person thus took on a particular valence in the hands of community service providers; they translated the active self not in terms of neoliberal self-sufficient individuality, but, rather, in terms of individual *assertiveness*. Here, clients were encouraged to defend their roles as mothers, as active members of their *whanau*, and as rights-bearing members of a community-minded (if not communitarian) Aotearoa/New Zealand. Feminist activists and faith-based providers articulated this somewhat differently—the latter wanted women to eschew individual satisfaction and indulgence (via consumerism) in favor of motherly devotion to children, while the former advocated for an assertion of the right to parent—but both translated the enterprising self as something markedly different from a self-sufficient monad.

This profound attention to women's roles as mothers was coupled with a deep concern with issues related to racism and cultural difference. Although a few lamented the supposed dysfunctionality of Indigenous culture, and of Maori culture in particular, the vast majority condemned the welfare system for failing to recognize or build on the strengths of Maori and Pacific Island cultures, situating this failure in the context of a wider social system marked by a historically enduring privileging of Pakeha persons, culture, and institutions.

Community service providers' institutional locations outside of the welfare system and their relatively greater access to the everyday realities of poverty and welfare afforded them the opportunity to develop unique policy knowledges that differed from those of both welfare providers and official policy makers. Although they were concerned about "welfare dependency," community service providers meant something very different by it than welfare providers. Rather than constructing it as a property of poor persons or as an artifact of an overly lenient welfare system, they situated it squarely in terms of inadequate welfare provisioning and in relation to a dysfunctional society, whether their readings took the form of pining for a golden past, lamenting the detriments of consumerism, or puzzling over shifts in the gender division of labor. They focused, like their counterparts in Riverview, precisely on what welfare providers neglected to attend to; and they located the real problem not in persons, but in the welfare system and the social patterns it reflected and reproduced.

Reconfiguring Poverty, the Poor, and Policy

Once set in motion, policy is translated and assembled not only by those officially charged with its implementation, but also by an array of community service providers who have as much contact with single mothers on welfare as do welfare providers, if not more. Welfare mandates and workplace requirements and environments exert considerable pressure on welfare providers, comprising more or less restrictive conditions of possibility for their translation and assemblage work. Community service providers are also limited by the agendas and resources of their organizations; but, less tethered to the state, they have somewhat more leeway in their interpretations of policy. Positioned at the crossroads where state, politics, society, competing values and agendas, and disenfranchised poor persons meet, they play a crucial role in the realization or interruption of official policy agendas.

As I have already noted, community service providers occupy a unique position vis-à-vis state welfare agencies. They sit alongside their counterparts in welfare offices, as fellow providers of services to the poor; and they sit in-between their clients and the welfare office, as intermediaries. This unique positioning has several characteristics. The first concerns the nature of the interactions that they have with their clients. The romantic idea that community service providers are structurally more aligned with their clients—located in agencies "closer" to clients than state bureaucracies, often having gone through what their clients are going through and therefore more sympathetic to them—clouds more than clarifies ethnographic realities. Many community service providers, like their counterparts in the welfare office, have to impose eligibility requirements and quotas: clients may be restricted in how many times they can go to the food bank; how many counseling sessions they may have; how much legal assistance, clothing, or furniture they have access to; and so on. More importantly, while community service providers often function as advocates, they, and the agencies they work for, can also embody forms of governance, engaging in surveillance and employing a range of techniques of self designed to change who their clients are as persons. Thus while providers in Kingston encouraged their clients to stay on the DPB as long as necessary in order to be able to fulfill their roles as mothers, they also deployed a range of psychology- and Christian-based approaches designed to inculcate dominant neoliberal models of personhood and/or neoconservative models of family formation. Similarly, in Riverview, community service providers criticized the welfare bureaucracy's expectations that clients display "will and determination," while simultaneously valorizing the "learning process" that needs to (or should?) happen in order to build that will and determination. However couched in terms of "compassion" and "helping," these interventions nevertheless represent attempts to improve the lives of single mothers on welfare by altering their orientations to the world, and, most importantly, to themselves.

At the same time, my engagements with all three groups indicate that interactions between poor single mothers and community service providers have a different valence than those between welfare mothers and street-level bureaucrats in welfare offices. The welfare mothers I worked with were uniformly less afraid of community service providers than of welfare providers, and they felt considerably more comfortable in seeking their assistance—in no small measure because they are not official representatives of the state, but also because women felt that they had more choice in approaching them (e.g., there was more than one family services organization in town). It was to community service providers that welfare mothers turned when they needed help in understanding welfare requirements, when they needed to cry about the meanness of their case managers, when they found that their welfare checks would not stretch to cover their bills, or when they were looking for used clothing or furniture or, sometimes, congenial company (which is not to say that they got all of these). Indeed, community service providers were often partially included in poor mothers' personal networks, alongside friends and family.

For their part, community service providers reported more intense emotional involvement in individual clients' lives than did welfare providers. This is not surprising, given that they spent considerably more time with their clients, listening to more stories, hearing more about their clients' ups and downs, and meeting with them in a range of venues. They were also more privy than welfare providers to the details of how welfare mothers struggled to make do in their day-to-day lives, and of how, specifically, welfare checks stretched or fail to stretch. This is not to say that community service providers were always receptive and never challenging or judgmental. Nor is it to say that they have unmediated access to clients' lives. Welfare mothers most certainly have agendas when they go to community service agencies—they are looking for sympathy and/or material support—and these agendas no doubt influence their presentations of self. Among the single mothers I worked with, however, the need to engage in particular forms of facework was of a lower order of magnitude when it came to meetings with community service providers as opposed to welfare providers; again, in contrast to welfare offices, community service agencies were never a last-ditch effort—there were always other possibilities.

A second notable artifact of community service providers' positioning is that it awards them unique avenues of insight into what the welfare system does and does not do. In the constructions of the community service providers with whom I worked, the welfare system *did* put undue pressure on recipients, and it *did not* provide adequate means of survival, treat clients with respect, or take into account the full dimensions of their lives: the centrality of children and of their roles as mothers, race and racism, and cultural difference (read by community service providers in both positive and negative ways). Third, and related, their positioning encouraged community service providers to situate the welfare system in the larger society in which it is embedded, and which, from their perspective, it reflects. Their diagnoses of the welfare system were thus part and parcel of diagnoses of society as suffering from the negative repercussions of capitalism, materialism, consumerism, racism, individualism, and an inability to recognize that not everyone could rise to the occasion in the ways demanded by welfare mandates. From their vantage point, community service providers saw welfare providers as contributing to rather than ameliorating the problem, since they reproduced and exacerbated society's mistreatment of the poor—whether that be in failing to provide clients with adequate information about their entitlements, discriminating against them on the basis of race/ethnicity, pushing them beyond their capacities, or promoting "welfare dependency."

This did not mean that community service providers were not grateful that the welfare system existed—they were; rather, it meant that they nevertheless found it woefully inadequate. Indeed, they translated the entire system through a lens of deficiency, in terms of what it failed to provide, and of what it did not, or refused, to see. Thus while community service providers translated policy requirements—the "hard," or mechanical rules and regulations—in a relatively straightforward manner, they translated them within radically different frames, dismissing as empty rhetoric government assertions that its policies were designed to help to the poor. Instead, they read through claims about empowerment, dignity, and self-respect for the poor to highlight what they saw as their governments' primary agendas: balancing the budget, shrinking the role of the state in the provision of social services, strengthening the economy, and creating a competitive workforce. This was equally the case in post-2002 Aotearoa/New Zealand as in the context of austerity in Alberta. Community service providers considered these agendas illegitimate, since they did not, in their view, contribute to the elimination of poverty. This general reading was, of course, refracted through the particular lenses of the feminist, faith-based, ethnic, and youth-oriented organizations for which community service providers worked. Via these very different routes, however, they ended up in the same place.

Community service providers' particular framings of policy led to an assemblage of approaches to policy that were, above all, tactical and strategic. The translation work they did for their clients was not limited to helping them fill out forms, crucial as that was; in addition, in constructing welfare mandates as illegitimate and provisioning as inadequate, they presented policy as in need of manipulation. "This is how the system works," community service providers would tell the women who came to them, "this is what you have to do, this is how you must act, and these are the questions you must ask when you go to the welfare office." Community service providers of course did not look in on the welfare system as outsiders, but, rather, as co-participants in the social systems in which welfare programs were embedded. Thus, as I indicated earlier, they adhered to certain aspects of dominant discourses of the person, mothering, children, and work. But they always coupled these dominant discourses with expressions of other values: the right of all persons to respect and fair treatment, critiques of consumer culture and of systems that value money making above all else, and so on. These couplings resulted in the unique assemblages of independent individuality and collectivity, in Riverview; and of individuality, community, and entitlement, in Kingston. In the hands of community service providers, then, the active society and the active self were transformed such that welfare recipients were positioned as victims who pointed to rather than embodied what was wrong with society.

Given these readings, community service providers had a much greater tendency than did welfare providers to report resisting official policy directly. Welfare providers certainly have mechanisms for pushing back, for giving critical feedback to official policy makers, although such feedback is more or less solicited and sanctioned depending on where an organization fits along the service-control continuum I discussed in chapter 2. But community service providers seem to have even more opportunity and leeway to "talk back," in spite of their dependence on the state for funding: they can petition government decision makers directly, their organizations can release media reports critical of government, they can phone or visit individual welfare providers to pressure them to give more to their clients, and they can help clients fill out forms and accompany them to the welfare office. All the community service providers I interacted with made use of one or more of these approaches on a regular basis. And while welfare providers were by no means uncritical of policy, community service providers were considerably more vociferous in their opposition, more biting in their criticism. This should come as no surprise: although in one respect "passing along" policy mandates, in another respect community service providers and the organizations for which they worked were structurally situated in opposition to, or at least at an angle to, the welfare bureaucracy. They existed because the welfare bureaucracy was doing the wrong thing, or not doing enough of the right thing. Their job, then, in addition to filling the gaps, was to point to them. This pointing-to took various forms, depending on providers' political, social, and religious orientations. Again, however, despite these variations—as well as the variations and sometimes contradictions in how they approached poor mothers and provisioning, as I have described above—community service providers' pointing converged in both tenor and direction.

In translating policy in particular ways, community service providers thus create it. Their creations are assemblages, cut-and-paste constellations comprised of their knowledges of how the welfare bureaucracy operates, of the larger cultural systems within which policy frames are embedded, and of what they know of their clients' lives and of the results of particular policy practices on those lives. As yet an additional set of hands through which policy moves, their unique policy productions provide different vantage points on, as well as for, the poor single mothers on welfare who call on them in their efforts to make ends meet.

Notes

1. As Fraser (1989) indicates in her discussion of the transformation of needs into administrable form as they are legitimized and taken up by the authorities, co-optation may be inevitable when states get involved. Thus, to follow her example, the work of shelters for battered women, originally established and run by feminist activists, is transformed as shelters are taken over by "expert" social workers and become dependent on funding from government agencies: social workers, with their psychological perspectives, serve to depoliticize battering; while government funders place their own constraints on shelter-related activities.
2. "Reserve" refers to parcels of land set aside for Indigenous groups, which were historically forcibly relocated and restricted to such parcels. The US term is "reservation."

Chapter 4

WORKING WITH POLICY IN "REAL LIFE"

Welfare Mothers' Engagements

∝∞

> [I]t is important to consider the ways in which "governmen-
> tal" action may attempt to manage social formations, may
> attempt to subject them to regulation, and may attempt to
> fix the meanings of words and the identities of subjects. But
> that does not mean that these attempts succeed. (Clarke
> 2004: 70)

At the end of the travels I have explored so far in this book—travels
across time in Aotearoa/New Zealand and Alberta, across national and
provincial boundaries in globalized policy networks, and through sites of
production, implementation, modification, contestation, and rejection
in huge edifices of bureaucracy and social provisioning—are poor single
mothers on welfare, the recipients of enormous amounts of political, academic, and activist attention, theorization, and diagnosis, if not of adequate means to live. As I argued in the Introduction, welfare mothers
have played a key role in neoliberal imaginaries. In debates about fiscal
responsibility, the role of the state, and the proper configuration of social
relations, they have served as negative object lessons; and both they and
the welfare programs they rely on have been scapegoated as problems for
the economy and for society: drains on the public purse, and negative
social and moral exemplars. Poor single mothers embody precisely what
"we" don't want to be (Kingfisher 1999, 2002b), and, as such, they be-

come useful projects to work on (Kingfisher 2007b). The work that we do on them and enjoin them to do on themselves via welfare reform provides one example of how, through particular policy regimes, we produce culture: structures of sentiment, ways of being human, and forms of organizing ourselves socially, economically, and politically.

I have placed poor single mothers last in my policy travelogue for two reasons. First, although policy translation and assemblage occurs simultaneously in a number of sites by means of the situated engagements of a range of actors, these sites and agents are not all equal. I therefore locate poor single mothers last in order to underscore (rather than reinscribe) their place at the bottom of the social hierarchy—last in line, as it were (although they are of course first in line in policy constructions that target poor persons rather than the conditions of possibility for poverty). I also hope to reprise the point, outlined in the preceding chapters, that the relationship between the state and its policy targets, far from direct, is mediated by a range of persons and institutional structures, all of which always also transform that which they transmit. Thus it is not surprising that the translations of poor single mothers contain traces of the meanings produced by an array of providers, both official and unofficial. It is equally not surprising that the women selectively disassembled and reassembled these meanings in keeping with their own everyday knowledges. In this sense, there is a good argument to be made for tracking policy "downstream," as it were, as long as we avoid positing each translation as determining the next and keep in mind the goal of "understanding ... policy 'reinvention' as a continuous, multi-site process" (Peck and Theodore 2012: 27).

A Note on Data and Methods

I have organized this chapter in a way fundamentally different from how I organized the preceding two chapters. This reflects, first of all, the data to which I had access. As I outlined in chapters 2 and 3, my interactions with welfare and community service providers were in many cases restricted to interviews, the majority of which took the form of one-on-one conversations. There were exceptions to this, particularly in the case of community service providers. But, in general, my encounters with both groups of providers were not robustly ethnographic. My inability to engage in more traditional forms of participation observation with providers reflected both their time restrictions and the privacy regulations of their agencies. However, although I was unable to participate in events in which providers interacted with their clients or among themselves (e.g., staff meetings or tea breaks), two community service organizations—Aboriginal Alternatives in Riverview, and Parent Connection in Kingston—gave me access to their clients. In both cases, I was able to have ongoing interactions with welfare mothers, individually and in groups, in a range of contexts. The result was a set of engagements that were significantly more informal than events called "interviews," however unstructured, and which provided relatively greater access than I had with providers to the nuances of how the women translated welfare policy and assembled their ways of being in the world. The richness of the data produced, particularly in the course of the women's interactions with each other,[1] was enhanced by the opportunities I was awarded, via participant observation, to develop relationships with them that entailed personal, meaningful, emotional ties.

In addition to reflecting the contexts in which I was able to interact with research participants, my organization of this chapter reflects the unique content of the data, in light of which I group the women in Riverview and Kingston together. My reason for this is simple, although it reflects a not-so-simple phenomenon: in key areas, the women in both sites reported remarkably similar experiences and expressed astoundingly similar views. This convergence is simultaneously striking and mundane. Its banality reflects the obvious point that the women shared certain structural locations in cultural contexts characterized by family resemblance: they were all single mothers struggling to care for their children more or less on their own; they were all poor; they were all recipients of stigmatized financial assistance in historical periods marked, in both cases, by radical reconfigurations of the welfare state in social contexts in which neoliberalism and strands of neoconservatism had a great deal of purchase; and, as nonideal persons, they were also all subjects of state interference designed to alter who they were as persons. The shared discursive patterns I outline below therefore make some sense.[2]

It is precisely the differences in the situations of the two groups of women, however, that renders the convergences in their experiences and expressions striking as well as mundane. Regardless of the family resemblances between the two sites, each has its own unique historical, cultural, ethnic, and political compositions and trajectories. The structure of the welfare regimes in each location also diverged significantly, particularly with regard to workfare requirements. Nor were the women in Kingston and Riverview part of a global social movement that works to construct common frames of understanding and coordinated political approaches—they were not plugged into any global networks, and they certainly did not have any contact with each other. Nevertheless, they shared most of their views, often articulating them in remarkably similar fashion. These shared discursive patterns provide yet another entry point into the broader tensions between convergence and divergence that serve as one focus of this book.

With few exceptions, my grouping together of women in Riverview and Kingston entails grouping together First Nations, non-Native, Maori, Pacific Island, and Pakeha women. This is not to claim that there were no differences among them. As I discuss below, non-Native and Pakeha women, for example, were more likely to express career-related desires, while First Nations, Maori, and Pacific Island women were more likely to emphasize the importance of family and community. There were also differences in how the women constructed the causes of poverty, how they diagnosed the problem with men, and how they experienced their interactions with welfare providers and the welfare system more generally that correlated loosely with ethnicity. However, the boundaries between the groups were more fluid than I had expected, and in many cases the differences were not absolute but rather differences of degree—and sometimes surprisingly small degrees at that. And, although certainly not irrelevant, these differences pale in comparison to the convergences in the women's views that cut across the various ethnic, cultural, and geographic divides that otherwise separated them.

Aboriginal Alternatives and Parent Connection

Aboriginal Alternatives, in Riverview, is a homeless shelter for poor single women who are undergoing some kind of "transition"—most typically, from the reserve to town, or out of abusive relations or drug addictions. Aboriginal Alternatives can accommodate ten women and their children, who are permitted to stay in the shelter for up to a year. The various programs offered, in addition to individual counseling and advocacy, include workshops on self-esteem and job skills, and a Head Start program for the children. Residents share the cooking and cleaning, and pay rent (from their welfare checks) to supplement the funding Aboriginal Alternatives receives from the city and province. Although designed to meet the specific needs of Indigenous women (all staff were First Nations), Aboriginal Alternatives is open to all, and during my fieldwork two of the ten residents were non-Native. (It nevertheless took me considerable time—three years—to gain access, because, I was later told, staff were suspicious of yet "another non-Native" who was interested in the lives of their clients.)

I engaged in three types of activities at Aboriginal Alternatives. First, as suggested by staff, and in keeping with their emphasis on group activities, I organized regular discussion sessions. For each session, scheduled at times convenient to the majority of the women, I supplied food, mostly of the kinds the women told me they liked but did not have access to on a regular basis—various cheeses and fancy crackers, fresh fruit (their favorite), and nuts—as well as cookies and other treats. The food provided the physical focus for our discussions, and the women were always grateful for the leftovers. During these sessions, which usually lasted about two hours, we sat around a large table in the boardroom, ate, and talked. Each time we met, we started with a question: What is the good life? What are your goals? What does it mean to be a mother? What does it mean to be a father? How do you juggle having a job and being a mother? What do children need? What do you need? What are your biggest challenges? Sometimes, especially early on in my time at Aboriginal Alternatives, I came up with the opening question, but eventually the women took over and determined their own topics of conversation, often wrapping up one discussion group by formulating the opening question for the next. Regardless of who set the topic, once the conversation got going I had very little input, as I was more interested in where the women themselves decided to take their talk. As a result, conversation tended to range over a variety of topics at any given meeting, weaving in and out of various aspects of their relationships with men, their extended families, paid labor, the state, their children, themselves, and each other. Children wandered in and out of the room, coming in to get food, check in with their mothers, and periodically contribute a few words to the conversation before returning to their play.

When I asked the women what I could do in return for the time they were giving me at the discussion sessions, they asked what skills I could teach them. I offered to teach either yoga or meditation, and they voted unanimously for latter because, they said, they wanted to learn how to better cope with stress. So, once a week, I held meditation classes, each time working on a different approach (sitting versus lying down, breathing versus visualization). Since there was no daycare available at Aboriginal Alternatives, I hired babysitters to look after the children during these sessions. Although I also provided written instructions for each type of meditation so that the women could practice on their own if they liked, staff told me that no one ever asked for these instructions, guessing that the women preferred the structure and sociality of the organized sessions. Finally, the more organized interactions I had with the women in discussion and meditations sessions were contextualized by a more generalized "hanging out," particularly during meal preparation and sharing in the evenings, and in the lounge during the daytime, where there was always one or two people sitting around, usually with the TV on in the background. Sometimes we chatted, sometimes we played with the children, and sometimes we just sat, saying nothing.

At the end of my five months at Aboriginal Alternatives, the women held a going-away party for me. They baked a cake and pooled their money (of which they had very little, being homeless) to get me a set of wind-chimes and a coffee cup, both with Native motifs. In the card they gave me, each woman thanked me for listening to them—a gesture I found both heartbreaking and revealing: being validated by so few, they were surprised and grateful that someone was interested enough in their lives to spend some time with them.

My work at Aboriginal Alternatives was informed and supplemented by participant-observation at the one of the three food banks in town, where I spent two summers as a volunteer and also served as a board member; by interviews with residents at the YWCA, which houses a women's shelter and rooms for low-income women; and by interviews and discussion groups with women who contacted me in response to ads placed in grocery stores.

As in Riverview, my work in Kingston, Aotearoa/New Zealand, focused on and radiated out from one key site. Parent Connection is the only one of seven Community Houses in Kingston, funded by the city council and the New Zealand government, geared exclusively to the needs of low-income single parents.[3] It offers counseling services (clients may choose to work with either a Pakeha or Maori social worker), workshops on self-esteem, budgeting, and parenting; legal advice (from a lawyer who visits once a month); welfare advice (from a welfare case manager who visits once every two weeks as well as from Parent Connection staff); and advocacy. Parents can also come in on a daily basis to pick up free bread and pastries donated by local grocery stores and bakeries, or to get clothing and household items from the opportunity shop.[4] Finally, Parent Connection holds "morning tea" three times a week from 10:00 a.m. to noon, during which children are attended to by staff trained in early childhood education so that their parents can relax and chat with each other. Not only does morning tea fit cultural convention but, more importantly, as explained to me by staff, it also gives women a break from child care, setting the stage for the provision of mutual support and information sharing. The goal of morning tea, then, was to provide an antidote to the (social and informational) isolation experienced by many poor single mothers, especially those with very young children.

In contrast to Aboriginal Alternatives, where I had to create discussion groups, morning tea at Parent Connection provided a naturally occurring event into which I could insinuate myself. As at Aboriginal Alternatives, I brought copious amounts of food to the teas (Parent Connection provided the coffee, tea, and milk) so that the women could take leftovers home, and we sat around a large table in the lounge and talked. And again, as at Aboriginal Alternatives, conversation ranged across topics, as women discussed child care and mothering, relationships with their immediate and extended families, financial issues, dreams and aspirations, and the trials and tribulations of being on welfare. Children came in and out of these conversations, and the women themselves would often leave for a few minutes at a time to change a diaper, make a cup of tea, or speak with a staff member. I spent my mornings at Parent Connection regularly for two blocks of eight weeks during the (Aotearoa/New Zealand) winter, bracketing morning tea with "hanging out." Although women tended to participate in Parent Connection activities for only several months at a time, some were present across both fieldwork periods, and I became close with a few of them. And again, as at Aboriginal Alternatives, at the end of each research period the women formally thanked me (in this case, with gifts of Marmite, a popular Kiwi sandwich spread) for taking an interest in their lives, which, again, I read not only as friendliness but also as a marker of their low status and isolation.

I told each woman I met at morning tea that I would be interested in interviewing her individually, if she was inclined to tell me her story in detail. Most women did not take me up on this offer, preferring, perhaps, the congeniality of morning tea. Several did, however—and certainly more than did at Aboriginal Alternatives—and I have included some of their stories in my analysis. With the help of community service organizations serving Maori and Pacific Islanders, I was also able to interview and have discussion groups with women not directly associated with Parent Connection. These were few, however, when compared with the number of welfare mothers I met in Riverview outside of Aboriginal Alternatives.

Policy Meets the "Real World"

As I spent time with women on welfare, a bundle of phenomena emerged as central: children, men, welfare, independence, employment, and self/identity. Together, these composed an assemblage of what was important to them. While welfare and community service providers recognized (more or less) the complexities of their clients' lives, they nevertheless tended to be fragmentary in their in-the-moment exclusive emphasis on housing, child care, employment, and so on, depending on women's immediate needs and program foci. Poor single mothers themselves, of course, did not disarticulate pieces of their lives from each other, but rather saw and lived them as inextricably tied. My goal, accordingly, was to attend to the women's whole lives, and to the policy worlds (Shore and Wright 2011: 2) that they inhabited.

In working with poor single mothers, welfare and community service providers, and policy mandates, it became clear to me that welfare
mothers were being subjected to competing visions of welfare, work,
mothering, and personhood. First, they encountered the contradictions
embedded in policy and in the dominant ideologies informing it. One of
the most glaring discrepancies here concerned the messages the women
received regarding the kinds of persons they should be: on the one hand,
in keeping with neoliberal philosophies, they were expected to be independent individuals; and, on the other hand, in keeping with neoconservatism, they were told that their primary function was to be mothers
and care-givers. The former message was most pronounced in the Alberta
reforms, which reconfigured welfare mothers as genderless self-sufficient
individuals (Brodie 2002, 2008), and required them, accordingly, to behave as autonomous monads. The neoconservative approach, in contrast,
placed women in the home as dependent housewives, primary caregivers,
and key agents of socialization for children. Given its maternalist history, the weakness of actual work requirements in the 1991 and 1996 reforms, and the explicit nod to the importance of parenting in the 2002
reforms, neoconservative constructs of gender roles were most evident in
Aotearoa/New Zealand—but they were also present in Alberta, albeit in
muted form. The Klein administration, unable to simultaneously assert
that poor single mothers were individuals (and thus able-bodied workers)
and promote traditional nuclear family formation, nevertheless indirectly
promoted the latter as a solution to poverty:

> While the government's efforts to implement a workfare scheme have sug-
> gested that single women with children are presumed to be workers rather
> than mothers, the absence of adequate childcare facilities, the low wage
> jobs in which many of the these women are employed and the province's
> insistence on maintaining the minimum wage at $5.00 per hour, the sec-
> ond lowest in Canada[5], suggest that the only way for these women to at-
> tain a reasonable standard of living is to attach themselves to an employed
> man or return to their parental home. (Harder 1996: 60)

More recently, Harder and Trimble (2005) indicate that the continuing
inadequacy of child care in Alberta, the requirement that welfare recipients pursue child support from the fathers of their children, and tax legislation favoring single earner nuclear families is indicative of an ongoing
structural disfavoring of women in general, and of poor single mothers
in particular. In other words, while the Alberta reforms were explicitly
designed to encourage recipients' engagement in paid labor, the wider
cultural context has been one that disproportionately awards moral ap-
proval and material benefits to traditional nuclear families. Along with its

clear market orientation, then, the Klein administration also buttressed neoconservative approaches to economic and social organization, simultaneously encouraging independent individuality and heteronormative family formation. In parallel fashion, as I described in chapter 2, New Zealand policy officially supported women in their parenting roles while simultaneously deploying an approach to Personal Development and Employment Plans that stressed self-sufficient, independent individuality. My discussion in chapter 1 of the divergences between Alberta and Aotearoa/New Zealand regarding larger cultural patterns related to individualism and mothering thus does not mean that opposing tendencies were not also present in each context.

In addition to inconsistencies within policy itself, and in the larger social arena occupied by policy, poor single mothers were confronted by contradictions both among and between welfare and community service providers. The information given by one welfare provider might not match that offered by another, and, even more frequently, welfare and community service providers offered women diametrically opposed perspectives and types of information. For example, here is a sample of the kinds of contradictory messages and advice the women I worked with received from the two categories of provider: you should stay on welfare as long as you can in order to look after your children at home; you should get a job; the welfare office is here to help; the welfare office is racist; here is an information session that will tell you everything you need to know about the services available to you through the department; case managers never tell you everything that you're entitled to; our carefully crafted budget will allow you to meet all your needs; welfare never gives you enough to live on.[6]

The women's bundle of interests, in the context of the opposing messages and demands they were subjected to, raised a series of questions. Most generally, how do poor single mothers engage with policy, and to what effect? How, for instance, do they negotiate the contradictory terrain between neoliberal tenets of independent individuality and neoconservative models of women as natural mothers and caregivers? Given the existence of multiple (albeit unequal) possibilities, how do they come to "invest" in particular subject positions and not others, particularly when those subject positions may be inimical to their material and social well-being (see, e.g., Moore 1996)? And how do they make sense of the different messages and information they receive from welfare and community service providers in light of their own everyday knowledges, gleaned from personal experience and shared with each other in settings such as Parent Connection and Aboriginal Alternatives?

In the remainder of this chapter I explore these questions, with particular attention to what welfare mothers in Kingston and Riverview seemed to have translated directly, uncritically and without question, on the one hand; and what they challenged, contested, and refused, on the other hand. I also argue, however, that even the women's uncritical "absorption" of particular ideologies and practices did not always result in behavior compliant to the welfare bureaucracy or dominant society. On the contrary, in some cases their appropriation of dominant ideologies led instead to challenges to certain programmatic prescriptions, regardless of whether they can be construed as deliberately and explicitly resistant. In other words, poor single mothers translated even that which they adopted unquestioningly in ways reflective of their situated knowledges, in the process transforming what they adopted into something slightly, or, in some cases, radically different from their "original" form.

Convergence: Independence, Work, and Mothering

If the women I worked with had encountered contradictory messages about the kinds of persons they should be—enterprising and self-sufficient individuals versus stay-at-home mothers and housewives—what I encountered was women who had translated both messages into taken-for-granted absolutes that were complementary rather than contradictory: they simultaneously aligned themselves with the ideas of personal fulfillment accomplished via independent individuality, *and* of women as "natural" mothers and caregivers. However, the women translated these messages, received from welfare and community service providers as well as from society at large, in such a way that they could claim the valorized statuses associated with both independence and motherhood while also avoiding the pitfalls of paid labor and relationships with men.

The women's adoption of neoliberal models of the person focused on self-fulfillment via self-sufficiency was most evident in their discussions of paid work, in which they voiced a desire to have "careers" and constructed paid labor as a central marker of full personhood. In a group discussion at Aboriginal Alternatives on the topic of men's and women's roles, for instance, Sandra gave voice, in the most mundane way, to the notion that paid labor is a fundamental aspect of being a person: "I was dating this older guy ... and I was working and I got hurt at work, and I was off work for three weeks and he refused to let me go back to work. He told me that I needed to stay home and every day I had to have dinner ready, the house had to be clean. ... I left him ... I just up and left. I'm sorry, I have to work." "I'm sorry, I have to work," was not just Sandra's response to an overly demanding partner, but also an expression of a basic characteristic of her self; as such it serves as an example of translation as internalization. The following exchange, from a discussion of the "good life" at Aboriginal Alternatives, is even more telling. The speakers, Martha (M), Tiara (T), Krystal (K), and myself (C), have just established that a supportive family is crucial to the "good life":

C: What other kinds of things might you need for a good quality of life?

T: A job.

C: Okay, a job.

T: A job you enjoy.

C: Okay … a job you enjoy, and so what is a job, what does that give you? You get the pleasure from doing the job? You earn a certain amount of money?

T: Independence.

C: Okay.

M: Self-worth.

C: Yeah, okay.

T: Confidence …

C: Yes?

K: Self-esteem.

C: Self-esteem, right, from being able to do something … on your own, eh?

K: mm huh

Fully in keeping with neoliberal models of the self, the women construct paid labor as a key component of positive identity. It provides not only income, but also confidence, self-esteem, and, ultimately, self-realization and fulfillment. Indeed, I was the only one among the participants in this exchange to specifically mention *money* as an important reason for having a job. Tiara refers to independence, which presumably is enabled by the money earned from a job, but she places equal weight on enjoyment and confidence; and Martha and Krystal are most interested in self-esteem. It is worth underscoring that this exchange did not occur in the context of a job training workshop put on by state agents who had control over the women's finances,[7] but while we were sitting around a table, relaxed, eating, and surrounded by children engaged in various playtime activities. What was being voiced seemed to me to be genuine, heartfelt sentiments.

Women in Kingston, whose assertions of autonomy, like those of women in Riverview, were always accompanied by expressions of desires to "do something" with their lives, expressed similar views. Indeed, in Kingston, the positive value of work and career was such that some women voiced support for the Personal Development and Employment Plans (PDEPs) that they were required to construct with the help of their case managers at the welfare office. In a conversation at Parent Connection one day, for instance, Allison argued that the PDEP meetings were "good in a way; it's making you sit down and set goals for yourself to achieve and it's all up to you, so you actually do it, and it's all for you." Wendy concurred, referring to her specific goals of "getting my own home … [and] getting study [an education] so I was able to go into the workforce." Neither woman questioned the welfare bureaucracy's regulation of self; on the contrary, they valued it as something useful, since it supported their own quests for personal development. They looked positively on the idea of having a "plan," and saw themselves as projects to be worked on, selves to be realized. As in Riverview, paid labor was here constructed as a key component of identity, not just a source of income. In both sites, then, women consistently expressed interest in engaging in career-related projects-in-the-world, and they were all determined to realize their "full potential" and to find fulfillment through paid labor. Worker-citizenship (Korteweg 2006) was thus in some ways expressed as commonsense. This kind of "good" translation would be considered laudable by many welfare providers, and certainly by the policy elites who wrote welfare legislation in both Alberta and Aotearoa/New Zealand: expressing desires to work, and enumerating the profoundly life- and soul-enhancing benefits of employment could easily be read as an index of the successful transformation of welfare bums into enterprising individuals.

The women's individualized understandings of the causes of poverty further index the hegemony of the neoliberal approaches to the person embedded in policy. In reflecting on their own poverty, most women, even in the group contexts of Aboriginal Alternatives and Parent Connection, did not mention the gender division of labor, societal patterns in domestic abuse, inadequate education systems, or other structures of economic inequality. (Only one woman mentioned "Ralph Klein and selling out all our utilities.") Their concerns, rather, had to do with *their* relationships with *their* abusive partners, or *their* inability to get a good job, or *their* need to get a good education in order to possibly secure a better job. These individualized frameworks for thinking about their situations were completely in keeping with the neoliberal narrative of poverty: the women tended to focus, as do policy experts and many welfare providers, on lack of education, low self-esteem, bad habits of various sorts, and an inability to budget. When referring to their personal experiences of entering poverty (as opposed to abstract "causes of poverty"), the women also reproduced neoliberal ideologies of self-examination and responsibilization, often narrating their experiences as being the outcome of the "bad choices" they had made. As Mandy, in Riverview, put it: "I was younger, too, and I started making really bad choices with my husband. Then I got out of that relationship and so, now I kind of got my head together. ... So, I think people really need to be looked at where they are coming from because some people create their own circumstances that they are under." Insofar as the women constructed their personal experiences as personal, rather than as illustrative of any kind of social pattern, they represented a class in themselves rather than for themselves (Bourdieu 1990; Young 1997; see also Kingfisher and Goldsmith 2001).

First Nations women provided the one exception to this pattern. Although as quick as non-Native Albertan and Aotearoa/New Zealand Pakeha women to point to issues of addiction, self-esteem, and bad relationships with bad men when discussing what causes and perpetuates poverty, they nevertheless sometimes situated these patterns of addiction and "bad choices" in historical and contemporary contexts of racism. As I discuss further below, First Nations women also pointed to racism when diagnosing problems with the men in their lives.

The women's more or less "good" translation of the neoliberal tenets informing welfare mandates met its limits, however, in the realities of paid work, which, coupled with raising children single-handedly, told a different story. Echoing feminist and other critical scholars (Davies et al. 2001; Lochhead and Scott 2000; Wacquant 1999), the women knew well that employment in itself—especially the kinds of employment to which they had access—was no way out of poverty for mothers with dependent children. This was particularly the case in Riverview, where welfare recipients were subjected to strict work tests. Hester, for instance, told me that she had been unable to make ends meet despite holding down three jobs simultaneously. Others mentioned the need to work under the table, or to lie about their health or finances to their welfare providers—activities they told me they deplored but nevertheless felt compelled to undertake in order to survive. Yet others spoke of the difficulty of getting any job at all in the face of clashes between shift work and child care availability. Given the realities of low-wage work, the requirement in Alberta that welfare recipients make looking for a job a full-time pursuit made little sense to women in Riverview, especially since such requirements ignored their parenting work. As Susan put it: "They [welfare] ask you to do a full-time day, as if you're working a full-time job, to go looking for a job, job hunting. But yet then if you've got kids they won't provide any child care for you." Indeed, as I described in chapter 2, when I attended the mandatory orientation session for welfare applicants in Riverview, the facilitator responded to one woman's question about child care costs by asserting that from the point of view of the welfare department, employment was always superior to unemployment, even if there was no financial gain once child care costs were subtracted. This was not a message that women on welfare could easily accept.

Although women in Kingston were not officially subjected to work tests, they nevertheless reported experiencing enormous pressure to find jobs. At Parent Connection one morning, Stella and Kim, both of whom had been on the DPB since before the 2002 reforms, told me that their case managers were now putting *more* pressure on them than previously to take whatever jobs were available. As Kim put it, "They've gotten a lot harder.... They do try to get you to go to work." Stella recounted an interaction she had with providers at the welfare office after she had turned down a job offer: "I told them that ... I think I've changed my mind (about taking the job), and they sort of said, 'No, once a job is offered to you, you take it.' I said, 'No, I don't take it.'" In Stella's view, her knowledge that the welfare department could not actually force her to take a job—knowledge, she pointed out, that not all beneficiaries had—was the only thing that enabled her to avoid succumbing to such pressure. Nevertheless, both women also reported having the kind of PDEP meeting that the providers I discussed in chapter 2 described: "They just ask you where you want (to go in life) ... what you want to do ... are you still happy ... doing what you're doing ... do you have any plans for the future?" The more facilitative and holistic approach advocated by the 2002 reforms was there, then, but this did not prevent recipients from also feeling compelled by their case managers to engage in paid work.

At morning tea a few days later, Kim prompted two other women, Yvonne and Venetia, to tell their stories of being pressured to engage in work or training activities. Yvonne recounted how she had been told she had to seek employment when she was twenty-nine weeks pregnant and with two young children at home. "There's not a job out there for twelve weeks," she reported telling her case manager, who then, Yvonne acknowledged with gratitude, backed down. Venetia's story was simply bizarre: her case manager insisted that she participate in a training course, so she found herself on a canoeing trip when she was six months pregnant. "It sucked," she said, inciting laughter from the rest of us. "You're pregnant ... (and) the canoe is uneven ... about the worst trip ever, it fucking blows." When I asked her what the goals of the course were (thinking she would say something about self-reliance, or persistence in the face of hardship), she replied, "I don't know." From where she sat, Venetia had no say in whether she had to take a training course or in even in choosing which one to take, and she had no idea of the purpose of the exercise. Her case manager was adamant, and Venetia felt that there was nothing she could do but acquiesce.

In both Riverview and Kingston, then, there was a contradiction between the almost unanimous desire for being out in the world and having
careers, on the one hand, and a rejection of actual paid labor (or training
courses), on the other. While the women had adopted received neoliberal
assertions that paid work is a crucial component of positive subjectivity, their everyday experiences, heavily influenced by the exigencies of
childrearing and the realities of the labor markets to which they had access, served to temper dominant discourses equating employment with
independence.

This convergence of views across the two sites regarding paid labor was
met with a second: in both Kingston and Riverview, the women negotiated the contradiction between their desires for and the realities of paid
work by adopting neoconservative models of women as natural mothers
and caregivers, which they took as much for granted as they did neoliberal models of independent individuality—and which, significantly, provided legitimate grounds for their opposition to workfare. In Riverview,
the women's adoption of the mothering role took the form of fantasies of
being able to be stay-at-home mothers. (Sandra, whose rejection of the
wife-at-home model with which I opened this section, was the exception
that proved the rule—but only in terms of temporality; see below.) In a
conversation with Maggie and Cynthia, for instance, who I met through
my volunteer work at a food bank in Riverview and who shared an apartment and child-raising duties, Maggie insisted that she had no interest
in going out to work and placing her children in daycare. "I'd rather stay
at home with my own kids," she said—a phrase she repeated four times,
accompanied by wistful sighs, in the course of less than one minute. Cynthia concurred, saying that she would like to "have little parties for the
kids ... and bake cookies;" she giggled at the sheer delight of this fantasy.
For their part, women in Kingston complained that having a job meant
that "you never see your child 'cause then you're always working," as
Yvonne put it. In the views of the women at Parent Connection, the tasks
involved in being a mother and caretaker—including not only spending
time with children, but also washing, cleaning, cooking, and so on—were
more important than any paid job. *These* were what had to take priority,
not earning an income. Sally, who I met through one of the women at
Parent Connection, accordingly made it her business to know both her
entitlements and obligations as a beneficiary. The mother of four, she was
a strong advocate for choice regarding employment: "Women fought to
be able to go to work," she said, and they should not be "punished" for
choosing to work. "But," she added by way of qualification, "if you want to
stay at home and be an earth mother that should equally be an option"; in
fact, such women should "be honored for ... bringing up the next genera-

tion." She argued that children were necessary to the nation in general and to the economy in particular, indicating that "anybody who's got half a brain understands that somebody has to stay at home and bring them up." Indeed, in spite of advocating free choice in this matter, Sally admitted that she had a hard time imagining that mothers would actually *want* to go out to work: "If you're not gonna stay home and bring up your child, then why did you have it?"

These two convergences led to a third: in both Kingston and Riverview, the women dealt with the contradictions between their stated desires to participate in paid labor, the realities of paid work, and their assertions that they were first and foremost mothers by placing mothering and paid labor in a clear temporal sequence: they were mothers *now*, as they should be; and they would *also* pursue their careers and join the paid labor force—only *later*, once their children were old enough (considered to be school age among women in Riverview and eighteen years old among Kingston mothers). It was this strategy of deferral that enabled the women to simultaneously embrace paid labor as a foundational component of valued subjectivity and assert that their primary focus at this point in their lives was to be mothers. Their situated knowledges of the rigors and joys of parenting, and of the rigidities and inadequacies of the workplace, resulted in a unique articulation of aspects of neoliberalism with aspects of neoconservatism, a cut-and-paste effort to assert a valorized place for themselves in societies that tended to deny it to them.

Independence and Men

This disassemblage and reassemblage of bits and pieces of neoliberalism and neoconservatism was also evident in how the women framed the role of men in their lives. When women discussed the primacy of mothering and the importance of staying at home with their children until they were old enough to be able to handle a mother with a career, men were conspicuously absent; the women simply evicted from their narratives the father of the neoconservative nuclear family model. Thus there were no invocations of fathers barbequing, mowing the lawn, taking out the rubbish, or working on cars—let alone contributing financially—when Maggie and Cynthia related their white-picket-fence, stay-at-home fantasies. To be sure, a few women dreamed about finding partners, but they quickly qualified their musings as fantastical. Martha, in Kingston, for instance, said, "I am smarter than that, but you feel … kind of alone or something and you think 'Here's somebody who cares.'" The women were also cognizant of the social validation provided by attachment to a man in couplist societies. Thus Harriet, in Riverview, said, "Even if you are divorced, you are more validated than a single parent because a single parent, maybe it was just a one night stand." Significantly, however, and across the board, the portions of conversations in which fantasies of domestic bliss figured were separated in both time and tone from those in which the real men with whom the women had relationships were discussed, as if they fell into mutually exclusive categories.

The women had good reasons for being wary of relationships with men. Having previously adopted nuclear family models—the vast majority had attempted, or had wanted to attempt, to live in conjugal families (de jure or de facto)—the women found that by and large men tended to abdicate their roles as partners and parents. The centrality of welfare in their lives thus reflected the centrality of men in their lives. Their everyday knowledge of men as inadequate, obstructionist, or even harmful was, accordingly, foundational to how they encountered the welfare system and how they translated its mandates.

Abuse was a key component of this everyday knowledge of men. The following two stories provide examples of the severity of the physical abuse suffered by some of the women at Aboriginal Alternatives and Parent Connection:

> Ruby, a 36-year-old Native woman with four children, had been receiving welfare while staying at Aboriginal Alternatives for the last ten months. As we were waiting for the other residents to join us for a discussion group one day, Ruby walked me through her list of health problems, which included arthritis in both her knees and a variety of back troubles. She also told me that she needed corrective surgery on two of her fingers. When I asked her what for, she casually, almost matter-of-factly, told me that six months previously she had used her hand to block a kick to her face by her partner, and two of her fingers had been smashed. She held up to her hand show me how the fingers dangled and then told me that she had finally broken up with him the night before our meeting. Trying to mask my surprise that she had waited six months after such an event to leave her partner, I expressed sympathy for the injury as the other residents started arriving for our discussion session. When I returned to Aboriginal Alternatives two days later, Valerie, another resident, told me that Ruby's ex, in retaliation for the break-up, had cleaned out their joint bank account, leaving Ruby and the children with no funds whatsoever; and, given that they had just deposited that month's funds into the account, the welfare office was unwilling to provide further support. As Valerie relayed these events to me, two of Ruby's children stood nearby, weeping. Several months after finishing fieldwork, I found out that Ruby and her children, who had gone beyond the one-year limit on staying at the shelter, were found sleeping in the alleyway next to Aboriginal Alternative's garage.

Diane, a 24-year-old Pakeha mother of two children under the age of six, attended morning tea at Parent Connection regularly for a month during the winter of 2004. What most stood out to me when I first met her was that she had no front teeth, top or bottom; I assumed this was the result of some kind of infection combined with a lack of access to adequate dental care. Diane was shy and reserved, but still wanted to talk, and so one day we left the tea room and went upstairs to a private room, where she told me her story. After growing up in an abusive household, witness to her father's regular and severe beatings of her mother, Diane eventually found herself with an abusive partner who routinely beat her in front of relatives, friends, and neighbors, who did nothing to intervene. He pulled her hair, punched her in the face and stomach, and eventually kicked out all of her front teeth (she had lost some molars as well). The kicks to the face were what finally drove her to leave him, and she had since been in and out of various programs—including a halfway house for people with anger management, since she had developed violent tendencies towards her children. Her children had been taken away from her on a temporary basis a number of times, but were soon to be placed in permanent foster care, and her future access to them would be limited and supervised.

Other women had encountered less dramatic but nevertheless debilitating forms of financial and/or emotional abuse. Many complained that, far from providing protection from poverty, relationships with men were often precisely what *generated* the poverty in which they were now mired. Marlene, for instance, who I met at the food bank in Riverview, had been married for a year when she had her daughter, after which she became a stay-at-home mother. Her husband began to spend less and less time at home, and Marlene soon realized that he was having an affair. When they finally split up, Marlene was plunged into poverty, primarily because of the debt he left her with: he had maxed out their joint credit cards buying gifts for his girlfriend, and had also trashed an as-yet-to-be-paid-for car on which she was listed as primary owner. She thus began her new life as a single mother on welfare owing over $10,000, added to which her ex-husband's child support checks frequently bounced. When she found out that her ex was marrying his new girlfriend, Marlene drove over to their house on their wedding day to drop off a thank-you card for the new wife, "for taking him off my hands." Although unique in her creative parting gesture, Marlene's situation in general is representative of that in which many of the women I encountered found themselves.

A number of women spoke of bad experiences with men who promised the world and delivered nothing, or who created more work for them because of their negligence and sloppy habits. The following excerpt from a group discussion at Aboriginal Alternatives regarding men's and women's roles is typical of the women's constructions of men. Toward the end of a lengthy conversation about the traditional gender division of labor, I asked Tiara (T), Ellen (E), and Ruby (R) what they thought men wanted. The response was fast and unequivocal:

R: They want to stay home.

C: That was simple.

R: In front of the TV on their butt or in front of the computer all day.

E: Yes.

T: They want to stay home and be waited on, they want to stay home and watch TV or play on the computer.

E: All day.

R: Men want to be pampered.

T: Yah.

R: They want mothers, eh.

E: In this day and age.

R: They want mothers.

T: In this day and age?

E: Yup.

C: Okay.

R: They want mothers, they want mothers.

Comments Mandy made during a focus group of mostly non-Native women at my home are equally instructive: "My daughter's dad still lives with his parents and he has no respect for nothing because nothing will ever happen to him, he will not be kicked out of his house, he will not lose his brand new car ... so he doesn't need to [do anything]. ... There's no consequences in this boy's life." Mandy made these observations while recounting a narrative about how her children's father hung up on her when she called to ask for money: "I'm yellin' and screamin,' I said, 'BUT I HAVE NO MONEY I HAVE NO FOOD AND THESE KIDS ARE EATING CRACKERS FOR CRYIN' OUT LOUD SEND ME SOME MONEY!' No. Click." As I translated it, Mandy's argument was that her children's father had never had to face the consequences of his actions, with the result that he took no responsibility whatsoever for his children's well-being and was, in fact, completely immune from even the *sense* that he might have any obligations vis-à-vis his children at all.

Thousands of kilometers away at Parent Connection in Kingston, women said the same thing, although in perhaps slightly stronger terms.

After listening to a group of women assert that they did not want a man around "all the time," I inquired as to why; Lena and Harriet responded as follows:

L: I think … they're just weird.

H: They're just a-holes [laughs] they're just …

L: [laughs]

C: They're … what?

H: Arseholes.

C: Oh, assholes. [laughs]

L: They're just messy and they pee me off and they're lazy and, you just get the house clean and they come in and just dump everything.

H: Yeah.

C: Yeah.

In this exchange the three of us cooperate to produce an elaboration of men as "weird" "arseholes"—messy, lazy, inconsiderate of others, and, by implication, self-absorbed. Earlier in the same conversation, Martha (who did not participate in this portion of the exchange) had said, "It doesn't help [to be with a man] because then you end up with two child[ren]—the actual child and the man child." Crossing the globe to return again to Riverview, I encountered the same sentiment, as voiced by Ellen at Aboriginal Alternatives: "I'm just tired of raising overgrown kids," she lamented. "They always come to us and drain us broke and then they say that we overspend." As she put it on another occasion: "It's hard when you have a spouse that is a yoyo. … It's like he's a child, it's like raising my kids *and* him, disciplining him, forcing him to work." Her ex, she said, was ten years older than her and yet "he still doesn't know what he wants in life."[8]

Divergence

Discussion of the reasons why men were so inadequate took one of three directions. As I described above, some women talked about what was wrong with men as if they just came that way, reflecting essentialist models, or, perhaps, a disinterest in the causes of men's behavior as opposed to the realities of it. This group comprised non-Native women in Riverview, and women of all ethnicities in Kingston. A second strand of thought, also outlined above, diagnosed men's problems as reflective of poor socialization—the negative repercussion of the "me" generation, of too much coddling. The women who expressed this view, lamenting a golden past when men were men and took proper care of their families, tended to be non-Native (in Riverview) and Pakeha (in Kingston).

Finally, there were women who claimed that men were inadequate as a result of the disablements of racism. Although voiced by only a few Maori and Pacific Island women in Kingston (in contrast to community service providers there, as discussed in chapter 3), First Nations women in Riverview were unanimous in expressing the view that Indigenous men had been debilitated by racism in general, and by the residential schooling system in particular.[9] In their view, residential schools interrupted the cycle of socialization: "When you think about kids getting snatched away and ... the parents don't have their kids to parent," Valerie explained during a group discussion one day, it becomes clear that young adults emerging from residential schools "don't know how to parent." As the conversation continued, however, we became confused: if women coming out of residential schools could find some way to manage, how come men could not? We decided to address our confusion by inviting a staff member's husband—who, along with his siblings, had attended residential school—to participate in one of our discussion sessions. Adam came the following week, and he explained to us that boys in residential schools suffered not only physical and sexual abuse similar to that suffered by girls, but also, and specifically, emasculation; as a consequence they lost not only a capacity to parent, but also the capacity to form intimate relationships of any sort. Many of the people Adam knew from residential school "tried to make it in the world, start a relationship, and a lot of them ended up in the streets," taking solace in alcohol and other drugs. Finding themselves in a situation in which "nobody ever learned how to say 'I love you,'" and which was designed "to only bring the Indian people to a certain level and they can never go beyond that," he said, young men came out of residential schools to confront not only high unemployment, but also women who seemed to be coping on their own by being providers as well as nurturers—both of which further undermined men's sense of masculinity. And although he argued that men needed to "choose" to make something of themselves, Adam claimed that they needed familial, social, and spiritual support in order to do this. Ironically, however, such support was sorely lacking precisely because of the damage caused by residential school, as well as by ongoing racism.

The women initially challenged Adam's assessment: since they had worked hard to look after their children, why could their men not do the same? Again, women had suffered in residential schools, too. But they were eventually convinced by his emphasis on emasculation, and they certainly agreed with the issue of ongoing racism, which they experienced alongside their men. They spoke in this regard of racist stereotypes that made it difficult for them to access services and that produced in them a profound sense of dispiritedness. In their view, racism was the biggest obstacle to their "making it"—to everything from finding affordable housing to getting and holding down a job. And they encountered racism in the welfare office as well as in society at large. As Tiara put it, "One of the biggest problems is because it's so stereotyped, well, we're 'What's the point?' you know, 'What's the point, we're gonna be classified anyways?'" The women expressed a generalized sense of otherness, which they took as foundational to the kinds of personal problems that they claimed (in keeping with the majority view in Riverview and Kingston, and with the neoliberal narrative more generally) resulted in falling prey to poverty—problems like poor self-esteem, low levels of education, drug abuse, or imprisonment in abusive relationships.

Convergence, Continued: Men as Perpetual Children

Regardless of how they contextualized men's inadequacies, however, the women were unified in the view that men were fundamentally flawed as persons. Men were seen in this regard as incapable of handling even the most basic aspects of parenting. One day at Aboriginal Alternatives, for example, Malinda described how her son's father could not cope with even disposable diapers: "I'd get home after work [and] the baby at the time would be soaked, right, *soaked*." "They're dumb," she continued, "they're stupid." Ruby challenged her by claiming, "The fathers just don't want to *do* it, that's all"—in other words, the problem was not stupidity, but a lack of commitment. In contrast to other occasions when the women criticized men, Malinda's description and Ruby's counterclaim were met not with laughter but with quiet sadness and resignation.

Women at Parent Connection were similarly exasperated by men's inability to attend to the basics of everyday life. Lynn, for example, once told the story of what happened when she left town to look after her ailing mother, leaving her son in the care of his father (with whom she was living at the time): "I went away for a week ... and Jason was about sixteen months old. I come back and the house was completely trashed. He [her ex] had done the washing but left it in the washing machine wet, all the dishes from Monday were still on the bench [counter] ... Friday, and it was like, 'Oh my gosh' ... I said 'I'm not cleaning it.'" Although her partner had not been abusive, Lynn said, he was more of a hindrance than a help; she therefore saw no reason why she should stay with him.

The women certainly did not consider men to be their equals. As Braewyn, a grandmother who had been a single mother herself and whose daughter, now also on the DPB, was a regular at Parent Connection, put it, "I think that single moms are a lot stronger than the males. ... Men can go out and do their work, but they can't take what's emotionally stressful." Kim (K), Yvonne (Y), and Lena (L) concurred:

K: With the male species. [uproarious laughter]

C: I guess they're not our species?

K: Their nature is selfish and ... the female nature is giving.

Y: Selfless.

K: Yeah, yeah, I don't know how we even live together really.

L: Nah.

Y: God they're different, aren't they.

K: Completely different.

On the basis of these varied—yet uniformly negative—experiences and constructions, the women rejected long-term relationships with men. Sally, the Kingston mother of four mentioned above, for instance, had had numerous relationships with men over the years, but never considered moving in with one. As she explained it to me, "I don't dislike men or anything, but I just find that they're not willing to make the sacrifices that women are." In some cases, then, the excision of men from the women's imaginings and practices of motherhood and family was explicit. Venetia, at Parent Connection, to give another example, put it like this: "I think that a man on their own feels they've gotta have a partner whereas a woman would (be fine) without it. I mean, a man is lost without a partner but ... women'll survive. ... A man is not a necessity in your life. ... In some countries ... the husband is just the sperm provider." In other cases, men's absence was assumed, left unspoken. Kim, for instance, a regular at Parent Connection whom I got to know well over the course of two research trips, had two children, fathered by the same man. It never occurred to her, however, to actually live with him; and she never even bothered to articulate this until I asked her, pointedly, after the birth of her second child, about the nature of her relationship with her children's father. She told me that she simply had "no interest in setting up house" with him. Although she liked him well enough, she saw herself and her two children as a separate unit.

The women often joked about men in disparaging ways, as if, now that they knew what men were *really* like, any desire to actually have a long-term relationship with one was beneath them. One day at Parent Connection, I was telling Yvonne (Y) and Marika (M) about my mock intake interview at the DPB office (discussed in chapter 2), during which two case managers had asked me why I was no longer with the hypothetical father of my hypothetical children. They laughingly constructed an imaginary conversation with a case manager:

Y: You should have said you dumped him.

M: You dumped him. [laughter]

C: "I dumped him."

Y: And then they'd want to know why. ... "Why did you dump him?"

M: "I don't like his hairstyle anymore."

Y: "He (has) funny shoes."

M: "He leaves the top off the toothpaste."

Y: "He leaves the top off the toothpaste." [heavier laughter]

M: "Yeah, (he) leaves the toilet seat up all the time."

Y: "Yeah, and the toilet paper, toilet roll on the wrong way." [laughter]

C: Isn't that interesting.

M: I mean if you're not happy, you're not happy, I mean, that's not good to just stay somewhere when you're not happy.

Women at Aboriginal Alternatives also joked about men. On my final day there, the women baked a cake for me, and, as we snuck in bites between howls of laughter, Betty read us an email she had received on the topic of men:

Men are like laxatives, they irritate the crap out of you. Men are like bananas, the older they get the softer they are. Men are like bad weather, nothing can be done to change them. Men are like blenders, you need one but you're not quite sure why. Men are like chocolate bars, and they usually head straight for your hips. Men are like government bonds, they take sooooo long to mature. Men are like mascara, they usually run at the first sign of emotion. Men are like popcorn, they satisfy you, but only for a little while. Men are like lava lamps, nice to look at but not very bright [etc.].

The women's previous attempts to live with men, coupled with their derisive jokes and their current determination to avoid long-term relationships with them, reflected a shifting consciousness: from an attempt to fulfill societal (and their own personal) values regarding the importance for women of having a partner, to a rejection of this value on the basis of their actual experiences with men. The women thus added a proviso to neoconservative notions of women's proper role as mothers: they would support it, as long as one key ingredient of the heteronormative family, the male head of household, be left behind—unless, of course, men's personalities changed so that, as Samantha at Parent Connection put it, they were "exactly like a woman but with the male anatomy." "What we need," Venetia added, "is a gay man but not gay."

Perhaps the most interesting pattern in the women's productions of men's character is their construction of men as childlike. "They want mothers" and "overgrown kids" clearly index this, as does Mandy's reference (in Riverview) to her children's father as "this boy." Men were variously portrayed as lazy, irresponsible, thoughtless, and entitled; but it strikes me that they were above all viewed as immature, and that the women felt that it was this fundamental immaturity that produced their irresponsibility and self-centeredness. This dovetails in interesting ways with the neoliberal argument that welfare recipients will be best able to become responsible, self-sufficient, and autonomous via the discipline provided by welfare cuts and exposure to the realities of the market; that is, by facing the real-life consequences of their own actions—which is something that the men my research participants had been involved with had, in the women's views, never done. In this formulation, a life in which one can do whatever one wants with no negative consequences, or in which one has no motivation to do anything besides sit in front of a TV or play computer games, is infantilizing, robbing one of the opportunity to become a fully-fledged adult person.

The women I worked with, then, used their everyday knowledge of men to disassemble the neoconservative marriage model. They adopted uncritically the idea that women are "natural" mothers, but rejected those aspects of the neoconservative model that extend women's caretaking role to the care of *men*. Instead, and despite dominant constructions of welfare dependence, the women constructed *themselves* as independent individuals and they celebrated their independence from men who fell far short of being the "natural" breadwinners of neoconservatism. Thus the flip side of their disparaging remarks about men was their positive references to doing things their own way: "I really enjoy [being a single mom]," Martha said at Parent Connection one morning. "I've always done most things by myself and I wouldn't change it. At the end of the day I don't know if I could cope if I actually had a partner." Marilyn, also at Parent Connection, further underscored the importance of avoiding compromise when she talked about her intake interview at the welfare office: "They [the welfare office] … wanted to know real particulars and stuff [about the breakdown of her relationship] and I thought, does it really matter? I wasn't happy with him, I wasn't happy there, it wasn't abusive or anything like that, I just wasn't happy. … I didn't wanna be there anymore." Marilyn's invocation of personal, individual fulfillment reflects a particular reading of neoliberal valorizations of individuality, one that allows her to challenge the neoconservative emphasis on nuclear family formation expressed by her welfare provider. Independence, then, was not only about self-sufficiency, but also about being one's own self without limitation, about choosing for oneself how one wants to live one's life, or, as Marilyn claimed, about being "happy." The women accordingly constructed "family" as comprising mothers and children, whose circle could expand to include, when they were available, relatives and close friends who fulfilled kin-like roles. Children's fathers were not a significant part of this reconfigured family.[10]

In the end, in both sites women's primary concern with regard to men was, first and foremost, to be independent from them. Men would not help them raise their children, and men would not help them get out of poverty—quite the opposite; in short, men would not make their lives easier in any way. As one young mother in a Kingston program for teenage parents put it, "She's *my* baby and *I'll* support her." Her daughter's father had no place in the picture. Nor did the women feel particularly lonely without men in their lives. As Mele at Parent Connection put it, "I love being home alone," to which Yvonne added, "I know people in relationships who are desperately lonely, you know, 'cause you're in a house with somebody but they have no communication." Back at Aboriginal Alternatives, Moira, mirroring Mele, said, "I don't need that other half or something, I am a whole already."

There are some interesting things happening here in terms of translation. The women translated, easily and directly, messages about independent individuality and women's "natural" role as mothers and caregivers, constructing both subject positions as equally desirable and appropriate. What they translated without a hitch, however, were *ideas*. Their translations of these ideas into *practice*, on the other hand, were partial, and in both cases left behind key elements of the "original" package. In translating neoliberal philosophies in which independent individuality is inextricably tied to employment, the women dropped the implied temporal frame of *now*, deferring their accomplishment of individuality via employment to sometime in the future. And in translating neoconservative models of women-as-caregivers, they dropped the key figures of the wife and of the male head of household. They were, in other words, highly selective in what they chose to take up. Their choices reflected their situated knowledges—based on real live embodied experiences, as opposed to neoliberal and neoconservative models—of the labor market and of men. Ideas about getting a job and about marriage were thus limited, in practice, by actual jobs and men that fell short of meeting basic requirements, let alone fantastical expectations regarding financial prosperity or nuclear family bliss.

Welfare as Capricious (Just Like Men)

The women's experiences with men carried over into their encounters with the welfare office. Where Wendy Brown (1995) has provided insightful analyses into the "man in the state"—the notion that women can receive support from either a conjugal partner or the state but not simultaneously from both—my research provides insight into women's understandings of men and the state as essentially the same, insofar as both were experienced as consistently undependable and capricious, reinforcing each other in cumulatively damaging ways to leave poor single mothers in a permanent state of insecurity. From where the women I worked with sat, the issue was not so much the man *in* the state as the man *and* the state.

All the welfare mothers in Riverview and Kingston, without exception, experienced welfare, like men, as inadequate. First, and most obviously, welfare provisions fell woefully below what was needed to survive, let alone thrive. At Parent Connection one day, for instance, I asked Kim, Yvonne, Mele, and Terry how they spent their welfare checks. Terry took the lead in answering: rent was paid to the landlord, and what she had left—about $60.00 a week—went to food, utilities, and clothing for herself and her two children. That was it. The other women concurred: every penny was spoken for. They nevertheless then launched into a discussion of how they acquired extras, beyond the bare necessities. Yvonne described how she went about the business of buying her daughter a pair of attractive (Disney-type) mittens: "I had to save up for two weeks. ... You have to always plan ahead." Mele interjected, "If there's something that you want that costs ten dollars I'm sure you can get it cheaper somewhere for five dollars." "Right, you look around," agreed Kim. "I mean, I do a lot of shopping in op-shops," Mele concluded. Movies, sporting events (as participant or spectator), and eating out—basically, any activities associated with relative as opposed to absolute frameworks for thinking about poverty and citizenship—were usually out of the question.

One day at Aboriginal Alternatives, Tiara (T), Moira (M), Ruby (R), Althea (A), and I (C) walked through how the women spent their money, using Althea (who had two children) as an example:

A: I have to have $200.00 for groceries, now we get $898.00 [from welfare].

C: You get $898.00 total [a month]?

A: Yuh.

C: So.

A: And they told me $500.00 has to cover my rent and my utilities.

C: $898.00, so $500.00, so that leaves you $398.00, $500.00's supposed to be rent and utilities.

A: Yuh.

C: And then $398.00 is everything else?

A: Yes.

C: Food.

M: Food.

T: Clothing.

R: Medicine, phone.

M: Diapers.

R: Everything.

C: Diapers.

T: Milk.

M: Everything.

C: Yah.

M: Gas if you have a car, insurance then if you have a car, all those kinds of things.

C: And that's for a single parent with two children?

A: Mmm.

C: Any of you have one child?

T: $743.00.

C: Okay, $743.00 with one child.

The women insisted that welfare providers had no idea of the costs of day-to-day living: "They don't look at the rent, they don't," said Tiara, and Moira added: "Have they been in a grocery store? Like, have they *gone* anywhere? They haven't seen *anything. They don't know!*" The inadequacies of welfare benefits thus left the women scrambling to make ends meet by shopping in second-hand stores, frequenting food banks, engaging in under-the-table work or other illegal activities, and so on. When I asked what would be a reasonable amount of money for someone with two children, they decided on $1,500.00, "for you just to survive," Moira said.

Workfare requirements were similarly considered unreasonable. One woman in Riverview, Leanne, relayed a desperate story of trying to meet job search requirements while living in Calgary:

I used to take the bus and then they [welfare workers] say, "Okay, go and get all these resumes done and do this and do this," and you've gotta go all over the city for like, say, every day all over the place, right? And you're dragging your kids and they're screaming and they're pooping and they're doing everything you can imagine and ... it's enough to drive you absolutely haywire, so then you almost like just lose your whole thing and say, you know, "Some people just sit on this welfare and they don't do anything," I'm so, like, "I can't do this anymore," ... You just lose it, it's just so ... frustrat[ing] ... and you feel like, "I can't even take care of my kids, I can't," you know, like, and you feel like your kids are in the hot sun and you have no money to give 'em a drink or something and you're out and ... they're pooping and you ... got no diaper wipes and you don't know where the bathroom ... is.

The Parent Connection women's stories of how they were pressured to find jobs, recounted earlier in the chapter, expressed a similar sentiment, although in less harrowing terms, given the lack of official coercion in the New Zealand welfare system at the time. When translated from abstract formulae into "real life," then, both benefit rates and workfare requirements were patently—palpably and desperately—inadequate.

These deficiencies were accentuated by the predictably unpredictable and undependable nature of welfare mandates and providers. Because policy mandates seemed to shift for no evident reason that the women could discern (a point to which I return below), and because different providers told them different things, the women could never be quite sure of what was happening. The result was an ongoing sense of precariousness. One day at Parent Connection, for instance, Dawn described how her case manager had asked her a series of questions about her relationship with her ex-partner. Mele stepped in to say that her case manager had never asked anything about her relationships with men. Then Terry recounted how her case manager had not only asked questions about men, but had also required that Terry produce a written statement regarding the status of her relationship with her daughter's father. The women all knew that they were not supposed to be in long-term relationships with men (which they all claimed they did not want, at any rate) while receiving welfare; but the particulars of how often a man could spend a night (which many of the women did desire on occasion) seemed to be left to the whim of their case managers,[11] and the women never knew in advance what was okay to reveal and what was not. In the end, Mele said, "maybe it just depends on who you have" as a case manager—something that was unpredictable and completely out of the women's control.

Once, when I commented at morning tea that some women had complained to me that case managers were not always clear about what clients are entitled to, Patricia, a current beneficiary who used to work for the welfare office answering phones, underscored the arbitrary way in which providers treated different clients differently: "When they [case managers] actually go in and apply for the job they are actually told everything that they need to do [e.g., inform beneficiaries of their full entitlements] … but they don't always do it. … They pick and choose who they want to help and when they want to help and … it's not fair. Unless you get someone who has … had those life skills and experience and who … [has] been through that hardship … you won't get their help at all. … So they pick and choose. They bend the rules for some people … [and for] others they wouldn't." When I asked Patricia on what grounds she thought case managers decided who to help and who to hinder, she said, "I don't know, honestly I don't know," adding, "It's quite terrible, that's why I … finished working for them, I never went back." Sally, on the other hand, saw something more systematic:

> There's a whole culture within [the welfare department] of … the deserving and undeserving poor, so you go in there and you're Maori and your child has a snotty nose with no shoes on they're not gonna tell you anything … whereas if you go in there and you're well dressed and your child is well dressed and you're articulate … they tend to be a little bit more wary of you so they're more careful, and they still don't tell you your rights or anything—you have to work that out for yourself, you have to go in there knowing what's available to you 'cause they won't tell you, they'll constantly … forget, constantly, constantly, constantly, that they're civil servants, that they're there to serve the public, they think that somehow they're more superior than we.

Management practices of constantly changing welfare provider assignments without notifying beneficiaries contributed, in Sally's view, to this not-telling. This would never happen in any other sector; even a car insurance company, she said, would have the courtesy to send a letter notifying a change of representative. She argued that the frequent reassignment of case managers was "an action of disempowerment," undermining beneficiaries' ability to develop sustained relationships with providers, further eroding the possibility of getting clear and consistent information from them. In the end, Sally said, beneficiaries were often left in the dark about their entitlements, as well as about the actual requirements of the system and how to best manage them. By way of example, she referred to the requirement that beneficiaries name the father(s) of their children so that the state can appropriate child support payments to offset the costs of distributing benefits. Clients who refused to provide this information stood to lose a certain percentage of their benefit. Sally, however, knew that if a woman provided a fictitious name, the department would be unable to locate the "father"; she would then receive full benefits, since in such cases the problem was attributed to the department, not the client. Sally lamented the lack of savvy on the part of most beneficiaries, and attributed this in part to a bureaucratic culture that failed to give beneficiaries their due as persons. She complained bitterly of the lack of transparency of the system, and of how difficult it is to find information. She herself went on the Internet, looked up welfare legislation, read it, and brought it with her to her meetings with her case manager. Some information, however, was not available online but restricted to those with access to the welfare department computer system. As well-educated and determined as she was, Sally nevertheless often felt at the mercy of her case manager's whim.

Women in Riverview were in the same position. "They don't tell you [the information] unless you know it," Jessica said one day, when we were discussing the extra support for baby supplies provided by the welfare department. "How are you supposed to find out about these things?" "You find a nice worker," Moira advised her, "or talk to the supervisor"—to which Ruby countered, "A supervisor won't tell you it either, they don't explain nothing." The women agreed that who their provider was determined whether they were treated with respect or got everything to which they were entitled. They then started listing, by name, the few welfare providers who were "nice"—"I think she's a really nice lady and she was so understanding"—versus the majority, who were "awful"—giving rise, as Ellen put it, to "this sick feeling with my stomach, I just felt like turning around and walking back out." Later, when we had a few minutes alone, Ellen told me how disoriented she felt when she went to the welfare office for the first time: "When I did go to SFI I really got a hard time. When I first went there ... I had to fill all the papers and it wasn't, it's really not easy. You can't just go in and, you know, get help. They just gave you a lot of runaround. [They asked for] things that you wouldn't know. Things they just want you to do and a lot of paperwork to be filled out." Ellen had never encountered this kind of bureaucracy before. She could not understand many of the forms, and she was not sure what, exactly, was expected of her. Reflecting on this experience, she said, "They weren't very understanding ... that I was a single parent with a child, with a little boy, and that I needed help. ... The lady I saw there ... I found her really stubborn and you know she kind of raised her voice." To give another example, Sandra, who moved to Riverview to get away from a bad relationship in Calgary, had to deal with welfare providers in both sites. She told me that the different providers she was working with gave her conflicting information regarding the department's coverage of her moving expenses; until she convinced her provider in Riverview to call her provider in Calgary, she was unable to find out what steps she needed to take in order to receive the support she needed.

As Sally, above, observed, being on the receiving end of conflicting, incomplete, or confusing information resulted in a lack of clarity among the welfare mothers regarding actual requirements and entitlements. A conversation with Terry and Vivian at Parent Connection illustrates the pattern. We had been discussing the pressure case managers put on beneficiaries to find jobs, when Terry and Vivian had the following exchange about work tests:

T: They do try to get you to go back out there [into the workforce].

V: Right, but you don't have to.

T: You don't have to.

V: Not until they're fourteen [years old].

T: Not until they're fourteen.

V: It's either fourteen or sixteen, I think it's fourteen.

T: Okay.

V: Which is fair enough because by then, you know, they're pretty, you know.

T: Right.

V: Independent.

This exchange took place more than a year after work tests had been eliminated. I encountered similar confusion the following year, when two women told me that the rules required them to return to work when their youngest child turned seven.

This confusion concerning eligibility requirements, work tests, and entitlements ran across my two research sites. Initially, I was puzzled, especially since staff at Parent Connection and Aboriginal Alternatives went out of their way to circulate information on these matters. As I noted in chapter 3, for instance, staff at Parent Connection gave their clients a checklist to take with them to the welfare office; there were also numerous posters on the walls at both Parent Connection and Aboriginal Alternatives—as well as at food banks and various other community service agencies—with information on welfare recipients' rights and obligations. Reflecting on Ellen's remark that she could understand neither the forms nor eligibility requirements—a complaint I heard from many women, Native and non-Native, Maori, Pacific Islander, and Pakeha—I wondered if at one level the women did not know how to translate some of what they were encountering, if it was not a truly foreign language, especially since the clues they were given for how to decipher this language were themselves inconsistent and often puzzling. Three patterns I have already noted are relevant here. First, welfare providers, some of whom were more forthcoming than others, were rotated frequently; second, the information and perspectives supplied by community service providers often did not align with what the women were told at the welfare office; and, finally, policy itself was subject to recurrent change, making it almost impossible to keep up. The workfare requirements that Terry and Vivian were confused about provide a case in point with regard to the latter. In Alberta, workfare stipulations shifted considerably in just over a decade: from when a recipient's youngest child was two years old in 1990, to six months old in 1993, and then up to a year during the time of my study. In Aotearoa/New Zealand, the age of the youngest child shifted from eighteen years prior to 1996, to fourteen (for full-time work) and seven (for part-time work) in 1996, then back up to eighteen in 2002. It is worth wondering, incidentally—as did some of the women I encountered—on what basis such lines are drawn, since when Alberta and Aotearoa/New Zealand are placed side by side, and if other countries are included as well, it becomes evident that such lines are profoundly arbitrary. Women in Kingston were shocked and horrified when they heard about the work requirements in Riverview, while women in Riverview were shocked and jealous when they heard about conditions in Aotearoa/New Zealand. But the arbitrariness was evident to the women without the aid of comparative analysis, just by virtue of the shifts they experienced over the course of their engagements (and those of their friends) with their local welfare offices. The women also complained, accurately, that, as Kim at Parent Connection put it, "All these government departments, they don't communicate." Not only were there disjunctures between government offices in one domain, say, welfare, and another, e.g., housing, but the connections between government departments and other service providers, such as food banks, organizations providing budgeting and parenting advice, church groups, and so on, were also often poor.

How to keep up with the details of these shifts when information is uneven, piecemeal, contradictory, and in some case incomprehensible, and when one is living in day-to-day economic and social crisis, becomes a daunting task indeed. It should come as no surprise, then, that this vast terrain of changing governmental and nongovernmental approaches, policies, and agendas was confusing to the women I worked with. They discussed strategizing—trying to find out the details of rules and regulations, and attempting to discern where welfare providers were "coming from," as Yvonne at Parent Connection put it—but they were also acutely aware that, to a certain extent, what they received from the welfare department was luck of the draw, and that, in most cases, just as with men, what they received was inadequate.

Discussion

Like policy makers who translate policy frames and programs from other times and/or places in accordance with their own emergent conditions and agendas, and like welfare and community service providers, who similarly translate policy mandates in ways that reflect their institutional restrictions and enablements, poor single mothers actively engage with what they encounter when they approach the welfare bureaucracy and community service agencies as supplicants. Although translation is always subject to constraint—related to political expediency, the requirements of the workplace, existing resources, and discursive possibilities—the limitations faced by poor single mothers on welfare are particularly burdensome. Given that their agendas have to do with the basic economic and social survival of themselves and their children, they have very little room in which to move: manipulations of and resistances to welfare program requirements can go only so far, and there is only so much to be had from community service agencies.

In contending with the various material constraints they encountered, the women I worked with took whatever opportunities they could in light of the information and avenues available to them. They did their best to get a clear sense of program stipulations and entitlements so that they could be sure to get as much as possible from their providers and so that they could avoid succumbing to pressures that did not have official authorization; and they supplemented the support provided by the welfare department with provisionings from community service agencies, cutting and pasting resources from all possible sources. These efforts are instances of translation and assemblage: the women worked to understand the mechanics of the system and to piece together what they needed to survive. In addition, given that they were subjected to persistent and sometimes extreme forms of pressure and coercion designed to change not only their behavior, but also who they are as persons and how they interact with their children, men, the state, and society more generally, the women worked as intensively with those aspects of policy addressing personhood and social relations. While they may have had difficulty understanding various forms and procedures, and keeping up with shifting mandates and incomplete and sometimes contradictory information, they very accurately read the normative assumptions contained within welfare programs: the assertions and desires related to personhood, motherhood,

gender, the family, heterosexual relationships, adulthood, personal fulfillment, and so on, that welfare programs were designed to inculcate. My
focus in this chapter has been precisely on these engagements with "soft"
policy. The women's translations and assemblages of the these elements of
policy, I would argue, both provided a frame for going about the business
of making ends meet and served as a form of protest against the intrusions
into and assaults on the self embodied in policy mandates and delivery
practices. The women's work, then, was about carving out possible spaces
of social and psychological, as well as material, well-being.

As I described above, the women translated certain assumptions informing welfare policy seamlessly, appropriating and adopting them as
their own. They were unquestioningly aligned with the neoliberal model
of the individual. They looked down on dependence in adults, condemned
irresponsibility, and valued motivation, determination, and persistence.
They similarly adopted as commonsensical neoconservative models of
women as natural mothers and caretakers. These ideas translated well
and easily—the equivalences of meaning desired by policy mandates were
well established and well received. There is nothing particularly surprising about this: given that neoliberalism and neoconservatism represent
contemporary iterations of discourses of individualism and gender roles
that have a long history in Euro-American culture, it is likely that they
would have some currency, particularly among poor single mothers, who
are, after all, the specific targets of reforms that work to actively promote
these practices of personhood.

As I also noted above, however, "good" translations of these ideas were
limited by the women's practical knowledges of men, of the inadequacies
of welfare provisions, of the unreasonable nature of work expectations, of
the sexist and racist realities of the workplace, and of the capriciousness of
both policy and the various providers engaged with it. These knowledges
served as scrutineers of neoliberal and neoconservative philosophies,
throwing into relief the contradictions within and between them and underscoring the extent to which they were divorced from "real life"—at
least as experienced by poor single mothers on welfare. Two things happened in this space of interaction between models and realities. First,
as noted, the women accommodated the models, internalizing them as
commonsense and axiomatic. But, and second, in the process they disassembled and reassembled them in ways that made sense in the context of
their lived realities.

I begin with the ideal neoliberal person: independent, self-sufficient,
motivated, enterprising. That the neoliberal model of the self is not only
historically and culturally specific, but also deeply gendered, becomes evident when we attend to the forms of dependence that are stigmatized in

the model versus those that are erased: while women's reliance on state financial support counts as "dependence," negatively valued, men's reliance on, for instance, women as caretakers (the "good woman behind every successful man") does not fall into the category of dependence, or, indeed, into any named category at all. It remains underground and unrecognized in both dominant discourses and policy prescriptions. In this highly gendered distinction between dependence and so-called independence, poor single mothers, unable to be fully independent, are not-quite persons. It is, at one level, their particular *gendered* locations and *gender-specific* roles that leave them open to judgment and to various forms of state intervention. The women I worked with, however, reversed these unarticulated gender relations by claiming that they, as *women*, and as *mothers* in particular, display the traits of self-sufficiency, responsibility, and motivation so valued in neoliberal discourse. *They* are the ideal neoliberal individuals, not men: *they* have no interest in sitting around all day, in being waited on—indeed, in being mothered—but, rather, have developed, by means of their specifically gendered roles as mothers, the qualities so valorized in neoliberal-inflected discourses informing welfare policy. In addition, the women constructed themselves not only as more responsible and motivated than men, but also as more *adult* than men. In a neoliberal cultural framework, adults are "naturally" utility maximizing, self-sufficient, and enterprising, having experienced dependence and gone through the process of learning to become independent during childhood and adolescence. Children are, in this sense, full-persons-in-the-making. The women accepted this characteristic of their children as natural, but were highly critical of it in the men they encountered, who were, after all, fully grown and therefore reasonably expected to behave accordingly. The women's constructions of men as childish, then, took on a particular valence: they were not as-yet persons, but, rather, *failed* persons. Significantly, this mirrors neoliberal criticisms of welfare recipients as irresponsible, lazy, and specifically unadult in their dependence, inability to defer gratification, and so on. In claiming that men are somehow deficient persons, the women effectively redirected the criticisms to which they are subject as welfare recipients away from themselves, and on to men, providing the grounds for a resistance to the injuries to self that accompany their stigmatized social locations (see, e.g., Foucault 1980; Goffman 1963; Kingfisher 1996a, 1996b).

The women thus disassembled the gendered components of neoliberal discourses of personhood, and articulated a model of the proper person that fit with their knowledges of real live men and of their own practices as hardworking, motivated, and responsible mothers. This disarticulation and rearticulation of gender and personhood in turn provided the grounds for the women's rejection of the neoconservative marriage model. For that model to operate successfully, men have to be responsible; they have to be motivated and hardworking—in a sense, they have to be proper *neoliberal* persons. The neoconservative nuclear family model is, then, partially based on the masculinist neoliberal model of the person. Accordingly, if men fail to be proper neoliberal persons, they cannot be proper heads of idealized neoconservative nuclear families. The women I worked with thus simultaneously engaged both neoliberalism and neoconservatism: they declared themselves too independent to want to be married, and men insufficiently neoliberal to make good heads of nuclear families.

The women's rejection of the neoconservative model of the family was partial, however: they ejected men from the model, but held on to ideologies of mothering, which, as I indicated above, were crucial to their engagements with neoliberalism. This "successful" translation of ideologies of women as mothers also provided grounds for the rejection (philosophically, if they were unable to do so in practice) of workfare. Specifically, it gave women the grounds on which to insert a temporal delay in the neoliberal requirement (and in their stated desires) to engage in paid labor.

This work of disassemblage and reassemblage represents a kind of "talking back" (Lendvai and Bainton, forthcoming), an instance of selecting and inventing from the materials—the ideas, the discursive frameworks—which the women are presented with and with which they have to work (Pratt 1991: 36). The contradictions between woman as natural mother and the individual as independent and self-sufficient may have caused immense problems for the women, caught betwixt and between, but it was also precisely these tensions that provided them with the space to move, to "talk back." The hegemony of the neoliberal model of the person allowed them to evaluate men as inadequate and thus to deconstruct the neoconservative marriage model; their acceptance of motherhood as natural provided grounds to argue against workfare and to relegate their financial dependence on the state to the margins of their selfhood; and, finally, their explicit insertion of a temporal sequence permitted them to claim to be, simultaneously, proper neoconservative mothers *and* proper neoliberal individuals.

The women's translations of the dominant frameworks of personhood and gender informing welfare policy thus did not lead to the kinds of actions that the state might have desired. The women did indeed take the value of independence for granted, but, given their practical experiences and the knowledge they constructed in light of those experiences, they applied this naturalized goal of independence to men first, and only secondarily to the state, on the grounds of the importance of mothering—no doubt to the lament of welfare bureaucrats. They certainly translated and took on as their own both neoliberal and neoconservative tenets of personhood and gender roles; but when articulated with their other knowledges and with their practical agendas, the result was something very different—as unreasonable and "off" in translation from the perspective of the official architects of policy as were levels of provisioning and workfare requirements, or pressures, from the perspective of the mothers.

I am not arguing that theirs was always a deliberate, explicitly articulated analysis of the neoliberal and neoconservative aspects of policy, or that they always made conscious tactical or strategic decisions about what to adopt in order to resist. The women were sincere in their expressions of neoliberal individuality, and they took mothering seriously—there was nothing superficial or crudely political here. Rather, my claim is that the women translated neoliberal and neoconservative policy mandates and frames through the lens of their own situated knowledges and resources: an assemblage of what they received by way of information and attitude from welfare and community service providers, coupled with their own experiences with and understandings of parenting, men, work, children, and the realities of living on welfare. Although there are clear traces of welfare providers' information and attitudes in the women's talk, the result of the women's own interpretive work was a constellation of understandings that did not simply reflect the intentions of policy mandates as communicated (albeit in complicated ways) by welfare providers; nor did the women take up in their entirety the range of messages transmitted by community service providers. Not only that, but their assemblages included a great deal *more* than those of welfare and community service providers. For instance, although community service providers attended to children, women's roles as mothers, and racism to varying degrees— and much more so than did welfare providers—neither welfare nor community service providers gave primacy of place to women's relationships with *men*, which, as I described above, were central to their encounters with policy. In actually *living* them, the women were required to engage with, and so were much more adept at describing, policy worlds in their entirety.

Clarke (2004: 70–71) argues that governing is an "uneven and partial process that has to proceed through alliances, compromises and conflicts in which subjects succumb, sign up or comply—but also resist, or are recalcitrant and troublesome. As a result, its attempted subjections are likely to be less than comprehensive and only temporarily settled." It can never be assumed, in other words, that policy shifts, and the normative assumptions they embody and promote, will eventually take on the valence of common sense among policy targets in any pure, unidirectional, predetermined, or complete fashion. Even at the bottom of the heap—or perhaps especially at the bottom of the heap, precisely because of their marginality (hooks 1984)—people have some power to decide what and how to translate; and, indeed, they must exercise such power, given the need to articulate policy messages with lived realities. What I hope to have pointed to here is something akin to the complexity Clarke underscores: not a clear-cut distinction between succumbing, signing up, and complying versus being resistant, recalcitrant, and troublesome, but, rather, a complex terrain of both succumbing and resisting, unfolding in particular contexts in which agents have access to a range of often competing knowledges that they must assemble together in order to make ends meet (literally and ideologically). Once translated, then, aspects of policy mandates and the various discourses that inform them combine with other discourses and practices in all sorts of unanticipated ways. In the case of the welfare mothers I worked with, the result was a series of adoptions, reversals, and deferrals that were in some ways precisely what policy elites wanted, and in others precisely the opposite of what they might have hoped for. The attempted subjections of poor single mothers in Kingston and Riverview were successful, on the one hand, and clearly "less than comprehensive" on the other.

Notes

1. My goal at both Parent Connection and Aboriginal Alternatives was to capture "naturally occurring" talk, that is, talk generated for reasons other than the presence of a researcher. On the surface, I was limited in this endeavor—at Aboriginal Alternatives due to the orchestrated nature of the discussion sessions and to my status as non-Native (although this was somewhat ameliorated by the presence of two non-Native residents and by my status as the single mother of a Native child); at Parent Connection due to my status as a foreigner with a distinct, heavy accent, which made me stand out as an object of curiosity; and in both sites due to the presence of my tape recorder. Nevertheless, my transcripts indicate that "radio shows"—performances oriented to the tape recorder—were at a minimum; in addition, the wide-ranging nature of the conversations, which I did not attempt to keep "on topic," and the women's conversational tendency to bounce off each other—to orient to each other rather than to me once discussion got going, and to switch topics freely to suit the needs of the conversation rather than those of my research—indicate that these events were somewhat closer to naturally occurring conversation than to interview talk.

2. At one level, convergences among welfare and community service providers similarly reflect their shared structural positionings and commonalities in the issues with which they were faced. There was, however, considerable variation in the *content* of

welfare and community service providers' translations and assemblages across the two sites. This was not the case with the welfare mothers I encountered.

3. Although Parent Connection was open to all low-income single parents, I encountered only one single father during my time there.

4. Opportunity shops, or "opp shops," are charity stores, many faith-based, that sell used clothing and household items. There was an op-shop attached to the church on whose property Parent Connection was situated.

5. The minimum wage at the beginning of my study was $5.90 per hour, the lowest in the country (Arthurson 2005); when I completed research in 2006, it was at $7.00 per hour.

6. As I watched women spin in circles trying to make sense of all of this, I was reminded, painfully, of my time in the hospital just after the birth of my son. As shifts changed, so I received wildly opposing instructions from the nurses: you should feed your baby on demand; you should feed him only once every four hours; you must keep your child in the bed with you when you sleep; you must never let the baby sleep with you; let visitors handle your baby so that he grows up to be socially oriented; don't let people pass the baby around or he'll be overstimulated. All of these pieces of advice were framed not as advice, but as hard-and-fast rules, sometimes even as matters of life and death. These diametrically opposed bits of advice were only complicated further when I came into contact with lactation consultants in addition to nurses. As I reflected on this parallel set of experiences, I realized that women on welfare occupied this kind of confusing and contradictory terrain consistently, for years, rather than months or weeks, at a time.

7. See Korteweg (2006) for a discussion of how precisely this kind of speech is in fact required by participants in such workshops in the United States.

8. The above transcript excerpt and portions of the analysis are from Kingfisher 2006.

9. The residential schooling system, established in the 1840s and phased out only in the late 1960s, operationalized an assimilationist policy by taking Native children from their homes and placing them in boarding schools where they were forbidden to speak their native languages and subjected to various forms of abuse.

10. Portions of the above paragraph are from Kingfisher 2006.

11. This was, in fact, reflective of official New Zealand policy, since the 2002 reforms left investigations of beneficiaries' relationships with men to the discretion of case managers.

TRACING POLICY

Process/Power

∝∞

Blandly defined in contemporary contexts as something along the lines of "a course or principle of action," and evoking images of "administration" and "management," the etymology of *policy* implies something much more encompassing and powerful. As described in the Oxford Dictionary online, *policy* makes its entry into late Middle English "from Old French *policie* 'civil administration,' via Latin from Greek *politeia* 'citizenship,' from *politēs* 'citizen,' from *polis* 'city.'" Dean (2005: 258–69) thus usefully points to historical connections between *policy*, *polity*, and *police* (in its broadest sense of "order"). This considerably more expansive sense of policy as about the organization of society and its members dovetails with current anthropological approaches that theorize it as a key building block of culture, in many contexts as foundational as, for example, kinship, or exchange. Policy, in other words, is world making (Bourdieu 1990). Thus welfare reforms in both Aotearoa/New Zealand and Alberta were designed to produce specific kinds of persons who operate in particular ways in relation to forms of social organization similarly produced via policy. There is nothing superficial about such attempts to remake persons and reconfigure state-market, public-private relations; it represents, on the contrary, a radical intervention targeting the very underpinnings of society and sociality. At the same time, however, policy requires the cooperation of myriad actors, each of whom is institutionally and socially located and affected differently, and each of whom operates in relation to particular sets of restrictions, agendas, and resources for action, both material and interpretive. The possibilities for interruption and unevenness are thus enormous. This tension between powerful intent, on the one hand, and contingent process and outcome, on the other, constitutes the social life of policy.

Divergences

Throughout this book, I have followed a particular sequence of discussion, moving from convergence to divergence. I have repeated this pattern at almost every juncture in tracing the travel of the NZ Model to Alberta, exploring constructions of policy among welfare and community service providers, and outlining translations of policy among welfare recipients. My metamessage, consistent through all these "stops" in my travelogue, has been that while some things travel well, others do not. I could have easily reversed the sequence of discussion to begin with what did not travel well, and then turn to focus on, and highlight, what did. The metamessage would have been different: even though some things do not travel well, others do.

My choice to emphasize divergence over convergence represents an attempt to intervene in mainstream models of policy as an objective entity that is constructed in linear, rational fashion and then transferred *in toto* as it moves across jurisdictions and is applied mechanically in sites of implementation and reception. This mainstream approach reflects both theoretical and methodological failures. Theoretically, it reveals a failure to *people* policy and to situate it in the *social*, despite the irony of working with a topic that is profoundly about both. The corresponding and simultaneous methodological failure is one of a fundamental neglect of policy as comprised of a range of social relations and forces as well as technical processes, a neglect that indexes an indifference to what happens to and with policy in specific contexts as well as to the power struggles that are inherent to any kind of project that addresses "social problems." Referring to Harold Lasswell's (1951) pioneering work in the establishment of the policy sciences in the mid-twentieth-century United States, Fischer (2003: 4) diagnoses the problem as follows:

> In contrast to the multidisciplinary methodological perspective outlined by Lasswell, the field has been shaped by a more limiting methodological framework derived from the neopositivist/empiricist methods that dominated the social sciences of the day. This has generated an emphasis on rigorous quantitative analysis, the objective separation of acts and values,

and the search for generalizable findings whose validity would be independent of the particular social context from which they were drawn: that is, a policy science that would be able to develop generalizable rules applicable to a range of problems and contexts. In no small part, this has been driven by the dominant influence of economics and its positivist scientific methodologies on the development of the field.

"Studying through" (Shore and Wright 1997; Wedel et al. 2005; Wright and Reinhold 2011), or "following the policy" (Peck and Theodore 2012; Shore and Wright 2011), provides one antidote to this kind of detached approach. Focused on tracing what happens as policy travels from official sites of production to sites of implementation and reception, "studying through" embraces contextualization over decontextualization, situatedness over abstraction, and uneven multisitedness over homogenous universalism; it draws attention to ethnographic realities as opposed to models. This methodological approach simultaneously opens the theoretical door to conceptualizing policy as translated rather than transferred or implemented, as assembled not "scientifically" and once and for all, but ongoingly, in power- and value-laden, often piecemeal fashion by various invested agents in specific contexts.

Although I pointed to the importance of attending to convergences in the Introduction, divergences—partialities, rejections, and alterations—provide more obvious markers of policy as translation and assemblage than convergences, which may reinforce mainstream models by giving the impression of seamless travel and articulation. And in the story I have followed here, there were indeed numerous divergences. First, as I outlined in chapter 1, while New Zealand rhetorics of reform were picked up with some zeal by the Alberta government, the specific programs with which those rhetorics were articulated differed markedly in Alberta when compared to New Zealand, where workfare stipulations were considerably more generous and where workfare itself had a shelf life of only six years. The gender regime of Aotearoa/New Zealand as it was embodied in welfare reform, the negative impacts of Rogernomics and Ruthanasia, and the policy shifts that occurred after Helen Clark's election were all ignored by the Klein government. These were not minor footnotes, moreover, but fundamental aspects of New Zealand policy developments. The result in Alberta was a policy framework that drew only on those bits and pieces of the NZ Model that fit the Klein administration's specific agendas.

Similarly, in chapter 2, I stressed that welfare providers, crucial to the realization of policy mandates, are also in a position to arbitrate—to add, delete, or cut-and-paste in ways that deliberately or inadvertently challenge the underlying assumptions of government mandates, if not always their practical application. Thus in Riverview, the "toughness" of the Klein reforms was refracted through the lens of providers' constructions of clients' needs—which from their vantage point included not only the firm hand of discipline, but also a higher minimum wage, less pull-yourself-up-by-your-bootstraps rhetoric, accessible child care, and an understanding of each person's unique circumstances. In Kingston, similarly (although in reverse order), the "love" of the 2002 reforms was embraced, but, again, only partially, reflecting both the double valence of the reforms themselves and the endurance of the previous regime's ideology. In addition, in both sites welfare providers drew attention to what was missing, or ignored, in state frameworks, pointing to government shortcomings and thereby resisting the notion that state experts knew what they were talking about—that they were, in fact, experts. The state's (attempted) vertical encompassment (Ferguson and Gupta 2002)—the flow of policy from official policy-making centers (Edmonton, Wellington) down through welfare offices—did not proceed unimpeded. Welfare providers were more (in Riverview) or less (in Kingston) limited in terms of practical action, but in all cases they developed everyday policy knowledges that challenged, to varying degrees, the frameworks of policy elite.

As my discussion in chapter 3 implies, the very fact that community service agencies exist and that welfare mothers are often dependent on them for material and social support tells us that policy movements from official sites of production to sites of reception (that is, into recipients' lives) are not insulated from other forces or inputs. Although differing wildly in their political orientations, addressing poverty in relation to feminist, faith-based, Indigenous, and youth-oriented agendas, among others, there were some remarkable similarities in the patterns of divergence from policy frames expressed by the community service providers I worked with. Most notably, they shared a strong tendency to read through welfare policy to what they saw as its true missions: to serve state budgets rather than to eliminate poverty (even in the supposedly enlightened Clark era in Aotearoa/New Zealand), and to buttress a perverted social system—the artifact of materialism, consumerism, income inequality, racism, and/or cultural inadequacy—that created the need for welfare in the first place. They also tended to translate policy with reference to their central positioning of children and of women's roles as mothers—both ironically sidelined by welfare providers—as well as in relation to race and cultural difference—again, ignored by the vast majority of welfare providers. Equally important to their translations of policy was their knowledge of the material inadequacies of provisioning and of the psychological assaults with which it was often accompanied. Distinguishing between policy requirement and policy justification, community service providers translated the first directly while challenging the second outright. "Soft" policy—the ideologies informing particular eligibility or work requirements—did not make it through these channels unscathed. Neoliberal models of independent individuality, in particular, were transformed by community service providers as they read them in relation to, and against, models of community and of mothering.

Finally, in chapter 4, I outlined how welfare mothers, the recipients of messages from the range of agents associated with the welfare state as well as from society more generally, adopted but also profoundly transformed the dominant discourses informing welfare mandates. Most notably, while women in both Riverview and Kingston were strongly in favor in independence, they were in favor of independence from men, not from the state. In their hands, then, the very grounds of independence as well as the objects from which persons were ideally independent were radically shifted. Instead of hankering for independence from the state, the state itself, in the form of welfare programs, became the means by which they could gain independence from men and fulfill their roles as mothers. Constructing mothers instead of male monads as the embodiment of the responsibility and motivation valorized in neoliberal models of the person, the women made claims against the state for better support and inserted a temporal delay in their professed desires to pursue fulfillment through employment. In doing so, they turned neoliberal and neoconservative models on their heads, deferring and deflecting criticism in ways that allowed them to survive (albeit often barely) both ideologically and materially.

As Latour (1986: 268) claims, "tokens" (orders, ideas, claims, etc.)—here, policy mandates—do not "move in the same direction as long as there is no obstacle." Rather, they move through *people*, "who slowly turn … [them] into something completely different as they [seek] to achieve *their* own goals" (1986: 268; emphasis in original). Transmission via diffusion is here transmuted into transformation via translation and (re)assemblage; far from deterministic and unidirectional, translation "inevitably includes the possibility of retranslation, of redefining and resisting, of 'talking back' to dominant understandings" (Lendvai and Bainton, forthcoming; Rubel and Rosman 2003). Translation also often occurs in contact zones, "social spaces where cultures meet, clash, and grapple with each other" (Pratt 1991: 34). Although not always the case—the NZ Model was not imposed on Alberta; far from it—these zones are frequently marked by unequal power relations. This certainly holds at points where welfare providers, community service providers, and welfare recipients meet state mandates. Translation here involves processes of transculturation, "whereby members of subordinated or marginal groups select and invent from materials transmitted by dominant or metropolitan culture" (Pratt 1991: 36). Thus shifts and transformations that occur as items move can be far from simple errors of transmission. They can also represent active manipulation and dissent: "As the aphorism says, traduttore-traditore, from translation to treason there is only a short step" (Callon 1986: 224).

These processes of transformation and talking back index the enablements and constraints that provide the conditions of possibility for translation and assemblage. In the story I have told here, these include the political positionings of governments looking for external experts to legitimate their agendas in light of received cultural formations; the location of welfare workers on the boundary of state agencies and populations, simultaneously translating institutional categories into something applicable to human beings, and human beings into types or needs that are then administrable; the complicated positioning of community service providers, who mediate not only between their clients and the organizations for which they work, but also between their clients and the welfare office; and, finally, the circumstances of welfare mothers, subject to a range of often contradictory and competing requirements and advice, all of which they have to articulate with the complex realities of juggling being on assistance, mothering, and staving off the injuries inflicted on them by virtue of their status as social pariahs. Only by following through on studying through—on tracing policy as it moves through official sites of construction, implementation, and reception, each peopled by invested actors and marked by specific agendas and particular possibilities of production—can we hope to gain insight into the ethnographic realities that produce policy and that are produced by it.

Convergences

While divergence may place translation and assemblage into relief, this does not mean that translation is always about transformation and rejection; nor does it mean that power is unable to operate effectively even as it changes hands. Alterations do not necessarily prevent dominant meanings from getting through, and even ideas that are appropriated and redeployed in particular contexts in relation to specific agendas that are markedly different from those of policy elites can carry some of their original force.

It is thus worth looking at what traveled well. The government of Ralph Klein may not have adopted New Zealand approaches to mothering and workfare, and it may have failed to attend to the temporal unfolding of the NZ Model, but it did pick up crucial features of the model:

the need to exercise both comprehensiveness and speed in undertaking restructuring, the foregrounding of debt elimination as the central concern of government, and a vision of a golden past of enterprising rugged individualism. These frameworks are at the very heart of neoliberal approaches to restructuring the welfare state.

Similarly, while welfare providers dropped some portions of their governments' framings of reform, they carried through others, in particular, active society models of the person and of welfare provisioning—also key components of a neoliberal package. In both Riverview and Kingston, welfare providers took it as axiomatic that the "responsibility" and "self-sufficiency" engendered via employment provided *the* solution to poverty. They also embraced the shift from passive to active welfare, manifested in Alberta in Client Investment Plans and the surveillance of providers, and in New Zealand in Personal Development and Employment Plans and Enhanced Case Management.

Community service providers, too, channeled certain aspects of dominant discourses. For the most part, they rejected neoliberal constructs of the self insofar as these undercut women's roles as mothers and the primacy of community. They similarly challenged the ideas that anyone and everyone could function as a self-sufficient monad (even when this rejection reflected culture-of-poverty approaches), and that economic engagement—that is, employment—was the solution to poverty. But they placed a high value on independence and self-direction: independence from external pressures, such as those exerted by welfare providers or dominant society; and self-direction in choosing one's own path. Significantly, community service providers often encouraged their clients to resist external pressures whenever possible so that they could pursue one particular "self-chosen" path: motherhood. This was in keeping with the neoconservative and maternalist ideologies embedded in policy. But in counseling their clients to be assertive in their pursuit of these apparently natural and obvious priorities, community service providers were also encouraging the development of enterprising selves—selves who are willing to take risks to opportunistically pursue their own interests. Although more critical of the welfare system than welfare providers, then, community service providers articulated certain aspects of neoliberal individualism *and* of neoconservative/maternalist constructions of women as mothers.

Welfare mothers also adopted and asserted dominant models of personhood and gender roles; indeed, their taking-for-granted of these models serves as a diagnosis of their hegemony. They deployed—wittingly or not—neoconservatism against neoliberalism, mothering against employment; but in many ways they accepted the fundamentals of both neoliberalism and neoconservatism: the need to be enterprising and self-directed, the critical role of employment in self-fulfillment (and, indeed, the primacy of the idea of self-fulfillment itself), the overriding importance of independence (albeit from men, but independence nevertheless), and the centrality of mothering.

These relatively smooth travels are remarkable: across a range of contexts, in the hands of a range of differently (and sometimes oppositely) situated actors, certain ideas had the power to resonate. On the other hand, perhaps this is not surprising: as I pointed out in chapter 4, active models of society and self, however unique their 1980s and 1990s renditions, are also reiterations of discourses of individualism and independence that have a long history in Euro-American culture. Nor are maternalist ideologies anything new. Neoliberalism and neoconservatism thus do not represent complete ruptures with previous philosophies of personhood or of gender, but mark, rather, their escalation and extension into new arenas and populations. These continuities underscore the need to attend to two patterns. First, they underscore the need to attend to the positive resonances of dominant discourses. Stuart Hall (1988: 167) highlights this necessity in an essay on Thatcherism when he refers to the

> momentous historical project ... [t]o win over ordinary people to [the Thatcherite version of regressive modernism], not because they're dupes, or stupid, or because they are blinded by false consciousness. Since, in fact, the political character of our ideas cannot be guaranteed by our class position or by the "mode of production," it is possible for the right to construct a politics which does speak to people's experience, which does insert itself into what Gramsci called the necessarily fragmentary, contradictory nature of common sense, which does resonate with some of their ordinary aspirations.

Second, we need to recognize that policy shifts of the sort that I have described here are not reflective of wholesale change. While paradigm shifts, à la Kuhn (1970), may entail a "jump" to a radically different frame (e.g., from one in which the Sun revolves around the Earth to one in which the Earth revolves around the Sun), policy shifts are messier, less clear-cut. To be sure, policy efforts to transform poor single mothers from unemployables into unemployed dependents do represent a sea change in approaches to provisioning and to constructions of gender roles. Moreover, in neoliberal regimes regulatory emphasis is no longer on the social or on structural relations of inequality, but shifts dramatically to focus on individuals and individual behavior, requiring various forms of policing and sanction to encourage employment, and with it (supposedly), independence. "Individualization," as Brodie (2008: 179) points out, "places steeply rising demands on people to find personal causes and responses to what are, in effect, collective social problems." Thus in Alberta under Ralph Klein and in Aotearoa/New Zealand under Rogernomics and Ruthanasia, poor single mothers were subjected to a doubly negative status—one associated with being unemployed, and the other with being (the wrong kind of) dependent. Nevertheless, new policy regimes, cut-and-pasted, always contain traces of previous regimes; policy shifts do not occur in a vacuum, but in relation to what came before. Thus in Alberta, the Klein Revolution sharply escalated what were in fact long-enduring, well-entrenched patterns in provisioning; while Rogernomics and Ruthanasia in Aotearoa/New Zealand were limited by an equally well-entrenched maternalism. Analysis of policy travels across sites and through the hands of various providers and recipients need to be similarly situated in relation to received formations and conditions of possibility.

In being situated in some relationship to what came before—as enhancement or opposition, or some combination thereof—policy developments and the various actors engaged with them draw on what is available to think with: popular discourses, emerging structures of sentiment, new and bold ideas that are in vogue, old and solidly entrenched ideas that have withstood the test of time. This can make it difficult, in the confluences that comprise policy, to delineate different strands, or bits and pieces, in order to position them in relation to origins. Nielsen (2011: 82) states in this regard that there is frequently "no easy way of knowing from where a rationality or a technology stems; often, there is no single point of origin and therefore no easy way to determine who or what is 'implementing' or 'appropriating' which logics, keywords or technologies from whom, how and where." Thus in his work with public health policy makers, for example, Freeman (2007: 485) found that a number of his interlocutors were unable identify where an idea came from: "It sort of became the thing, the obvious thing to do, at some point," one respondent says. Ideas can take flight from any number of locations, emerge from any number of contexts and epistemological frames, and circulate in such a way that they become something that is simply "in the air." This does not mean, however, that we should take this "in the air" for granted, since it points precisely to the conditions of possibility for temporal and spatial convergence. Thus it is important to avoid invoking the kind of inertia that Latour (1986: 266) describes as characteristic of diffusionist models of power, just as it is crucial to avoid assuming an unquestioning alignment among actors (1986: 268). On the contrary, convergence, like divergence, needs to be recognized as a social accomplishment, even if the processes involved in such concerted work leave fewer obvious traces than those involved in the production of divergence.

Global Neoliberal Policy Regime?

Drawing on what is *in the air* provides a quintessential example of the production of common sense, of hegemony. Is it the case, then, that the convergences I have outlined above signal the existence of a global policy regime? Most of what I have presented in this book argues no. Policy frames did not move smoothly and unimpeded from New Zealand to Alberta, or from official policy-making centers into the lives of recipients. On the contrary, they were challenged, repeatedly, and, in the case of welfare mothers, they were even upturned, transformed into a form of "reverse discourse" (Foucault 1980) that worked against dominant intentions. The nuances of policy unfoldings in Alberta and Aotearoa/New Zealand and among welfare providers, community service providers, and welfare recipients in both sites challenge any idea of simple repetition or total replication. Indeed, nuances of the type I have described here have provided one of the key entry points for analyses of neoliberalism's vulnerabilities and limits (Kingfisher and Maskovsky 2008). Clearly, we are dealing with something more complicated than a straightforward, unproblematic imposition resulting in uniformity.

Powerful ideas did get reinforced, however, and they did have traction across multiple sites. In this regard, welfare mothers' reverse discourse simultaneously points to the capillary nature of power (Foucault 1980), insofar as the women adopted dominant constructs of the person and of gender roles, constructs that were circulated in various forms through the lives and talk of welfare and community service providers as well. Hall's (1997) musings on homogenization through specificity with regard to global mass culture and capitalist forms of flexible specialization and accumulation resonate here, as does Roland Robertson's (1997: 77) reference to "the particularization of universalism" (which he couples, of course, with the "universalization of particularism"). To quote Hall at some length:

> We used to think ... that if one could simply identify the logic of capital, that it would gradually engross everything in the world. It would translate everything in the world into a kind of replica of itself, everywhere; that all particularity would disappear; that capital in its onward, rationalizing march would not in the end care whether you were black, green or blue so long as you could sell your labor as a commodity. It would not care whether you were male or female, or a bit of both, provided it could deal with you in terms of the commodification of labor.

> But the more we understand about the development of capital itself, the more we understand that that is only part of the story. That alongside that

drive to commodify everything, which is certainly one part of its logic, is another critical part of its logic which works in and through specificity. (1997: 29)

Hall goes on to argue that "in order to maintain its global position, capital has had to negotiate and by negotiate I mean it had to incorporate and partly reflect the differences it was trying to overcome" (1997: 32).

To cut-and-paste freely from wildly different thinkers, I am also reminded of Foucault's insight into resistance: "Where there is power, there is resistance, *and yet, or rather consequently, this resistance is never is a position of exteriority in relation to power*" (1980: 95; emphasis added). Resistance to policy mandates thus serves to remind policy makers of the need for their existence—meaning their existence as policy makers as well as the existence of the policies they produce—and of the need, perhaps, for more intrusion into and regulation of people's lives. If we need to attend to the limits of neoliberalism, capitalism, or any other powerful cultural formation, then, we also need to attend to the limits of "talking back" and of reverse discourse.

The materiality of policy—its objective facticity in the lives of those engaged with it—provides one such limit. The fact that policy providers and recipients translate and assemble policy in keeping with their knowledges and agendas does not mean that they have the power to impose their visions of reality. Welfare providers in Riverview were severely constrained by institutional protocols, in terms of which they were closely surveilled. Although they had more discretionary power—certainly enough to put pressure on beneficiaries to find work even though workfare no longer existed—welfare providers in Kingston were not free to do anything they liked. Similarly, community service providers in both sites were limited by the material resources to which they had access as well as by the (light) weight that their voices carried in the corridors of power. Finally, even though welfare mothers were able to translate and assemble policy in ways that permitted them to "get through," they did not thrive: their translations and assemblages did not alter the support they received from the welfare department, the pressures they were placed under by the welfare bureaucracy and its agents, the kind of housing in which they had to live, the limitations on the kinds and amounts of food they could eat, the personal relationships they were permitted have, or the social stigma to which they were subject. Nor did their orientations or the realities of the lives they lived travel back up the system to influence official decision makers. Theirs is a story of just getting by. That welfare mothers in Kingston and Riverview produced many of the same kinds of (and in some instances identical) translations and assemblages further indexes the power of the shared dominant discourses and institutional structures to which they were subject, and to the limited possibilities of rebuttal they offered.

If what we mean by a global neoliberal policy regime is absolute uniformity, then such a regime does not exist. If, on the other hand, what we are referring to is a dominant set of norms that have greater and lesser resonance in different sites—but always some resonance—then I would argue that such a regime does, in fact, exist. The Alberta iteration has been in place for some time now, and there are no indications that it will shift anytime soon. Nor were the progressive aspects of the Clark reforms of 2002 able to resist the encroachments of the Key government, which is heading right back into forms of Rogernomics and Ruthanasia. This certainly does not mean that the neoliberal policy regimes I have been describing here (or their neoconservative elements) are permanently settled. But we insult the victims of punitive and miserly welfare systems if we turn a blind eye to the realities they must endure in order to celebrate the creativity of their engagements with them.

Two Concluding Lessons

Throughout this book, I have been telling two parallel stories. The first has been about Aotearoa/New Zealand and Alberta. Here I have explored the emergence of models of welfare reform; their movement across cultural, national, and provincial space; and how this movement was articulated and experienced by those who were engaged with it—policy elites, welfare and community service providers, and single mothers on welfare. The New Zealand–Alberta story has allowed me, in turn, to tell a second story about policy processes more generally. Here I have worked to theorize policy as movable and mutable, and as not only an artifact of meaning and power relations but also a key means by which people create, carry along, contest, and modify them—in other words, as both a site of and a stake in power struggles (as Fairclough [1992: 67] writes in relation to discourse more generally). Together, these stories compose a travelogue: the tracing of particular (Aotearoa/New Zealand and Albertan, provider and recipient) practices and cultural formations, and the tracing of the kinds of processes of which social policies are constituted. Throughout, I have followed a specific thread of tension running through both stories: namely, that between convergence and divergence in relation to a global policy regime. In following this thread through my travels, I have learned two valuable lessons.

First, the various changes to policy frames that I have highlighted tell us that policy is not so much a thing that moves, passed along or rejected by the various actors with whom it comes into contact. Rather, it is a *process* with a *social life*, something that is always in-the-making just as it is always on-the-move (Freeman 2012; Nielsen 2011). As we travel along points of contact through which it moves, policy become increasingly complex: policy mandates themselves may be contradictory; but, in addition, contradictions and alterations often multiply as more and more hands become engaged in policy travels. As useful as the metaphor of travel that I have been using throughout this book may be, then, perhaps it is also worth pausing to recognize the limits of its commonsense invocations: images of a thing that circulates. Perhaps, on the contrary, travel creates the thing—which is never really a thing but an unfolding, emerging ensemble. This becomes abundantly clear when we attend to the productive work of all, not just some, of those implicated in the social life of policy.

Second, and in seeming contradiction to my first point, as much as the idea of unfolding, emerging ensembles—of translation and assemblage—is useful, we need to be careful to avoid fetishizing difference and change. While arguments about the inevitability of change in translation, as well as about the instability of meaning generally, usefully draw our attention to what is transformed into something else, or to what is left behind—in other words, to the nuances of contextual specificity—we need to remember to also attend to "good" translations, translations that seem to "work." Roger Douglas's slogan, *don't blink*, for example, articulated so seamlessly with Klein's agenda that I am not even sure we need to think in terms of "translation" here. Similarly, the active society models of the person I have followed in this travelogue, although shifted and repositioned by various interlocutors, nevertheless became near hegemonic (albeit in different forms) among even welfare mothers, who were the least likely to benefit from them. Well-oiled machines of uninterrupted movement are thus as important as sticky engagements (Tsing 2005), and since both require concerted effort, both deserve our attention. It may be easier to see the work involved in translation that involves change simply because the change is there to see: agents decide (within limits) what and how to translate, and what to link with what, in order to come up with some kind of assemblage that allows them to operate more or less effectively in their environments. But there is also work involved in producing alignments of meaning and purpose that can cut across different contexts and that have the strength and resonance to be taken up by any number of situated actors. And where there is no struggle or contestation, where "bits get stuck together for a long time" (Strathern 2011: 7) that tells us something, too, about the power policy draws on and the policy that power deploys.

Appendix 1

Key Moments in State Provisioning for Poor Mothers in Aotearoa/New Zealand

Date	Legislation	Provisions/Reforms
1911	Widows' Pensions	Support for widows. • Amended in 1936 to include deserted wives.
1926	Family Allowance	Allowance to wage-earning households. • Made universal in 1946. • Amended to include "illegitimate" children in 1964.
1938	Social Security Act	Increased support for widows and deserted wives.[1] Never-married mothers supported via "emergency" benefits.
1973	Domestic Purposes Benefit	Support for all poor single mothers.
1991	Richardson's "Mother of All Budgets"	Across-the-board benefit cuts.
1996	Tax Reduction and Social Policy Bill	Introduction of work test/work preparation requirements for the DPB. • Amended in 1998 to tighten work test/work preparation requirements.
2002	Domestic Purposes and Widows' Benefit Reform	Elimination of work tests, increase in benefit rates, introduction of Enhanced Case Management and Personal Development and Employment Plans.

Notes

1. The Act also included benefits for sickness, unemployment, and old age; and inaugurated a national health scheme.

APPENDIX 2

Key Moments in State Provisioning for Poor Mothers in Canada and Alberta

Date	Legislation	Provisions/reforms
Canadian Federal		
1944	Family Allowance	Allowance to families with children.
1966	Canada Assistance Plan	National standardization of assistance to all those in need, including single mothers.
1996	Canada Health and Social Transfer	Cuts to federal funding; devolution of welfare to provincial level.
Alberta Provincial		
1911	Mothers' Allowance	Provisions for widows and wives of men with disabilities.
1961	Social Allowance	Benefits for unemployed persons and families.
1990	Supports for Independence	Cuts in benefit rates, introduction of work tests.
1993	Family and Social Service Reforms	Benefit cuts, tightened work test and eligibility requirements.
2004	Alberta Works	Tightened work test and eligibility requirements, introduction of Client Investment Plans.

REFERENCES

Alberta Family and Social Services. 1990. *One Step at a Time: Supports for Independence*. Edmonton: Government of Alberta.

———. 1994. *Business Plan 1994–95 to 1996–97*. Edmonton: Government of Alberta.

———. 1995. *Business Plan 1995–96 to 1997–98*. Edmonton: Government of Alberta.

———. 1996. *Alberta Welfare Reforms Progress Report: March 1993—December 1995*. Edmonton: Government of Alberta.

Alberta Human Resources and Employment. 2004. *Alberta Works*. Edmonton: Government of Alberta.

Appadurai, Arjun. 1996. *Modernity at Large*. Minneapolis: University of Minnesota Press.

Armitage, Andrew. 2003. *Social Welfare in Canada* (4th ed.). Oxford: Oxford University Press.

Arthurson, Wayne. 2005. "Spare Change: Raising the Minimum Wage is only a Start." *Alberta Views*, April/May, no. 30: 33.

Asad, Talal. 1986. "The Concept of Cultural Translation in British Social Anthropology." In *Writing Culture: The Poetics and Politics of Ethnography*, ed. James Clifford and George E. Marcus. Berkeley: University of California Press.

Baker, Maureen. 1997. *The Restructuring of the Canadian Welfare State: Ideology and Policy*. Sydney: Social Policy Research Centre, Discussion Paper #77, University of New South Wales.

Baker, Maureen, and David Tippin. 1999. *Poverty, Social Assistance, and the Employability of Mothers: Restructuring Welfare States*. Toronto: University of Toronto Press.

Beaglehole, Ann 1993. *Benefiting Women: Income Support for Women, 1893–1993*. Wellington: Social Policy Agency, Department of Social Welfare.

———. 1994. "Benefiting Women: Income Support for Women, 1893–1993." *Social Policy Journal of New Zealand—Te Puna Whakaaro*, no. 3: 82–87.

Belgrave, Michael. 2004. "Needs and the State: Evolving Social Policy in New Zealand History." In *Past Judgement: Social Policy in New Zealand History*, ed. Bronwyn Dalley and Margaret Tennant. Dunedin, NZ: University of Otago Press.

Belshaw, Cyril S. 1976. *The Sorcerer's Apprentice: An Anthropology of Public Policy*. New York: Pergamon.

Bertram, Geoff. 1993. "Keynesianism, Neoclassicism, and the State." In *State and Economy in New Zealand*, ed. Brian Roper and Chris Rudd. Auckland and Melbourne: Oxford University Press.

Black, Julie, and Yvonne Stanford. 2005. "When Martha and Henry Are Poor: The Poverty of Alberta's Social Assistance Programs." In *The Return of the Trojan Horse: Alberta and the New World (Dis)Order*, ed. Trevor Harrison. Montreal: Black Rose Books.

Blau, Peter M. 1970. "Weber's Theory of Bureaucracy." In *Max Weber*, ed. Dennis Wrong. Englewood Cliffs, NJ: Prentice-Hall.

Bobrow, Davis G. 2006. "Social and Cultural Factors: Constraining and Enabling." In *The Oxford Handbook of Public Policy*, ed. Michael Moran, Martin Rein, and Robert E. Goodin. Oxford: Oxford University Press.

Boston, Jonathan. 1991. "The Theoretical Underpinnings of Public Sector Restructuring in New Zealand." In *Reshaping the State: New Zealand's Bureaucratic Revolution*, ed. Jonathan Boston, John Martin, June Pallot, and Pat Walsh. Oxford: Oxford University Press.

———. 1993. "The Challenge of Governance: New Zealand's Experience of Economic Liberalisation, 1984–91." In *Governing in the 1990s: An Agenda for the Decade*, ed. Ian Marsh. Melbourne: Longman Cheshire.

Boston, Jonathan, Paul Dalziel, and Susan St. John. 1999. "Rebuilding an Effective Welfare State." In *Redesigning the Welfare State in New Zealand*, ed. Jonathan Boston, Paul Dalziel, and Susan St. John. Auckland: Oxford University Press.

Bourdieu, Pierre. 1990. *In Other Words: Essays Towards a Reflexive Sociology*. Stanford, CA: Stanford University Press.

———. 1999. *Acts of Resistance: Against the Tyranny of the Market*. New York: New Press.

———. 2003. *Firing Back: Against the Tyranny of the Market*. New York: New Press.

Boychuk, Gerard William. 1998. *Patchworks of Purpose: The Development of Provincial Social Assistance Regimes in Canada*. Montreal: McGill-Queen's University Press.

Brodie, J. 2002. "The Great Undoing: State Formation, Gender Politics, and Social Policy in Canada." In *Western Welfare in Decline: Globalization and Women's Poverty*, ed. Catherine Kingfisher. Philadelphia: University of Pennsylvania Press.

———. 2008. "The New Social'isms': Individualization and Social Policy Re-form in Canada." In *Contested Individualization: Debates About Contemporary Personhood*, ed. Cosmo Howard. London: Routledge.

Brodkin, Evelyn Z. 1997. "Inside the Welfare Contract: Discretion and Accountability in State Welfare Administration." *Social Service Review* 71: 1–33.

Brown, Wendy. 1995. "Finding the Man in the State." In *States of Injury: Power and Freedom in Late Modernity*. Princeton, NJ: Princeton University Press.

Calgary Herald. 1994. "Hitting the Wall: What to Do When the Bills Come Due." Roman Cooney. 8 January.

———. 1994. "Klein 'Leading the Province to Ruin.'" Bob Bergen. 9 February.

———. 1994. "Klein Government Must Stick to its Tough Course." David Richards. 8 March.

———. 1994. "Alberta Strategies in U.S. Textbook." Don Martin. 12 March.

———. 1994. "Economic Revolution: Nine Years of Pain Bring no Gain." William Gold. 29 March.

———. 1994. "Downsize, Privatize, Immobilize." Robert Bragg. 13 April.

———. 1994. "Ex-official Paints Reforms as Failure." Sheldon Alberts. 7 May.

———. 1994. "Protest! Muted So Far, Opposition Has Been Most Effective When Aimed at Specific Targets." Sheldon Alberts. 29 May.

———. 1995. "World Spotlight Shines on Klein and Alberta: Views from Outside." Sheldon Alberts. 11 March.

———. 1995. "Even As a Boy, Premier Knew Which Strings to Pull." Carol Howes and Jeff Holubitsky. 15 March.

———. 1995. "Klein Revolution Will Be Spun in Ontario." Rod Ziegler. 19 July.

———. 1996. "One for the X-files: Thousands of Albertans Were Cut from Welfare Rolls, so Where Did They Go?" Don Martin. 21 November.

Callon, Michel. 1986. "Some Elements of a Sociology of Translation: Domestication of the Scallops and the Fishermen of St. Brieuc Bay." In *Power, Action and Belief: A New Sociology of Knowledge?* ed. John Law. London: Routledge & Kegan Paul.

Canada West Foundation. 1997. *Where Are They Now?: Welfare Reform in Alberta*. Calgary: Canada West Foundation.

Castles, Francis G. 1985. *The Working Class and Welfare: Reflections on the Political Development of the Welfare State in Australia and New Zealand, 1890–1980*. Wellington: Allen & Unwin/Port Nicholson Press.

City of Riverview. 2005. *Low-Income in Riverview: A Profile*. Riverview, AB: City of Riverview Community and Social Development.

Clarke, John. 2004. *Changing Welfare, Changing States: New Directions in Social Policy*. London: Sage Publications.

Clifford, James. 1997. *Routes: Travel and Translation in the Late Twentieth Century*. Cambridge, MA: Harvard University Press.

Cochrane, Alan, John Clarke, and Sharon Gewirtz, eds. 2001. *Comparing Welfare States*. London: Sage/Open University.

Collier, Stephen J. 2006. "Global Assemblages." *Theory, Culture & Society* 23, no. 2–3: 399–401.

Collier, Stephen J., and Aihwa Ong. 2005. "Global Assemblages, Anthropological Problems." In *Global Assemblages: Technology, Politics, and Ethics as Anthropological Problems*, ed. Aihwa Ong and Stephen J. Collier. Malden, MA: Blackwell.

Crapanzano, Vincent. 1986. "Hermes' Dilemma: The Masking of Subversion in Ethnographic Description." In *Writing Culture: The Poetics and Politics of Ethnography*, ed. James Clifford and George E. Marcus. Berkeley: University of California Press.

Czarniawska, Barbara, and Guje Sevón. 2005. "Translation Is a Vehicle, Imitation Its Motor, and Fashion Sits at the Wheel." In *Global Ideas: How Ideas, Objects and Practices Travel in the Global Economy*, ed. Barbara Czarniawska and Guje Sevón. Liber & Copenhagen: Business School Press.

Dacks, Gurston, Joyce Green, and Linda Trimble. 1995. "Road Kill: Women in Alberta's Drive Toward Deficit Elimination." In *The Trojan Horse: Alberta and the Future of Canada*, ed. Gordon Laxer and Trevor Harrison. Montreal: Black Rose Books.

Daly, Mary, and Katherine Rake. 2003. *Gender and the Welfare State: Care, Work and Welfare in Europe and the U.S.* Cambridge: Polity.

Davies, Lorraine, Julie Ann McMullin, William R. Avison, and Gale L. Cassidy. 2001. *Social Policy, Gender Inequality and Poverty*. Ottawa: Status of Women Canada.

Davis, Dana-Ain. 2004. "Manufacturing Mammies: The Burdens of Service Work and Welfare Reform among Battered Black Women." *Anthropologica* 46: 273–88.

———. 2006. *Battered Black Women and Welfare Reform: Between a Rock and Hard Place*. Albany, NY: SUNY Press.

Dean, Mitchell. 1995. "Governing the Unemployed Self in an Active Society." *Economy and Society* 24, no. 4: 559–83.

———. 1999. *Governmentality: Power and Rule in Modern Society*. London: Sage.

———. 2005. "Policy." In *New Keywords: A Revised Vocabulary of Culture and Society*, ed. Tony Bennett, Lawrence Grossberg, and Meaghan Morris. Malden, MA: Blackwell.

———. 2007. *Governing Societies: Political Perspectives on Domestic and International Rule*. Maidenhead, UK: Open University Press.

DeLanda, Manuel. 2006. *A New Philosophy of Society: Assemblage Theory and Social Complexity*. London: Continuum.

Deleuze, Gilles, and Félix Guattari. 1987. *A Thousand Plateaus: Capitalism and Schizophrenia*. Minneapolis: University of Minnesota Press.

Denis, Claude. 1995. "'Government Can Do Whatever It Wants': Moral Regulation in Ralph Klein's Alberta." *Canadian Review of Sociology and Anthropology/Revue Canadienne de Sociologie et d'Anthropologie* 32, no. 3: 365–83.

Dobbin, Murray. 1995. "New Zealand Nightmare." *Canadian Dimension* 29, no. 2: 21–24.

Dolowitz, David, and David Marsh. 1996. "Who Learns What from Whom: A Review of the Policy Transfer Literature." *Political Studies* 44: 343–57.

———. 2000. "Learning from Abroad: The Role of Policy Transfer in Contemporary Policy-Making." *Governance: An International Journal of Policy and Administration* 13, no. 1: 5–24.

Douglas, Mary, and Steven Ney. 1998. *Missing Persons: A Critique of the Social Sciences.* Berkeley: University of California Press and Russell Sage Foundation.

Douglas, Roger. 1980. *There's Got To Be a Better Way! A Practical ABC to Solving New Zealand's Major Problems.* Wellington: Fourth Estate Books.

———. 1993a. *Unfinished Business.* Auckland: Random House New Zealand.

———. 1993b. *Presentation by Sir Roger Douglas to the Alberta Taxpayers Association Forum on Public Debt.* Calgary: Alberta Taxpayers Association.

———. 1994. *The Politics of Economic Restructuring: The Art of the Possible.* An interview with Jean-Louis Maxim. *Insight.* Athabasca, AB: Athabasca University.

———. 1995. *Turning Pain into Gain: Lessons from the New Zealand Experience.* Presentation to the Atlantic Institute for Market Studies, Halifax, N.S. http://www.aims.ca (accessed 12 August 2004).

Dunér, Anna, and Monica Nordström. 2006. "The Discretion and Power of Street-Level Bureaucrats: An Example from Swedish Municipal Eldercare." *European Journal of Social Work* 9, no. 4: 425–44.

Easton, Brian. 1997. *The Commercialisation of New Zealand.* Auckland: Auckland University Press.

———. 1999. *The Whimpering of the State: Policy After MMP.* Auckland: Auckland University Press.

Edmonton Journal. 1993. "Don't Hesitate, N.Z. Deficit Fighter Advises." Joan Crockatt. 1 October.

———. 1993. "Cutback King Heading for Alberta." Rod Ziegler. 6 November.

———. 1994a. "Bedside Reading for Alberta Tories: The Books Behind the Budget." Joan Crockatt. 6 March.

———. 1994b. "Reinventing Alberta: Gurus around the Globe Inspire the Klein Revolution." Joan Crockatt. 6 March.

———. 1997. "Cancelled Speech Worth Listening to." Linda Goyette. 1 March.

Esping-Andersen, Gøsta. 1990. *The Three Worlds of Welfare Capitalism.* Cambridge: Polity Press.

Evans, Mark. 2004a. "Is Policy Transfer Rational Policy-Making?" In *Policy Transfer in Global Perspective,* ed. Mark Evans. Aldershot, UK: Ashgate.

———. 2004b. "Understanding Policy Transfer." In *Policy Transfer in Global Perspective,* ed. Mark Evans. Aldershot, UK: Ashgate.

———. 2004c. "In Conclusion—Policy Transfer in Global Perspective." In *Policy Transfer in Global Perspective,* ed. Mark Evans. Aldershot, UK: Ashgate.

Fairclough, Norman. 1991. "What Might We Mean by 'Enterprise Discourse'?" In *Enterprise Culture,* ed. Russell Keat and Nicholas Abercrombie. London: Routledge.

———. 1992. *Discourse and Social Change.* Cambridge: Polity Press.

Ferguson, James, and Akhil Gupta. 2002. "Spatializing States: Toward an Ethnography of Neoliberal Governmentality." *American Ethnologist* 29, no. 4: 981–1002.

Fischer, Frank. 2003. *Reframing Public Policy: Discursive Politics and Deliberative Practices*. Oxford: Oxford University Press.

Fisher, William F. 1997. "Doing Good? The Politics and Antipolitics of NGO Practices." *Annual Review of Anthropology* 26: 439–64.

Foucault, Michel. 1980. *The History of Sexuality, Vol. 1: An Introduction*. New York: Vintage.

Fraser, Nancy. 1989. "Struggle Over Needs: Outline of a Socialist-Feminist Critical Theory of Late Capitalist Political Culture." In *Unruly Practices: Power, Discourse and Gender in Contemporary Social Theory*. Minneapolis: University of Minnesota Press.

Freeman, Richard. 2006. "Learning in Public Policy." In *The Oxford Handbook of Public Policy*, ed. Michael Moan, Martin Rein, and Robert E. Goodin. Oxford: Oxford University Press.

———. 2007. "Epistemological Bricolage: How Practitioners Make Sense of Learning." *Administration & Society* 39, no. 4: 476–96.

———. 2009. "What Is 'Translation'?" *Evidence & Policy* 5, no. 4: 429–47.

———. 2012. "Reverb: Policy Making in Wave Form." *Environment and Planning A* no. 44: 13–20.

Goffman, Erving. 1963. *Stigma: Notes on the Management of Spoiled Identity*. Englewood Cliffs, NJ: Prentice-Hall.

Goldberg, G. Schaffner. 1990. "Canada: Bordering on the Feminization of Poverty." In *The Feminization of Poverty: Only in America?*, ed. G. Schaffner Goldberg and E. Kremen. New York: Praeger.

Goode, Judith. 2002. "From New Deal to Bad Deal: Racial and Political Implications of U.S. Welfare Reform." In *Western Welfare in Decline: Globalization and Women's Poverty*, ed. Catherine Kingfisher. Philadelphia: University of Pennsylvania Press.

Goodger, Kay. 1998. "Maintaining Sole Parent Families in New Zealand: An Historical Review." *Social Policy Journal of New Zealand* 10: 122–53.

Government of Alberta. 1993a. *Legislative Assembly Hansard*, 25 January.

———. 1993b. *Legislative Assembly Hansard*, 1 February.

———. 1993c. *Legislative Assembly Hansard*, 3 February.

———. 1993d. *Report to Albertans by the Alberta Financial Review Commission*. Edmonton: Government of Alberta.

———. 1994. *A Better Way: A Plan for Securing Alberta's Future*. Edmonton: Government of Alberta.

———. 1995. *A Better Way II: A Blueprint for Building Alberta's Future*. Edmonton: Government of Alberta.

———. 2001. *Low-Income Programs Review*. Edmonton: Government of Alberta.

Hajer, Maarten, and David Laws. 2006. "Ordering Through Discourse." In *The Oxford Handbook of Public Policy*, ed. Michael Moran, Martin Rein, and Robert E. Goodin. Oxford: Oxford University Press.

Hall, Stuart. 1985. "Signification, Representation, Ideology: Althusser and the Post-Structuralist Debates." *Critical Studies in Mass Communication* 2, no. 2: 91–114.

———. 1986a. "Gramsci's Relevance for the Study of Race and Ethnicity." *Journal of Communication Inquiry* 10: 5–27.

———. 1986b. "The Problem of Ideology—Marxism without Guarantees." *Journal of Communication Inquiry* 10: 28–44.

———. 1988. *The Hard Road to Renewal: Thatcherism and the Crisis of the Left*. London: Verso.

———. 1997. "The Local and the Global: Globalization and Ethnicity." In *Culture, Globalization and the World-System: Contemporary Conditions for the Representation of Identity*, ed. Anthony D. King. Minneapolis: University of Minnesota Press.

Harder, Lois. 1996. "Depoliticizing Insurgency: The Politics of the Family in Alberta." *Studies in Political Economy* 50: 37–63.

———. 2003. *State of Struggle: Feminism and Politics in Alberta*. Edmonton: University of Alberta Press.

Harder, Lois, and Linda Trimble. 2005. "The Art of Contradiction: Women in Ralph Klein's Alberta." In *The Return of the Trojan Horse: Alberta and the New World (Dis)Order*, ed. Trevor Harrison. Montreal: Black Rose Books.

Harrison, Trevor W. 2010. "Social Assistance and the Politics of Welfare Fraud Investigations: The Case of Alberta." In *Poverty, Regulation and Social Exclusion: Readings on the Criminalization of Poverty*, ed. V. Marie Johnston and D. Crocker. Halifax, NS: Fernwood.

Harrison, Trevor W., and Gordon Laxer. 1995. "Introduction." In *The Trojan Horse*, ed. G. Laxer and T. Harrison. Montreal: Black Rose Books.

Harrison, Trevor W., William Johnston, and Harvey Krahn. 2005. "Language and Power: 'Special Interests' in Alberta's Political Discourse." In *The Return of the Trojan Horse: Alberta and the New World (Dis)Order*, ed. Trevor Harrison. Montreal: Black Rose Books.

Harvey, David. 2005. *A Brief History of Neoliberalism*. Oxford: Oxford University Press.

Hass, Peter M. 1992. "Introduction: Epistemic Communities and International Policy Coordination." *International Organization* 46, no. 1: 1–35.

Heelas, Paul. 1991. "Reforming the Self: Enterprise and the Characters of Thatcherism." In *Enterprise Culture*, ed. Russell Keat and Nicholas Abercrombie. London: Routledge.

Helmer, Joanne. 1995. "Redefining Normal: Life in the New Alberta." In *The Trojan Horse: Alberta and the Future of Canada*, ed. Trevor Harrison and Gordon Laxer. Montreal: Black Rose Books.

Herzfeld, Michael. 1993. *The Social Production of Indifference: Exploring the Symbolic Roots of Western Bureaucracy*. Chicago: University of Chicago Press.

Hobson, Barbara. 1994. "Solo Mothers, Social Policy Regimes, and the Logics of Gender." In *Gendering Welfare States*, ed. D. Sainsbury. London: Sage.

hooks, bell. 1984. *Feminist Theory: From Margin to Center*. Boston: South End Press.

Hsu, Francis L. K. 1993. *Rugged Individualism Reconsidered: Essays in Psychological Anthropology*. Knoxville: University of Tennessee Press.

Hudson, Bob. 1993. "Michael Lipsky and Street Level Bureaucracy: A Neglected Perspective." In *The Policy Process: A Reader* (2nd ed.), ed. Michael Hill. London: Prentice Hall.

Human Resources and Development Canada. 1994. *The Context of Reform: A Supplementary Paper*. Ottawa: Government of Canada.

Innes, Judith. 2002. *Knowledge and Public Policy: The Search for Meaningful Indicators* (2nd ed.). New Brunswick, NJ: Transaction Books.

Jenkins, Richard. 2007. "The Meaning of Policy/Policy as Meaning." In *Policy Reconsidered: Meanings, Politics and Practices*, ed. Susan M. Hodgson and Zoë Irving. Bristol, UK: Policy Press.

Jesson, Bruce. 1987. *Behind the Mirror Glass: The Growth of Wealth and Power in New Zealand in the Eighties*. Auckland: Penguin.

Johnson, Björn, and Bo Hagström. 2005. "The Translation Perspective as an Alternative to the Policy Diffusion Paradigm: The Case of the Swedish Methadone Maintenance Treatment." *Journal of Social Policy* 34, no. 3: 365–88.

Jones, Liz. 2004. "Note on the 2002 Domestic Purposes Benefit and Widows Benefit Reforms." *Social Policy Journal of New Zealand* 12: 121–22.

Kelsey, Jane. 1993. *Rolling Back the State: Privatisation of Power in Aotearoa/New Zealand*. Wellington: Bridget Williams Books.

———. 1995. *The New Zealand Experiment: A World Model for Structural Adjustment?* Auckland: Auckland University Press with Bridget Williams Books.

———. 1999. *Reclaiming the Future: New Zealand and the Global Economy.* Toronto: University of Toronto Press.

Kingfisher, Catherine. 1996a. *Women in the American Welfare Trap.* Philadelphia: University of Pennsylvania Press.

———. 1996b. "Women on Welfare: Conversational Sites of Acquiescence and Dissent." *Discourse & Society* 7, no. 4: 531–57.

———. 1999. "Rhetoric of (Female) Savagery: Welfare Reform in the United States and Aotearoa/New Zealand." *National Women's Studies Association Journal* 11, no. 1: 1–15.

———. 2001. "Producing Disunity: The Constraints and Incitements of Welfare Work." In *The New Poverty Studies: The Ethnography of Power, Politics, and Impoverished People in the United States*, ed. Judith Goode and Jeff Maskovsky. New York: New York University Press.

———. 2002a. "Introduction: The Global Feminization of Poverty." In *Western Welfare in Decline: Globalization and Women's Poverty.* Philadelphia: University of Pennsylvania Press.

———. 2002b. "Neoliberalism I: Discourses of Personhood and Welfare Reform." In *Western Welfare in Decline: Globalization and Women's Poverty.* Philadelphia: University of Pennsylvania Press.

———. 2002c. "Where to Next? Against and Beyond Neoliberalism." In *Western Welfare in Decline: Globalization and Women's Poverty.* Philadelphia: University of Pennsylvania Press.

———. 2006. "What D/discourse Analysis Can Tell Us About Neoliberal Constructions of (Gendered) Personhood: Some Notes on Commonsense and Temporality." *Gender and Language* 1, no. 1: 91–103.

———. 2007a. "Discursive Constructions of Homelessness in a Small City in the Canadian Prairies: Notes on Destructuration, Individualization, and the Production of (Raced and Gendered) Unmarked Categories." *American Ethnologist* 34, no. 1: 91–107.

———. 2007b. "Spatializing Neoliberalism: Articulations, Recapitulations, and (a Very Few) Alternatives." In *Neoliberalization: States, Networks, Peoples*, ed. Kim England and Kevin Ward. Malden, MA: Blackwell.

———. 2009. "Off the Shelf and Into Oblivion?" In *Anthropology off the Shelf: Anthropologists on Writing*, ed. Alisse Waterston and Maria D. Vesperi. Malden, MA: Wiley-Blackwell.

Kingfisher, Catherine, and Michael Goldsmith. 2001. "Reforming Women in the United States and Aotearoa/New Zealand: A Comparative Ethnography of Welfare Reform in Global Context." *American Anthropologist* 103, no. 3: 714–32.

Kingfisher, Catherine, and Jeff Maskovsky. 2008. "Introduction: The Limits of Neoliberalism." *Critique of Anthropology* 28, no. 2: 115–26.

Kluckhohn, Clyde. 1951. "The Study of Culture." In *The Policy Sciences*, ed. Daniel Lerner and Harold D. Lasswell. Stanford, CA: Stanford University Press.

Korteweg, Anna C. 2006. "The Politics of Subject Formation: Welfare-Reliant Women's Response to Welfare Reform in the United States and the Netherlands." In *Analysing Social Policy: A Governmental Approach*, ed. Greg Marston and Catherine McDonald. Camberley, UK: Edward Elgar.

Kuhn, Thomas S. 1970. *The Structure of Scientific Revolutions.* Chicago: University of Chicago Press.

Langford, Tom. 2011. *Alberta's Day Care Controversy: From 1908 to 2009—and Beyond.* Edmonton: Athabasca University Press.

Larner, Wendy. 1997. "'A Means to an End': Neoliberalism and State Processes in New Zealand." *Studies in Political Economy* 52: 7–38.

———. 2000. "Post-Welfare State Governance: Towards a Code of Social and Family Responsibility." *Social Politics* 7, no. 2: 244–65.

Larner, Wendy, and William Walters. 2000. "Privatisation, Governance and Identity: The United Kingdom and New Zealand Compared." *Policy & Politics* 28, no. 3: 361–77.

Larner, Wendy, Richard Le Heron, and Nicholas Lewis. 2007. "Co-constituting 'After Neoliberalism': Political Projects and Globalizing Governmentalities in Aotearoa/New Zealand." In *Neoliberalization: States, Networks, Peoples*, ed. Kim England and Kevin Ward. Malden, MA: Blackwell.

Lasswell, Harold D. 1951. "The Policy Orientation." In *The Policy Sciences*, ed. Daniel Lerner and Harold D. Lasswell. Stanford, CA: Stanford University Press.

Latour, Bruno. 1986. "The Powers of Association." In *Power, Action and Belief: A New Sociology of Knowledge?* ed. John Law. London: Routledge & Kegan Paul.

Laws, David, and Maarten Hajer. 2006. "Policy in Practice." In *The Oxford Handbook of Public Policy*, ed. Michael Moran, Martin Rein, and Robert E. Goodin. Oxford: Oxford University Press.

Lee, Kevin K, and Cheryl Engler. 2000. *A Profile of Poverty in Mid-Sized Alberta Cities*. Ottawa: Canadian Council on Social Development.

Lendvai, Noémi, and David Bainton. Forthcoming. "Translation: Towards a Critical Comparative Social Policy Agenda." In *Handbook of Comparative Social Policy*, ed. Patricia Kennett. Cheltenham: Edward Elgar.

Lendvai, Noémi, and Paul Stubbs. 2006. "Translation, Intermediaries and Welfare Reforms in South Eastern Europe." Paper presented at the 4th ESPAnet Conference, Bremen.

———. 2007. "Policies as Translation: Situating Transnational Social Policies." In *Policy Reconsidered: Meanings, Politics and Practices*, ed. Susan M. Hodgson and Zoë Irving. Bristol, UK: Policy Press.

———. 2009. "Assemblages, Translation, and Intermediaries in South East Europe: Rethinking Transnationalism and Social Policy." *European Societies* 11, no. 5: 673–95.

Leve, Lauren, and Lamia Karim. 2001. "Privatizing the State: Ethnography of Development, Transnational Capital, and NGOs." *PoLAR: Political and Legal Anthropology Review* 24, no. 1: 53–58.

Li, Tania Murray. 2007. *The Will to Improve: Governmentality, Development, and the Practice of Politics*. Durham. NC: Duke University Press.

Lipsky, Michael. 1980. *Street-Level Bureaucracy: Dilemmas of the Individual in Public Services*. New York: Russell Sage Foundation.

Lisac, Mark. 1995. *The Klein Revolution*. Edmonton: New West Press.

Lister, Sarah. 2003. "NGO Legitimacy: Technical Issue or Social Construct?" *Critique of Anthropology* 23, no. 2: 175–92.

Little, Margaret. 1994. "Manhunts and Bingo Blabs: The Moral Regulation of Ontario Single Mothers." In *Studies in Moral Regulation*, ed. Mariana Valaverde. Toronto: Centre of Criminology, University of Toronto.

———. 1998. *"No Car, No Radio, No Liquor Permit": The Moral Regulation of Single Mothers in Ontario, 1920–1997*. Toronto: Oxford University Press.

———. 1999. "The Limits of Canadian Democracy: The Citizenship Rights of Poor Women." *Canadian Review of Social Policy* 43: 59–76.

Lochhead, Clarene, and Katherine Scott. 2000. *The Dynamics of Women's Poverty in Canada*. Ottawa: Status of Women Canada.

Malinowski, Bronislaw. 1926. *Myth in Primitive Psychology*. London: Norton.

Marcus, George E., and Erkan Saka. 2006. "Assemblage." *Theory, Culture & Society* 23, no. 2–3: 101–9.

Marsh, David, and J. C. Sharman. 2009. "Policy Diffusion and Policy Transfer." *Policy Studies* 30, no. 3: 269–88.

Maskovsky, Jeff, and Catherine Kingfisher. 2001. "Introduction, Special Issue on Global Capitalism, Neoliberal Policy and Poverty." *Urban Anthropology and Studies of Cultural Systems and World Economic Development* 30, no. 2–3: 105–21.

Mason, Robin. 2003. "Listening to Lone Mothers: Paid Work, Family Life, and Childcare in Canada." *Journal of Children & Poverty* 9, no. 1: 41–54.

McClure, Margaret. 1998. *A Civilized Community: A History of Social Security in New Zealand 1898–1998*. Auckland: Auckland University Press.

———. 2004. "A Badge of Poverty or a Symbol of Citizenship? Needs, Rights and Social Security, 1935–2000." In *Past Judgement: Social Policy in New Zealand History*, ed. Bronwyn Daley and Margaret Tennant. Dunedin, NZ: University of Otago Press.

Mead, Margaret. 1951. "The Study of National Character." In *The Policy Sciences*, ed. Daniel Lerner and Harold D. Lasswell. Stanford, CA: Stanford University Press.

Mertz, Elizabeth, and Andrea Timmer. 2010. "Getting it Done: Ethnographic Perspectives on NGOs." *PoLAR: Political and Legal Anthropology Review* 33, no. 2: 171–77.

Meyers, Marcia, and Susan Vorsanger. 2007. "Street-Level Bureaucrats and the Implementation of Public Policy." In *Handbook of Public Administration*, ed. B. Guy Peters and Jon Pierre. London: Sage.

Miller, Peter, and Nikolas Rose. 2008. *Governing the Present: Administering Economic, Social and Personal Life*. Cambridge: Polity.

Mishra, Ramesh. 1999. *Globalization and the Welfare State*. Cheltenham, UK: Edward Elgar.

Moore, Henrietta. 1996. *A Passion for Difference: Essays in Anthropology and Gender*. Bloomington: Indiana University Press.

Morgen, Sandra, Joan Acker, and Jill Weigt. 2011. *Stretched Thin: Poor Families, Welfare Work, and Welfare Reform*. Ithaca, NY: Cornell University Press.

Mosse, David. 2011. "Politics and Ethics: Ethnographies of Expert Knowledge and Professional Identities." In *Policy Worlds: Anthropology and the Analysis of Contemporary Power*, ed. Cris Shore, Susan Wright, and Davide Però. New York: Berghahn Books.

Murphy, Jonathan. 1997. "Alberta and the Workfare Myth." In *Workfare: Ideology for a New Under-Class*, ed. Eric Shragge. Toronto: Garamond.

Muscovitch, Allan. 1996. "Canada Health and Social Transfer: What Was Lost?" *CRSP. RCPS* 37: 66–75.

National Council of Welfare. 2006. *Welfare Incomes 2005*. Ottawa: Government of Canada.

———. 1997. *Another Look at Welfare Reform*. Ottawa: Government of Canada.

National Union of Public and General Employees. 1994. *If Pigs Could Fly: The Hard Truth about the "Economic Miracle" that Ruined New Zealand*. Ottawa: National Union of Public and General Employees.

Newman, Janet. 2006. "Constituting Trans-National Governance: Spaces, Actors and Vocabularies of Power." Paper presented at the 4th ASPAnet Conference, Bremen.

New Zealand Government. 2001. *Pathways to Opportunity. Nga Ara Whai Oranga: From Social Welfare to Social Development, A New Zealand Government Statement*. Wellington: Ministry of Social Development.

———. 2007. *The 2002 Domestic Purposes and Widow's Benefit Reform: Evaluation Report*. Wellington: Ministry of Social Development.

New Zealand Treasury. 1984. *Economic Management (Treasury Briefing to Incoming Government)*. Wellington: Government of New Zealand.

Nielsen, Gritt B. 2011. "Peopling Policy: On Conflicting Subjectivities of Fee-Paying Students." In *Policy Worlds: Anthropology and the Analysis of Contemporary Power*, ed. Cris Shore, Susan Wright, and Davide Però. New York: Berghahn Books.

Nolan, Melanie. 2000. *Breadwinning: New Zealand Women and the State*. Christchurch, NZ: Canterbury University Press.

O'Brien, Mike, and Chris Wilkes. 1993. *The Tragedy of the Market*. Palmerston North, NZ: Dunmore Press.

O'Connor, J., A. Orloff, and S. Shaver. 1996. *States, Markets, Families: Gender, Liberalism and Social Policy in Australia, Canada, Great Britain, and the United States*. Cambridge: Cambridge University Press.

OECD. 1990. *Employment Outlook 1990*. Paris: OECD.

———. 2005. *Economic Survey of New Zealand: Raising Female Labour Force Participation*. Paris: OECD.

Olds, Kris, and Nigel Thrift. 2005. "Cultures on the Brink: Reengineering the Soul of Capitalism—On a Global Scale." In *Global Assemblages: Technology, Politics, and Ethics as Anthropological Problems*, ed. Aihwa Ong and Stephen J. Collier. Malden, MA: Blackwell.

Ong, Aihwa. 2005. "Ecologies of Expertise: Assembling Flows, Managing Citizenship." *Global Assemblages: Technology, Politics, and Ethics as Anthropological Problems*, ed. Aihwa Ong and Stephen J. Collier. Malden, MA: Blackwell.

———. 2006. *Neoliberalism as Exception: Mutations in Citizenship*. Durham, NC: Duke University Press.

Ong, Aihwa, and Stephen J. Collier. 2005. *Global Assemblages: Technology, Politics, and Ethics as Anthropological Problems*. Malden, MA: Blackwell.

Osborne, David, and Ted Gaebler. 1992. *Reinventing Government: How the Entrepreneurial Spirit Is Transforming the Public Sector*. Reading, MA: Addison-Wesley.

Palmer, Howard, and Tamara Palmer. 1990. *Alberta: A New History*. Edmonton: Hurtig Publishers.

Peck, Jamie. 2001. *Workfare States*. New York: Guilford Press.

———. 2002. "Political Economies of Scale: Fast Policy, Interscalar Relations, and Neoliberal Workfare." *Economic Geography* 78, no. 3: 331–56.

———. 2011. "Geographies of Policy: From Transfer-Diffusion to Mobility-Mutation." *Progress in Human Geography* 35, no.6: 773–797.

Peck, Jamie, and Nik Theodore. 2001. "Exporting Workfare/Importing Welfare-to-Work: Exploring the Politics of Third Way Policy Transfer." *Political Geography* 20: 427–60.

———. 2010. "Mobilizing Policy: Models, Methods, and Mutations." *Geoforum* 41: 169–74.

———. 2012. "Follow the Policy: A Distended Case Approach." *Environment and Planning A* 44: 21–30.

Peters, Michael. 1997. "Neoliberalism, Welfare Dependence and the Moral Construction of Poverty in New Zealand." *New Zealand Sociology* 12, no. 1: 1–34.

Phillips, John. 2006. "Agencement/Assemblage." *Theory, Culture & Society* 23, no. 2–3: 108–9.

Pieterse, Jan Nederveen. 2009. *Globalization and Culture: Global Mélange*. Lanham, MD: Rowman and Littlefield.

Polanyi, Karl. 2001. *The Great Transformation: The Political and Economic Origins of Our Time*. Boston: Beacon Press.

Pollitt, Chris. 1993. "The Development of Management Thought." In *The Policy Process: A Reader* (2nd ed.), ed. Michael Hill. London: Prentice Hall.

Pratt, Mary Louise. 1991. "Arts of the Contact Zone." *Profession*: 33–40.

Pressman, Jeffrey L., and Aaron Wildavsky. 1984. *Implementation: How Great Expectations in Washington Are Dashed in Oakland* (3rd ed.). Berkeley: University of California Press.

Prottas, Jeffrey M. 1979. *People Processing: The Street-Level Bureaucrat in Public Service Bureaucracies*. Lexington, MA: Lexington Books.

Reichwein, Baldwin P. 2002. *Benchmarks in Alberta's Public Welfare Services: History Rooted in Benevolence, Harshness, Punitiveness and Stinginess*. Research Report prepared for the Alberta College of Social Workers, Edmonton.

Reinhold, Susan. 1994. "Local Conflict and Ideological Struggle: 'Positive Images' and Section 28." Unpublished D.Phil. thesis, Social Anthropology, University of Sussex.

Riccucci, Norma M. 2005. *How Management Matters: Street-Level Bureaucrats and Welfare Reform*. Washington, DC: Georgetown University Press.

Robertson, Roland. 1992. *Globalization: Social Theory and Global Culture*. London: Sage.

———. 1997. "Social Theory, Cultural Relativity and the Problem of Globality." In *Culture, Globalization and the World-System: Contemporary Conditions for the Representation of Identity*, ed. Anthony D. King. Minneapolis: University of Minnesota Press.

Rose, Nikolas. 1992. "Governing the Enterprising Self." In *The Values of the Enterprise Culture: The Moral Debate*, ed. Paul Heelas and Paul Morris. London: Routledge.

Rubel, Paula, and Abraham Rosman. 2003. "Introduction: Translation and Anthropology." In *Translating Cultures: Perspectives on Translation and Anthropology*, ed. Paula Rubel and Abraham Rosman. Oxford: Berg.

Rudd, Chris. 1993. "The New Zealand Welfare State: Origins, Development, and Crisis." In *State and Economy in New Zealand*, ed. Brian Roper and Chris Rudd. Auckland: Oxford University Press.

Sainsbury, Diane. 1996. *Gender, Equality, and Welfare States*. Cambridge: Cambridge University Press.

———. 2000. *Gender and Welfare State Regimes*. Oxford: Oxford University Press.

Sakai, Naoki. 2006. "Translation." *Theory, Culture & Society* 23, no. 2–3: 71–86.

Sangster, Joan. 2001. *Regulating Girls and Women: Sexuality, Family, and the Law in Ontario, 1920–1960*. Oxford: Oxford University Press.

Sassen, Saskia. 1996. "Toward a Feminist Analytics of the Global Economy." *Indiana Journal of Global Legal Studies* 4, no. 1: 7–41.

———. 1998. *Globalization and Its Discontents: Essays on the New Mobility of People and Money*. New York: New Press.

———. 2007. *A Sociology of Globalization*. New York: Norton.

Schön, Donald A. 1973. *Beyond the Stable State; Public and Private Learning in a Changing Society*. Harmondsworth, UK: Penguin.

Schram, Sanford. 1995. *Words of Welfare: The Poverty of Social Science and the Social Science of Poverty*. Minneapolis: University of Minnesota Press.

———. 2006. *Welfare Discipline: Discourse, Governance, and Globalization*. Philadelphia: Temple University Press.

Schwartz, Herman. 1997. "Reinvention and Retrenchment: Lessons from the Application of the New Zealand Model to Alberta, Canada." *Journal of Policy: Analysis of Management* 16, no. 3: 205–32.

———. 2000. "Internationalization and Two Liberal Welfare States: Australia and New Zealand." In *Welfare and Work in the Open Economy, Volume II: Diverse Responses to*

Common Challenges, ed. Fritz W. Scharpf and Vivien A. Schmidt. Oxford: Oxford University Press.

Shipley, Jenny. 1991. *Social Assistance: Welfare That Works. A Statement of Government Policy on Social Assistance*. Wellington: Ministry of Social Welfare.

Shirley, Ian, and Susan St. John. 1997. "Family Policy and the Decline of the Welfare State in New Zealand." *British Review of New Zealand Studies* no. 10: 39–62.

Shore, Cris, and Susan Wright. 1997. "Policy: A New Field of Anthropology." In *Anthropology of Public Policy: Critical Perspectives on Governance and Power*, ed. Cris Shore and Susan Wright. London: Routledge.

———. 2011. "Conceptualising Policy: Technologies of Governance and the Politics of Visibility." In *Policy Worlds: Anthropology and the Analysis of Contemporary Power*, ed. Cris Shore, Susan Wright, and Davide Però. New York: Berghahn Books.

Shore, Cris, Susan Wright, and Davide Però. 2011. *Policy Worlds: Anthropology and the Analysis of Contemporary Power*. New York: Berghahn Books.

Sklair, Leslie. 1998. "Social Movements for Global Capitalism: The Transnational Capitalist Class in Action." In *Civil Societies and Social Movements: Domestic, Transnational, Global*, ed. Ronnie D. Lipschutz. Aldershot, UK: Ashgate.

Smith, Paul. 2007. *Primitive America: The Ideology of Capitalist Democracy*. Minneapolis: University of Minnesota Press.

Soron, Dennis. 2005. "The Politics of De-Politicization: Neo-Liberalism and Popular Consent in Alberta." In *The Return of the Trojan Horse: Alberta and the New World (Dis)Order*, ed. Trevor W. Harrison. Montreal: Black Rose Books.

Stack, Carol. 1974. *All Our Kin*. New York: Harper and Row.

Stone, Diane. 2000. "Non-Governmental Policy Transfer: The Strategies of Independent Policy Institutes." *Governance: An International Journal of Policy and Administration* 13: 45–70.

———. 2002. "Introduction: Global Knowledge and Advocacy Networks." *Global Networks* 2, no. 1: 1–11.

———. 2004. "Transfer Agents and Global Networks in the 'Transnationalization' of Policy." *Journal of European Public Policy* 11, no. 3: 545–66.

Strange, Caroline, and Tina Loo. 1997. *Making Good: Law and Moral Regulation in Canada 1967–1939*. Toronto: University of Toronto Press.

Strathern, Marilyn. 2004. *Commons and Borderlands: Working Papers on Interdisciplinarity, Accountability and the Flow of Knowledge*. Oxon: Sean Kingston Publishing.

———. 2011. "Discussant Comments for Session on Tracing Policy: Translation and Assemblage." Presented at the AAA conference, Montreal.

Strong-Boag, Veronica. 1995. "'Wages for Housework': Mother's Allowances and the Beginnings of Social Security in Canada." In *Social Welfare Policy in Canada: Historical Readings*, ed. Raymond B. Blake and Jeff Keshen. Toronto: Copp Clark.

Stubbs, Paul. 2002. "Globalisation, Memory and Welfare Regimes in Transition: Towards an Anthropology of Transnational Policy Transfers." *International Journal of Social Welfare* 11: 321–30.

———. 2005. "Stretching Concepts Too Far? Multi-Level Governance, Policy Transfer and the Politics of Scale in South East Europe." *Southeast European Politics* 6, no. 2: 66–87.

Susser, Ida. 1982. *Norman Street: Poverty and Politics in an Urban Neighborhood*. New York: Oxford University Press.

Taft, Kevin. 1997. *Shredding the Public Interest: Ralph Klein and 25 Years of One-Party Government*. Edmonton: University of Alberta Press and Parkland Institute.

Taylor, Jeff. 1995. "Labour in the Klein Revolution." In *The Trojan Horse: Alberta and the Future of Canada*, ed. Gordon Laxer and Trevor Harrison. Montreal: Black Rose Books.

Taylor-Gooby, Peter, ed. 2001. *Welfare States Under Pressure*. London: Sage.

Thomson, David. 1991. "Society and Social Welfare." In *The Future of the Past: Themes in New Zealand History*, ed. Colin Davis and Peter Lineham. Palmerston North, NZ: Massey University Department of History.

Tsing, Anna. 2005. *Friction: An Ethnography of Global Connection*. Princeton, NJ: Princeton University Press.

Valentine, Charles. 1968. *Culture and Poverty: A Critique and Counterproposals*. Chicago: University of Chicago Press.

Venn, Couze. 2006. "A Note on Assemblage." *Theory, Culture & Society* 23, no. 2–3: 107–8.

Wacquant, Loic. 1999. "Urban Marginality in the Coming Millennium." *Urban Studies* 36, no. 10: 1639–53.

Waldegrave, Charles, and Peter Frater. 1996. "New Zealand: A Search for a National Poverty Line." In *Poverty: A Global Review. Handbook on International Poverty Research*, ed. Ed Oyen, S. M. Miller, and S. A. Samad. Oslo: Scandinavian University Press; and Paris: UNESCO.

Walters, William. 1997. "The Active Society: New Designs for Social Policy." *Policy and Politics* 25, no. 3: 221–34.

Wedel, Janine R., Cris Shore, Gregory Feldman, and Stacy Lathrop. 2005. "Toward an Anthropology of Public Policy." *Annals of the American Academy of Politics and Social Science* 600: 30–51.

Windybank, Susan. 2003. "Can New Zealand Fly Again? The New Reform Agenda." *Policy* 19, no. 2: 21–27.

Wirth, William. 1991. "Responding to Citizen Needs: From Bureaucratic Accountability to Individual Coproduction in the Public Sector." In *The Public Sector: Challenges for Coordination and Learning*, ed. Franz-Xavier Kauffmann. Berlin: De Gruyter.

Wright, Susan, and Sue Reinhold. 2011. "'Studying Through': A Strategy for Studying Political Transformation. Or Sex, Lies and British Politics." In *Policy Worlds: Anthropology and the Analysis of Contemporary Power*, ed. Cris Shore, Susan Wright, and Davide Però. New York: Berghahn.

Yeatman, Anna. 1990. *Bureaucrats, Technocrats, Femocrats: Essays on the Contemporary Australian State*. Sydney: Allen and Unwin.

Young, Iris Marion. 1997. *Intersecting Voices: Dilemmas of Gender, Political Philosophy and Policy*. Princeton, NJ: Princeton University Press.

INDEX